D0502027

12 —

The
Newfoundland

The Newfoundland's legendary benevolent character is mirrored by these three beautiful home-bred bitches from Margaret Willmott's Topmast Kennels, one of Canada's most successful. They are (left to right) Can. Ch. Topmast's Hello Dolly, Can. Ch. Topmast's Cotton Candy and Am., Can. Ch. Topmast's Prairie Lily.

The
Newfoundland

Companion Dog—Water Dog

Joan C. Bendure

HOWELL
BOOK HOUSE

New York

MACMILLAN • USA

Copyright © 1994 by Joan C. Bendure

All rights reserved. No part of this book may be reproduced or transmitted in any form or by any means, electronic or mechanical, including photocopying, recording, or by any information storage and retrieval system, without permission in writing from the Publisher.

Macmillan General Reference
A Simon & Schuster Macmillan Company
1633 Broadway
New York, NY 10019-6785

Library of Congress Cataloging-in-Publication Data

Bendure, Joan C.
    The Newfoundland: companion dog, water dog / by Joan C. Bendure.
        p.   cm.
    ISBN 0-87605-242-1
    1. Newfoundland dog.
    SF429.N4B46   1994
    636.7'3—dc20   93-2077

10 9 8 7 6 5

Printed in the United States of America

This book is dedicated to the memory of my son David, a young life with a bright future that was tragically and accidentally taken. I know that if there is another life, you and Shenanigans, Yankee and Chubby are fishing.

DAVID PAUL BENDURE

May 9, 1966–April 10, 1984

A CHILD LOANED

"I'll lend you for a little time a child of Mine," He said,
"for you to love the while he lives and mourn for when he's dead.
It may be six or seven years or twenty-two or three, but will you,
till I call him back, take care of him for Me?
He'll bring his charms to gladden you, and should his stay be brief, you'll
have his lovely memories as solace for your grief.

"I cannot promise he will stay, since all from earth return, but there are
lessons taught down here I want this child to learn. I've looked this wide
world over in My search for teachers true, and from the throngs that
crowd life's lanes I have selected you.
Now will you give him all your love, not think the labor vain, or hate
Me when I come to call and take him back again?"

I fancied that I heard them say, "Dear Lord, Thy Will be done. For all the
joy the child shall bring, the risk of grief we'll run.
We'll love him while we may, and for the happiness we've known,
forever grateful stay.
But should the Angels call for him much sooner than we planned
we'll brave the bitter grief that comes and try to understand."

DON LARSON 1974

Postage stamps from Newfoundland depicting the Newfoundland dog. The small, square half-cent stamp was issued in 1887 and has a Landseer head. The fourteen-cent stamp, top and bottom row center, pictured Ch. Westerland Sieger, bred by the Hon. Harold MacPherson and later owned by Waseeka Kennels. The other stamps are printed with Saint Pierre et Miquelon.

Contents

A litter of a dozen hungry puppies at mealtime at Bjørnebanden Kennels.   *Søren Wesseltoft*

Foreword

ITHAS BEEN nearly twenty years since Howell Book House has published a comprehensive volume concerning the Newfoundland dog. As all-breed handlers who have been associated with many Newfoundlands during that period, we have noticed ample changes in the breed. In our estimation those changes have more often than not been for the better. Regardless of specific breed differences from then until now, it remains the case that the fundamental restyling of the Newfoundland makes the publication of this book particularly important. Indeed, the thorough documentation of where a breed has been and where it currently stands is clearly beneficial in determining where it should be going.

We are particularly pleased that Howell Book House chose Joan C. Bendure to pilot this undertaking. Our association with Joan now goes back many years, having handled several of her dogs, both Newfoundlands and Portuguese Water Dogs, to their championships. As is the case with most successful breeders, Joan has breadth of knowledge concerning dogs in general and depth of knowledge concerning Newfoundlands in particular. Moreover, Joan's more recent flirtation with Portuguese Water Dogs serves her Newfoundland involvement well. Familiarity with multiple breeds usually results in a keener eye and a more balanced view of any one breed.

Though the breeding and exhibiting of quality dogs is certainly an important credential for any breed book author, other individual facets are equally important in developing a feel for the breed and the dog fancy in general. In this regard Joan excels, having devoted many hours to lesser-known activities, including the Erie County Canine 4-H program, the Erie Kennel Club, the Portuguese Water Dog Club of America, and perhaps most important, the Service Dog breeding program that has the responsibility of breeding and rearing dogs that are eventually used in assisting physically challenged persons. As you might guess, any one of these activities entails an investment of substantial resources, one that Joan has consistently been willing to make on a year-in, year-out basis.

We are confident that this book is going to entertain and inform a wide audience, ranging from the potential Newfoundland puppy buyer to the well-seasoned breed expert. It is therefore our pleasure to heartily endorse this work, one in which Howell Book House, Joan C. Bendure and the Newfoundland fancy at large can take justifiable pride.

ANDREA and TOM GLASSFORD

Acknowledgments

WRITING THIS BOOK would not have been possible without the cooperation of so many wonderful people in my life and in the Newfoundland world. Thanks are due first to my family, particularly my husband, Paul, who obviously has the patience and tolerance of a Newfoundland to put up with living with a dog fancier for so many years. Paul never knows who will be sitting at his dinner table or sleeping in the guest room; and then he has to suffer the embarrassment of having his wife referred to as the ''dog lady.'' Thanks also to our children—Tammy, David and Scott—who were so much help with the dogs and puppies over the years. I am sure there were times when they wished I had taken up gourmet cooking instead. But then again, how many other children had those big, beautiful black dogs for show-and-tell?

No one can be a dog breeder for long without the knowledge and compassion of good veterinarians. For that I must thank the doctors at Glenwood Pet Hospital, Dr. Doug Sorenson, Dr. Jack Zimmerly, Dr. Lee McVey and especially Dr. Ken Felix and Dr. P. J. Polumbo. It takes a special kind of vet to work with breeders. Dr. Felix is always willing to listen and explain, and give breeders all the options to let them decide. Unfortunately, Ken and I are about the same age, so I guess he will let me know when it is time to retire. Only a very special and dedicated vet like Dr. Polumbo would sleep on the floor with a Newf recovering from bloat.

Special thanks must go to:

Milan Lint, with whom I have enjoyed a long and lasting friendship, for all his help in writing this book. His mind is a memory bank that would rival any computer;

technical writer Jon Threlkeld for all his writing help and pushing me in
the right direction;

artist Dave Vitale for his wonderful illustrations; and

that wonderfully talented photographer Soren Wesseltoft, of Denmark, for
allowing me to use so many of his magnificent photos.

A special appreciation is extended to all the Newfoundland owners and breeders in the United States who allowed the use of their treasured pictures of their beloved dogs; as everyone knows, one picture is worth a thousand words.

Sincere thanks go to the warm and friendly members of the Newfoundland Club of England, especially Diane Sellers, Carol Cooper and Maggie Tyler, and all the Canadian Newfoundland breeders and exhibitors, particularly Jackie Petrie of Newfoundland for sharing information and important photographs.

I trust that Newfoundland breeders in all the countries of the world where the breed is known and loved will continue to work together on the breed's behalf in the future as they have in the past.

A very special thank-you must go to my editor, Seymour Weiss, of Howell Book House, for the time and patience he took to make me into an author. Seymour is obviously as tenacious as his Westies!

I only hope that future owners and breeders of these wonderful animals will enjoy reading this book and learning from it as much as I enjoyed writing it. This book reflects only one small part of the wonderful world of the Newfoundland, but if it makes being a part of that world more meaningful for you, I shall be well rewarded. As a Newfoundland person, always remember that you are part of a unique fancy and that you hold the future of an equally unique breed of dog in your hands.

JOAN C. BENDURE

The
Newfoundland

From Macgilvray's *History of British Quadrupeds* (1790) we have the above etching entitled "The Newfoundland Dog—Original Breed." The dog has a white muzzle and blaze, white chest and feet, a triangular head and sparse furnishings.

1

Origin and History
of the Newfoundland

T HE ONLY undisputable statement that can be made regarding the origin of the Newfoundland breed is that it originated in the easternmost Canadian province for which it is named. Most historians of the breed acknowledge the rather frustrating fact that little is to be found in the way of legitimate historical documentation. Most of what we have consists of anecdote, combined with speculation, intelligent guessing and, on the part of some writers, fanciful thinking. After briefly describing the land of this breed's origin and giving some background on canine evolution, I will put before you what I consider some of the more credible theories. From that, I invite you to draw your own conclusions.

LAND OF ORIGIN

Newfoundland is one of the Canadian Maritime provinces and consists of the large island of Newfoundland, along with some smaller ones, and Labrador, which is the easternmost portion of the Canadian mainland. The island of Newfoundland itself lies to the east of the Gulf of St. Lawrence and directly south of Labrador, separated by the Belle Isle Strait.

Its climate is northern maritime with cool summers and cold winters, often made all the more harsh by blasts of arctic air from the frigid reaches north of Hudson's Bay. The terrain is spectacular, characterized by rugged hills and mountains, icy cold lakes and streams and a jagged, rocky coastline.

1

DOMESTICATION—HOW THE CANINE
BECAME MAN'S BEST FRIEND

The association between humankind and the dog was probably the result of a gradual process beginning as far back as, perhaps, one hundred to two hundred centuries ago. As our relationship became closer and we became more sophisticated in the art and science of genetic manipulation, a wide variety of dog breeds evolved, ranging from the ancient Saluki to relatively recent types, of which the Newfoundland is one.

Many factors have influenced the breeding of dogs, resulting in a wide variety of physical and behavioral characteristics.

Contemporary dog breeds resulted from the selection of specific physical and behavioral characteristics. In the case of the Newfoundland, the evidence indicates that they were especially bred to be large, powerful, even-tempered working dogs who could be used for a variety of tasks that required strength, endurance, adaptability to a harsh climate and an innate ability to work cooperatively with their human masters. But beyond this reasonable conclusion, tracing the actual development of the Newfoundland breed becomes an exercise in drawing conclusions from stories, casual notes and incidental observations.

FOUNDATION OF THE NEWFOUNDLAND BREED

Around A.D. 1000, Leif Ericson explored Newfoundland, and according to some accounts was accompanied by a large black "bear dog" named Oolum; there is now universally accepted archeological evidence that his fellow Vikings temporarily colonized this land (which means they also brought with them their domesticated animals, including large dogs) for some sixty or so years. After that Newfoundland may have occasionally been visited by Greenlanders in search of timber. But it was pretty much forgotten until it was rediscovered by John Cabot, sailing under the English flag, in 1497.

During the sixteenth century, the cold Atlantic waters off Newfoundland became a popular fishing ground for Portuguese, Basque, French and English fishermen. Some of them established settlements complete with domestic animals, including dogs.

But the fact that the Europeans were not the first human inhabitants of this land should not be overlooked. There is evidence of ancient Native American (North American Indian) habitation as far back as 6500 B.C. on the west coast of the island of Newfoundland. These people also had domesticated canines, some of which are reported to have been fairly large, and it is safe to assume that these dogs interbred with the ones introduced by the Norse colonists.

The type of dog that resulted from this interbreeding was then genetically isolated for several hundred years until Newfoundland's rediscovery.

Let us first start out with what we do know. We do know that the Native American population in that region had dogs. From archeological information they appear to have been Spitz or of Northern type, with triangular-shaped heads, pointed muzzles, small, erect ears and curled tails. There is even some evidence that the North American Indians crossed their dogs with wolves. It is obvious, then, that if the native dogs of Newfoundland are behind the Newfoundland dog of today, there had to be a strong outside influence of other breeds.

We do know that the French, Basque, English and Portuguese fishermen, and the earlier Vikings, brought dogs with them, and we can be reasonably certain as to what type those were. Subsequent European, although primarily English, settlers who came to Newfoundland also brought their dogs with them. So there was a period, from 1500 to 1700, when dogs from all over Europe came to Newfoundland. In all probability they were bred to the dogs native to the island of Newfoundland.

Stetson, Drury and others subscribe to the theory that the genetic forerunner of the Newfoundland breed is the large black "bear dog" named Oolum, brought to the island by Leif Ericson. It is also believed that the Norse dogs were descended from the Tibetan Mastiff and that these dogs bred with the native stock that existed on the island at that time.

Later on, with the rediscovery and colonization of Newfoundland, a number of breeds were introduced that did include Great Pyrenees Mountain, Basque spaniels, sheepdogs of various kinds, and Portuguese Water Dogs. Dogs of these breeds mated with the descendants of the Norse black "bear dogs" and native forms as mentioned above.

These couplings, combined with the effects of geographical isolation, a harsh climate and the practical requirements of farmers and fishermen, have produced the large, heavily coated black dog that we know today as the New-foundland.

Aside from what I have explained so far, and since no accurate breeding records exist prior to the latter half of the 1800s, almost everything else we know of the development of the Newfoundland before that time is limited to speculation based on what are often fascinating stories and numerous incidental notes from diaries, journals and other documents.

There is also, to put it mildly, a very wide diversity of opinions as to which ancestral breeds contributed what characteristics to today's Newfoundland. I will mention several I believe are worthy of consideration as well as those I regard as more fanciful although interesting for, if nothing else, their creativity.

Let us first begin with the previously cited assertion by Stetson and Drury that the Newfoundland's ancestor was Leif Ericson's large black Norse "bear dog", which is believed to have been derived from the Tibetan Mastiff. These dogs were used in Norway for hauling and guarding.

While it is true that distant ancestry to the Tibetan Mastiff could account for the Newfoundland's size and, perhaps, its coat and coloration, there are two considerations that cast doubt on this theory.

The first is geography and the second is history. Tibet is thousands of miles from Scandinavia, and I am not aware of any historical evidence that suggests there was any significant communication between these two vastly distant regions up until the time of the Viking explorations to the New World. So, how could the Tibetan Mastiff get to Norway?

I believe that the Norse black "bear dog" may very well be one of the modern Newfoundland's ancestors, but its connection to the Tibetan Mastiff is nothing more than an unsubstantiated theory.

Others have suggested the Great Pyrenees as either a basic ancestor of, or complimenting the influence of the Norse dog on, the Newfoundland. Again, as with the Tibetan Mastiff, these authors could be looking too much at size and ignoring other characteristics that make the Pyrenees' influence doubtful at best.

It is true that French, and possibly Basque, settlers brought Pyrenees with them, but the physical characteristics of the modern Newfoundland suggests only a minimal influence.

Although the Pyrenees and Newfoundland are similar in overall size and general type, the Pyrenees possesses a significant characteristic that is almost nonexistent in the Newfoundland—the double dewclaw on each rear leg. While it is a required characteristic of the Great Pyrenees, it is almost never seen in the Newfoundland. In my own experience I have seen only one Newfoundland pup with a single dewclaw on one rear leg out of the hundreds I've observed. This fact makes it hard for me to believe that there exists a direct link between the Pyrenees and the Newfoundland.

Spaniels from the Basque region of northwestern Spain have also been suggested as a primary ancestor in combination with the descendants of the Norse dog.

What I find more interesting is what I consider strong evidence for a link between the Newfoundland and Portuguese Water Dog. It is well known that as early as the 1500s fishermen from Portugal operated in the rich fishing grounds off the Newfoundland coast and established fisheries there. They carried with them the genetic forerunners of what is now known as the Portuguese Water Dog. These dogs share many of the physical and behavioral characteristics of the modern Newfoundland.

There is an unmistakable closeness in a number of physical characteristics of the two breeds. There are very close similarities in the shape of their skulls, the webbed feet, and shape of the ear.

Another particularly outstanding similarity between the two breeds is the coloration of their coats—both breeds are generally black with varying degrees of white, but there are brown specimens as well. There are also certain behavioral characteristics that are common to both breeds. Both are gregarious animals who thrive on and need human contact. Both breeds love the water and are strong swimmers. Both breeds are intelligent, have a strong working instinct and are highly trainable.

Over the past years, having owned both Newfoundlands and Portuguese Water Dogs, the amazing similarity between the two breeds has convinced me that there is a strong possibility that the Portuguese Water Dog is an ancestor of the Newfoundland.

The relationship has also been noted in *The Newfoundland*, published by

Study of an eighteenth-century Newfoundland by Reinagle from Scott's *Sportsman's Repository*. This dog exhibits the well-developed brow of the Newfoundland, but still has a very flat skull compared with the Newfoundland of today. Note the typical cat-paw-shaped Newfoundland foot, which appears too large for the overall bone.

The Newfoundland Club of the United Kingdom, and *The Complete Portuguese Water Dog* by Kathryn Braund and Deyanne Farrell Miller (Howell Book House, New York).

THE LANDSEER CONTROVERSY

The history of the breed is also complicated by a continuing controversy as to just what exactly constitutes the Newfoundland breed. It is commonly accepted that the black Newfoundland and the Landseer are one and the same: simply color variations of the same breed, the Landseer being a white dog with black markings while the self-colored Newfoundland is typically an all-black, brown or gray dog, sometimes with small white markings.

I believe that, while the two have significant genetic commonality, there may have been a combination of different breeds from which each color evolved. I ask the reader to consider the following reliable historical information.

English settlers to Newfoundland brought with them dogs, very large ones, with primarily white and tan or black coloration, so-called estate or butcher dogs.

The black Newfoundland was exported, according to historical records, primarily from the islands of St. Pierre and Miquelon, which lie to the south of the island of Newfoundland. If nothing else, this suggests a significant geographical separation between the two.

I am not disputing that the black Newfoundland and the Landseer are today the same breed. But I am convinced that there are enough differences, based on physical characteristics and behavior, to consider the two as having some distinctly different breeds in their ancestry.

Again, let us consider what we do know.

As I have already mentioned, there was originally a geographical separation between the two, the Landseer having its origins on the main island and the black Newfoundland on St. Pierre and Miquelon.

The Landseer must also be consistently bred back to the black Newfoundland stock—every two or three generations—otherwise the Landseer starts to lose Newfoundland type. The bone becomes refined, the foot takes a somewhat hare foot shape, the head and muzzle become elongated and narrower and the body lacks substance. This is becoming less of a problem than it was, as Landseer breeders have consistently bred to the blacks to maintain type. For some time the two colors were kept separate. There is a good deal of black influence in Landseer pedigrees, but one does not generally find Landseer antecedents in the pedigrees of purely black Newfoundlands. Landseer breeders were also trying to avoid incorporating the brown or gray genes in their dogs' pedigrees.

Another characteristic that should be mentioned is that the coats of the two colors can be somewhat different. The Landseer coat is sometimes fine and cottony.

There can also be a difference in temperament between blacks and Landseers. While both are intelligent, people-oriented dogs, Landseers are generally

6

more active and alert. Some people will go so far as to say the Landseer is more intelligent. Genetically black Newfoundlands, while not exactly lazy, are usually more laid back than their two-colored peers.

The Landseer has made great strides in both popularity and quality in recent decades.

THE BREED'S STORY

The Newfoundland's existence, like that of so many of our other domesticated creatures, has been at the mercy of human whim. His strength, reliability as a useful and versatile beast of burden, cooperative disposition and intelligence have, all too often, been taken for granted. This breed's survival has frequently been threatened, on at least one occasion, by erratic government dictates in his homeland, as well as by the pressures of war and the fickle nature of human interest.

Although descriptions of what must be dogs of the Newfoundland breed appear as early as the seventeenth century and there was a flourishing commercial export of these dogs to Britain, the breed itself was not formally named until the latter half of the eighteenth century. George Cartwright is responsible for naming the breed about 1775, when he applied the name of the island to his own dog.

Ironically, only five years after the breed was formally named, the Newfoundland was almost exterminated in the land of its origin by governmental proclamation. In 1780 Governor Edwards limited legal ownership of the dog to one per family. The dogs were to be shipped out or destroyed. The rationale for this extreme measure was that it would, somehow, promote sheep raising. It was, however, a tragic failure because it had no effect on the island's sheep production but almost wiped out the Newfoundland breed in its homeland.

The only reason the breed survived (and just barely so) on the island was that the inhabitants ignored the decree: the Newfoundland dog was simply too valuable to destroy or export. He more than earned his keep: pulling heavy sledges, serving on fishing boats by retrieving objects (including human masters) and helping haul in fish-laden nets. So, many Newfoundlanders simply ignored the proclamation. But it would not be until the turn of this past century that the Newfoundland would once again begin to flourish in his native land.

By the late eighteenth century a number had made their way to the southern colonies (which later became the United States), despite the fact that many of the colonies had prohibitions against large dog breeds.

One American dog, QueQue, was owned by the patriot Samuel Adams. This remarkable dog gained some notoriety for himself during the British occupation of Boston by, as Drury says, harassing the redcoated troops "in every way possible." Perhaps the dog was attuned to his master's political sensitivities?

Another American Newfoundland, Scannon, accompanied Lewis and Clark on their famous expedition to the Pacific Northwest coast in 1802. He was not a mere mascot, but a valuable member of the party, assisting in hunting and retrieving game, and protecting expedition members from bears and other animals who might look upon humans as simply another link in their food chain. During the expedition some Indians dognapped Scannon with the apparent intention of converting him into canine cuisine. But a rescue party found Scannon in time, and his Indians captors had the good sense to surrender him, probably saving their own scalps.

In 1919 a small steamer, the *Ethie*, ran aground off Newfoundland's rocky coast. The surf and rocks made launching the lifeboats impossible, and the shore was too far to shoot a land line. A Newfoundland dog that just happened to be on board was given a line and swam to shore with it. The crew was then able to rig a boatswain's chair, and all on board were safely evacuated. No man could have made the shore: anyone foolhardy enough to make such an attempt would have been pulverized on the rocks by the pounding breakers.

During the first half of the 1800s the Newfoundland was also becoming known in parts of Europe, aside from England and the United States. In the 1830s and 1850s the legendary St. Bernard breed was in danger of extinction from disease and congenital defects, which were the result of too many years of inbreeding. The breed was saved from genetic oblivion by crossbreeding it with Newfoundlands, who were imported for that purpose.

Chroniclers of this period have also mentioned that both Napoleon I and his archenemy Lord Nelson had Newfoundlands. A number of heroic exploits have been attributed to these dogs, which probably contributed to the Newfoundland's reputation as, as Drury notes, "the hero dog."

On this side of the Atlantic the Newfoundland was contributing to the development of the Labrador and Chesapeake Bay Retrievers.

Although, as is the case with the Newfoundland, there are no reliable breeding records for this period, most of the early documentation cites the area around St. John's, which is on the island of Newfoundland, as the place where the Lab (the "Lesser Newfoundland") originated, rather than Labrador itself. And, although the Lab has a short coat and is smaller than the Newfoundland, Drury and others reasonably presume that the two, "had common ancestors but developed in the same area to be two distinct breeds with many common qualities."

The first recorded official showing of the breed occurred at the Birmingham (England) dog show of 1860, where six Newfoundlands were entered. Later, in 1878, the first registry of dogs was established, and from this point on the history of the breed can be documented with reasonable accuracy, at least in England. In 1886 the first breed club was established.

In the United States, despite the Newfoundland's popularity as a house pet during the 1890s, the breed was not granted official status by the American Kennel Club until 1914, when the first Newfoundland breed club, the Newfoundland Club of America, was recognized. Because the Club either kept few records or what records did exist have been lost, the reasons for its decline and dissolution are not known. In 1928 the Club lost membership in AKC for nonpayment of dues.

The Larger Newfoundland Dog (Youatt).

The St. John's or Labrador.

"The Larger Newfoundland Dog" by Orrin Smith (Youatt) and "The St. John's or Labrador" by G. Earl. These pictures are from *Stonehenge on the Dog* published in 1887. Stonehenge writes that there are several types of Newfoundland dogs, but states that the true island breed is considered a black dog, no more than 25 inches at the shoulder; however, in England they prefer dogs that are 30 or 31 inches, and Stonehenge believes that the larger Newfoundland is the correct type. He refers to the St. John's Newfoundland or Labrador as the small variety of Newfoundland; the color is always black, with a wavy, oily coat possessing no undercoat. The small variety was exported mainly to Hull, England. I would have to believe that the St. John's Newfoundland pictured had more influence on the black Newfs of England at the turn of the century than the larger Newfoundland. The Newfoundlands in the United States as recently as the 1960s had oilier coats, with much less undercoat than do the Newfoundlands of today.

9

"Leo," a top winning dog in England in the late 1800s, owned by Mr. S. W. Wildman (later by Mr. Howard Mapplebeck), from *Cassell's Illustrated Book of the Dog.*

Between 1922 and 1924 the North American Newfoundland Club was established. This organization wrote a Standard for the breed and staged the first recorded American water trials in 1929. (The British started them earlier.) But its history is also obscured by a lack of relevant documentation. Drury mentions that there was an unsuccessful attempt to merge with the present-day Newfoundland Club of America (which was founded in 1930) but that most of the members of the North American Newfoundland Club joined the latter organization.

World War I almost destroyed the breed in England. Food rationing made it impossible for breeders to continue their programs. But although only a few survived, twenty-two dogs registered in 1923, the quality of the breed remained high, which was fortunate, since the breed was also languishing on this side of the Atlantic, both in the United States and Canada. A number of English dogs were exported to fortify the weakened North American lines. It is interesting that even though the Newfoundland is one of relatively few dog breeds ever to be honored by its portrayal on a postage stamp (the Province of Newfoundland issued several versions), it was, according to a 1919 issue of *The National Geographic*, virtually on the edge of extinction: "It is a real pity that this noble, useful, and typically American dog should have lost popularity to such an extent that he is now almost never seen."

It is thanks to a small number of dedicated breeders that the Newfoundland is not only with us today but is also flourishing. Our present Newfoundland stock is actually descended from a small number of dogs.

Ch. Jonmunn Shakespeare II, bred by Dr. A. P. Munn. While the American Newfoundlands were of superior intelligence, excellent swimmers, healthy and loyal dogs, they were very much lacking in type. Shakespeare is an example of the lack of quality of the Newfoundlands in the United States prior to the importation of the Siki offspring from England around 1930.

2

Development
of the Newfoundland
in the United States

DESPITE THE FACT that, during the latter half of the 1800s, up until the turn of the century, the Newfoundland was one of the most popular American dogs, the registration records show very few Newfoundlands being registered in the United States and even fewer in Canada.

The first Newfoundland champion was Sam, in 1883. It would be thirty years before the next Newfoundland gained a championship. That was Major II, a dog of unknown parentage who was registered on his winnings.

Graydon's New Jersey Big Boy, a Landseer, was the third Newfoundland to win a championship in the United States. Graydon was the first imported Newfoundland to win his championship. Both his sire and dam were grandchildren of the famous English Ch. Shelton Viking, Best in Show Newfoundland of the 1908 Crufts Show.

At this time American-bred Newfoundlands closely resembled oversized contemporary Labrador Retrievers with curly, heavy double coats. They were small-bodied, had flat heads, with high-set ears, and elongated muzzles.

But what they lacked in beauty, they made up for in other ways, like superior intelligence, natural water instinct, hardiness and longevity.

It was only through the concerted effort of a very small number of dedicated breeders and fanciers that the Newfoundland breed in the United States escaped extinction.

Newfoundlands in Canada were not faring much better in the postwar years.

On the other side of the Atlantic in Great Britian, the breed had been kept going by a handful of dedicated people. And although after the war their numbers were small and the gene pool limited, the quality was high.

Newfoundlands in England had been bred for the physical traits that we now see in modern specimens: the massive head and body, heavy bone and rich, thick coats.

Then came the revitalization period of the Newfoundland breed in both the United States and Canada with the import of the Siki bloodline from England; one particular English champion, Siki, is credited with siring most of the English imports who revived the Newfoundland breed in the United States. What remained of the American lines was genetically overwhelmed by the English dogs.

In 1929 Miss Elizabeth Loring (later Mrs. Power), of Waseeka Kennels, "made a grand entry into the Newfoundland ring," according to Chern, with Ch. Seafarer, who was sired by Siki and out of Kaffi Girl.

Waseeka imported other Siki stock: Ch. Seagrave Blackberry, Ch. Harlingen Neptune of Waseeka and Harlingen Jess of Waseeka.

These, along with other English imports, laid the foundation for an ambitious and very successful breeding program, which made Waseeka the dominant Newfoundland kennel from 1929 well into the 1940s.

Other English imports that crossed the Atlantic to North America were Can. Ch. Shelton Cabin Boy and Can. Ch. Shelton Baron imported into Canada.

During the early thirties Mr. John Cameron of Ossining, New York, joined with Mrs. Eleanor Ayers Jameson to form Camayer Kennels to promote and improve the Landseers. Mrs. Jameson became interested in crossing blacks with the Landseers to strengthen Landseer lines. They aquired Ch. Oquaga's Sea Pirate, a top winning dog of the forties and fifties. Pirate, or "Pat," as he was called, was bred to all of their Landseers.

In 1944 Mrs. Jameson changed the kennel name to Seaward.

Nell Ayers, Mrs. Jameson's daughter, took over the kennel after the latter's death. Nell became active in the Newfoundland Club of America, serving as president for a period of time. Seaward went on to have the distinction of owning the top-winning Newfoundland in the history of the breed: Am., Can. Ch. Seaward's Blackbeard, ROM. "Adam," as Blackbeard was known, won two National Specialty Bests of Breed and in 1984 became the first and only Newfoundland to date to win Best in Show at the Westminster Kennel Club show. The judge was Kitty Drury.

Oquaga Kennels, founded in 1935, owned by Mr. and Mrs. Clifford F. Hartz, must be mentioned because of its significant contribution to the modern Newfoundland breed and the kennel's direct role in its resurrection. The Hartzes' original breeding was based on the Canadian Shelton line. In 1940 the Hartzes purchased Can. Ch. Laurel Brae's Gale, in whelp to her sire, Ch. Shelton Sea Diver. This produced only one puppy, Oquaga's Black Beauty, who in turn went on to produce many fine Newfoundlands.

"The Father of Champions," English Ch. Siki, whose offspring were imported into the United States during the late 1920s and early 1930s. While Siki himself was not an outstanding example of a Newfoundland, he was certainly a very prepotent sire that produced outstanding progeny. That progeny when crossed with the American-bred Newfoundland quickly improved the type of our dogs. Almost all Newfoundlands today can trace their pedigrees back to Siki.

CHAMPION SIKI

SIRE — Shelton King

- Gipsy Viscount
  - Zingari Chief
    - Gipsy Duke
      - Shelton Viking
      - Molly Bawn
    - Lady Melbourne
  - Hallside Crocus
    - Thornhill Top Gallant
      - Shelton Viking
      - Thornhill Rival
    - Hallside Roma
      - Pudsey's Scout
      - Easen Beauty
- Mollie
  - Omega
    - Shelton Viking
      - Lord Rosebery
      - Shelton Madge
        - King Stuart
        - Queenie
    - Shelton Madge
      - King Stuart
      - Seaweed
  - Tylehurst Lassie
    - Prince of Suffolk
      - Prince of Norfolk
      - Ladysmaid
    - Corona
      - Brookdale
      - Humber Snowflake

DAM — Rothwell Bess

- Gipsy Boy
  - Gipsy Baron
    - Fearless Foundation
      - Sir Alpha
      - Fearless Emblem
        - Shelton Viking
        - Black Columbin
    - Kista
  - Anchoria
    - Dondo
      - Lord Methuen
      - Jester
    - Louina
- Galphay Jess

15

Int. Ch. Seafarer, produced from a breeding of Siki to one of his daughters, was imported to the United States by Miss Elizabeth Loring (later Mrs. Power) of Waseeka Kennels. A top winner, he had four all-breed Bests in Show, many Group wins and Best of Breed at Westminster in 1931 and 1932.

Ch. Harlingen Neptune of Waseeka, a Siki son whelped in 1929 and imported from England. Neptune became an influential stud dog, siring ten champions, including the first two American-bred Best in Show Newfoundlands, and the first Obedience titlist.

It is dogs from the Oquaga line that are behind all the prepotent sires in the pedigrees of today's Newfoundlands: Ch. Dryad's Sea Rover, Dryad's Goliath of Gath, Int. Ch. Newton.

The Hartzes' knowledge and precise records allowed them to successfully linebreed and inbreed to quickly produce the type they desired. Unfortunately, in 1948 disaster hit the Oquaga Kennels. A distemper virus wiped out twenty-two of their twenty-four Newfs.

Many breeders offered them stock in the wake of their misfortune, and the kennel was restarted using breeding stock from the Waseeka and Coastwise Kennels. A number of champions resulted from this, among them Ch. Oquaga's Sea Pirate (owned by Seaward Kennels), Ch. Oquaga's Queen Mary and Ch. Oquaga's Molly Nine Mile, the foundation bitch for Barton and Anne Williams, Nine Mile Newfoundlands. Many kennels today can trace their bloodlines back to the Oquaga line.

Coastwise Kennels of California was started in the early 1940s by Mrs. A. B. Hilton, later to become Mrs. Major B. Godsol. Coastwise was based on the Waseeka bloodline and played a major role in the breed's revival.

Mrs. Godsol trained the first CD and CDX Newfoundland in this country, Ch. Mark Anthony of Waseeka, CDX. He was also the first Newfoundland to win a Group on the West Coast.

Mr. and Mrs. Godsol were both AKC all-breed judges and officers of the NCA.

Many dogs can trace their pedigrees back to Ch. Coastwise Steamboat Bill, Can. Ch. Coastwise Shore Leave and Ch. Coastwise Tugboat Annie.

Bing Crosby used Coastwise Newfoundlands for his breeding stock.

Midway Kennels, owned by Mr. and Mrs. Fred Stubbart, of Columbia, South Carolina, came on the scene during World War II. They imported entire litters from all over the world and kept the best specimens for breeding stock. Canadian stock became their foundation, which was later combined with linebred stock descending from the famous Siki offspring, Baron and Cabin Boy. This combination produced the memorable Am., Can. Ch. Midway Black Ledge Sea Raider in 1948.

Raider was co-bred by Zatha Hockridge, owner of Black Ledge Kennel in Nova Scotia, and was Best in Show in the United States at the Long Island Kennel Club in 1953. Raider became the foundation stud for Little Bear Kennels and was the first of nine consecutive generations of Best in Show or Group winners for the Little Bear establishment of Margaret and Vadim Chern.

Among other Midway champions were Ch. Stubbart's Greetings O'Lady, Midway Sea Queen, Midway Sea Raider, Midway Black Ace and Stubbart's Nelson.

Dryad Kennels, established by Mr. and Mrs. Maynard K. Drury, has been the most influential kennel for our present-day Newfoundlands. Kitty and Maynard were married in 1940 and started Dryad in 1943 at their Long Island

Impressive lineup of champions from Waseeka Kennels in the 1930s. Left to right: Ch. Seafarer, Ch. Waseeka's Sea King, Ch. Waseeka's Sailor Boy, Ch. Waseeka's Triton, Ch. Waseeka's Skipper and Ch. Waseeka's Pete the Pirate.

Ch. Oquaga's Sea Pirate, whelped in 1946, beautiful Group-winning dog during his time. "Pat" was owned by Seaward Kennels and was crossed to their Landseers to enhance the type.

Ch. Dryad's Coastwise Showboat, whelped in 1946, the first Newfoundland bitch to win a Best in Show. Owned by Mr. and Mrs. Major B. Godsol of Coastwise Kennels and later sold back to her breeders, Mr. and Mrs. Maynard K. Drury, Dryad Kennels.

home. The Dryad Kennel was based on the Waseeka and Coastwise bloodlines. Kitty's love affair with the Newfoundland breed had started many years before, when her grandmother presented her with her first Newfoundland, a dog named "Gyp," imported from Newfoundland. Kitty's first show dog was Ch. Harlingen Viking of Waseeka in 1928.

In the 1950s the Godsols, Mrs. Power and the Drurys decided that their dogs were not as good as they should have been. They had been linebreeding for many years and felt that an outcross was necessary. Mrs. Godsol went to Holland and imported two bitches, Saskie and Beatrice. They bred them to the best dogs they had available and then bred the pups from that, back into the line. The good dogs of today go back to that outcrossed line.

Dryad Kennels never kept a large number of dogs; they usually only had six or eight at a time. The foundation stock for Dryad Kennels was Waseeka Crusoe and Ch. Waseeka's Hesperus. The Drurys bred over fifty champions, including three all breed Best in Show winners.

Ch. Dryad Coastwise Showboat was the first Best in Show Newfoundland bitch. In fact, she won five Bests in Show in all and is the only Newfoundland ever to finish a championship without ever defeating another Newfoundland. She won three Groups to finish. Unfortunately, she never produced.

Some of the more notable dogs carrying the Dryad prefix were Dryad's Goliath of Gath, ROM; Ch. Dryad's Sea Rover, ROM; Ch. Dryad's George, ROM; Can. Ch. Dryad's Bounty, ROM; Ch. Dryad's Lord Nelson, UDT, ROM; Ch. Dryad's Strong Sea Pirate and multiple BIS winner and Heroic Newf Ch. Dryad's Flagship, ROM. Dryad was also the birthplace of many notable bitches, some that became the foundation dams for various kennels: Dryad's Gum Drop, ROM, and litter sisters Ch. Dryad's Christine of Glenora, ROM, and Ch. Dryad's Nancy of Glenora, ROM, that were the foundation for Edenglen Kennels. Dryad's Helen of Troy, CD, ROM; Dryad's Christmas Holly, ROM; Dryad's Lake Rova, ROM, owned by Jim Schmoyer; the ever-beautiful Ch. Dryad's Compass Rose, ROM, owned by Shipshape Kennel; Ch. Dryad's Candy's Duchess, ROM, of Tranquilus Kennels; Dryad's Kleine Baer, ROM, owned by Manzer; Ch. Dryad's Anthony's Penelope, ROM, owned by Halirock Kennels; and Ch. Dryad's Brigantine, CD, ROM.

Kitty and Maynard were both very active in the NCA, having both served as president and AKC delegate, working on many committees, and both were AKC-approved judges. Along with their busy dog activities they found time to raise and enjoy their five children. Together they founded and operated the Dryad Die Casting Company of Manchester, New York. After Maynard's death, Kitty continued running the company and raising Newfoundlands.

When Kitty retired from the die casting business she moved to her last home, Mark Twain Camp on Saranac Lake, New York. Upon retirement in 1973 Kitty transferred ownership of the Dryad prefix to her daughter Mary Drury Dewey of Conifer, Colorado.

Kitty celebrated her fiftieth anniversary in Newfoundlands with a huge dinner party in Lake Placid, New York, following the National Specialty in the fall of 1978.

Ch. Dryad's Sea Rover, ROM (Oquaga's Sea Diver II ex Dryad's Sultana), was a Group winner owned by Mr. and Mrs. Robert Lister of Shipshape Kennel. Rover is being shown here by his breeder, Mrs. Kitty Drury. Rover was a large, typey dog that will be found in the pedigrees of most of the current top producers.

Ch. Dryad's Lord Nelson, UDT, ROM (Dryad's Goliath of Gath ex Dryad's Lake Rova, ROM), foundation sire of Mrs. George McDonnell's Kilyka Kennel.

Ch. Shipshape's Sibyl, UDT, ROM (Can. Ch. Dryad's Bounty, ROM, ex Am., Can. Ch. Dryad's Compass Rose, ROM). Bred by Shipshape Kennels of Christine Lister. Sibyl is the foundation bitch of Betty McDonnell's Kilyka Kennel, the first Newfoundland bitch to earn all the Obedience titles, and is the all-time top producing Newfoundland bitch with fourteen champions, ten working titlists and two ROM offspring.

As the invitations came out, the phone lines were buzzing with everyone wanting to know who else had been invited to this very special party. An invitation was like your acceptance into the Newfoundland world.

Everyone was prepared to give a speech on Kitty and the wonderful Dryad dogs, but Kitty turned the tables on us as only Kitty could do. Kitty went from table to table, individually introducing everyone there and made special comments, without notes, about each person. Kitty wanted no special accolades for herself, she just wanted to enjoy a good time with her family and friends.

Kitty traveled all over the world judging but always reserved the month of August for her grandchildren.

Kitty was tragically killed on October 13, 1988, when her vehicle went off the road near Burlington, Vermont. She was on her way home from a judging assignment, and traveling with her was Ch. Dryad's Hesperus of Willowrun, known affectionately as Nanny.

Nanny exemplified all that Newfoundlands have been known for, as Joan and Roger Fosters' description of Nanny's reaction ''during a time of stress and confusion'' will attest.

> The car was demolished after it hit a rock ledge and flipped over. Somehow Nanny survived the accident. She never fussed and remained calm, quiet and friendly as she was freed from the car, winning the hearts of rescue workers, state troopers and the veterinarians who tended her. When we drove up to get Nanny, the veterinarian who stabilized her following the accident commented on how good she had been, and then he said, ''She has a sixth sense; she has been very sad.''

It was decided that Nanny would live with Jack and Carmen Drury and their children on the edge of the lake where she had lived with Kitty.

Mary Drury Dewey has carried on the Dryad Kennel by producing twenty title holders.

Little Bear Kennels, established in 1948 by Margaret and Vadim Chern, has been a very successful kennel, producing over one hundred champion Newfoundlands, National Specialty winners, Best in Show dogs, along with many Working Group winners and placers.

The Little Bear line was originally based on Midway and Black Ledge breedings with two later outcrosses: the Perryhow bloodline was introduced in the 1950s and the Newton line, through Dryad's Compass Rose, in the latter part of the 1960s.

Chern credits one particular Newfoundland, Am., Can., Ber. & Bahamas Ch. Newton, with inspiring the popularity of the breed during the 1960s. Newton won 15 Bests in Show, 55 Group Firsts, 138 other Group placements, 8 Specialty Bests, and 199 Bests of Breed. He became so well known that it was not uncommon to hear Newfoundlands accidentally referred to as ''Newtons.'' (An interesting and amusing aside to this occurred in 1968, when another champion, James Thurber, won Best in Show at Buffalo, New York, and the local paper carried the headline, ''Black St. Bernard Wins Best in Show.'')

Some of the top producing dogs and bitches that were owned or bred by Little Bear were Ch. Little Bear Canicula Campio, ROM; Ch. Little Bear's Roaring Main, ROM; Ch. Little Bear's Sargent Pepper, ROM; Ch. Bonnavista, ROM; Seastar of Perryhow, ROM; Ch. Little Bear Isolt of Irwindyl, CD, ROM, owned by Geraldine Irwin; Little Bear Primavista, ROM; Ch. Little Bear's Round Kim, ROM, owned by Ned Brower; Ch. Little Bear Cutty Hunk, ROM, owned by Nashau-Auke Kennel; and Little Bear Briny Deep, ROM, owned by Claire Ives.

In 1955 Margaret wrote *The Complete Newfoundland* and was almost finished with the updated edition, titled *The New Complete Newfoundland*, when she died while undergoing surgery in January of 1975. Margaret's husband, Vadim, completed the book. *The New Complete Newfoundland* is filled with delightful stories of Newfoundland antics, and Newfs with famous people.

After Vadim's death in 1980, the few dogs remaining and the Little Bear kennel name went to Virginia Wooster, who is continuing with the line today.

Irwindyl Kennels, owned by Mrs. Geraldine Irwin of Pennsylvania, began breeding and showing in the late 1940s, and produced many champions. The bloodlines were Kenmount, Perivale, Midway, and some Little Bear. Some outstanding champions were Lady Belle Isolt; Little Bear's Isolt Irwindyl, CD; Sir Lil Abner; Lady Guenievere, CD; Sir Aliking; Sir Aliduke; King Arthur; and Sir Lionel.

Harobed Hill Kennels was active in showing and breeding in the 1950s and has produced a number of champions based on Waseeka and Dryad stock. Among them are Harobed's Sheila Pike and Everloving Dino.

Kwasind Kennels of Syracuse, New York, owned by Dr. and Mrs. John D. Thompson, produced a number of champions starting in the early 1950s. Some of their champions were Jennie Cake Jennie, Princess Starfire, Feather in Her Cap, War Dance, St. Mary's O'Lady and Tao of Kwasind. They also owned Ch. Little Bear's Black Sambo, Ch. Little Bear's Tippo and Ch. Little Bear's Jiminy Cricket. Tippo's son, Little Bear's Royal Top Gallant, was exported to Denmark, where he became an outstanding show dog and sire.

Black Mischief Kennels of Le Roy, Kansas, owned by Alice Weaver, was also active in the early 1950s and produced champions based on Midway, Little Bear and Finnish bloodlines. Three outstanding Black Mischief champions were Christopher, Molly Brown and El Toro.

Temanend Kennels, owned by Captain and Mrs. Henri Rice have made significant contributions to the breed. Among their best known champions were Temanend Black Dolphin, Lady Nora, Price Henry, Misty Dawn and Snow Flurry.

24

The late Margaret Booth Chern, who along with her husband, Vadim, established Little Bear Kennels in 1948. Little Bear was the breeder of over 100 champions, a record that stood in the breed for many years, including numerous Best in Show, Group and Specialty winners. Margaret was also the author of two books on Newfoundlands.

Am., Can. Ch. Little Bear's James Thurber (Am., Can. Ch. Midway's Black Ledge Sea Raider ex Ch. Bonnavista, ROM), whelped in 1951. James had eight Bests in Show, the record for the breed until 1965. Bred by Little Bear Kennels and owned by Robert Dowling.

The 1960s saw the establishment of a number of kennels that have had a strong influence on the breed today.

Edenglen Kennels of Glenora, New York, owned by Willis and Helena Linn, was based primarily on Dryad bloodlines. The Linns' home and kennel had the most magnificent location, on the shores of beautiful Lake Seneca. A lovely crystal-clear stream flowed past the kennels and emptied into the lake. If you followed the stream a short distance, you came to a beautiful waterfall that cascaded into a pool below and then flowed out into the stream. Sitting on the porch watching the Newfs playing in the lake you truly thought you were in paradise.

Bill and Helena's foundation for their kennel were the top producing litter sisters—Ch. Dryad's Christine of Glenora, ROM, and Ch. Dryad's Nancy of Glenora, ROM.

Some of Edenglen's outstanding show dogs and producers included Am., Can. Ch. Edenglen's Banner, ROM, twice Best of Breed at the National Specialty; Ch. Edenglen's Beau Geste, ROM, and Ch. Edenglen's Oscar, ROM, both owned by the Dibbles of California; and Edenglen's Tucker, ROM, and Edenglen's Christopher Robin III, ROM. Both Tucker and Christopher were owned by the Linns.

Notable among the bitches was the gray Edenglen's Jenny Reitel, ROM, and Ch. Edenglen's Becky, ROM, owned by the Linns; Ch. Edenglen's Witch of Sojowase, ROM, owned by Sojowase Kennels; Ch. Edenglen's Prudence, ROM, owned by Shadybrook Kennels; Ch. Edenglen's Wistful Wendy, ROM, and Harbour Beem Ethie, ROM.

The Shipshape Kennels of Bob and Wilma Lister of Cape Cod, Massachusetts, was established in 1962 using dogs from the Dryad bloodline. The Listers owned and produced some of the most outstanding dogs in the Newfoundland breed: Ch. Dryad's Sea Rover, ROM; Am., Can. Ch. Dryad's Compass Rose, ROM, a Newton daughter out of Dryad's Christmas Holly; Ch. Shipshape's Cutty Sark, ROM; the all-time top producing bitch Ch. Shipshape's Sibyl, ROM, foundation bitch for Kilyka Kennels; Ch. Shipshape's Windsong; Ch. Shipshape's Cranberry Rose; Ch. Shipshape's Mighty Like a Rose; Ch. Shipshape's Spinnaker Rose; and Ch. Shipshape's Comin Up Roses.

Shipshape Kennels produced the foundation stock for the following kennels. Kilyka, Mooncusser, Nashua-Auke and Dalken Kennels.

The Tranquilus Kennels of Jim and Dot Bellows of Sterling, New York, were based on Dryad breeding stock. The Bellowses had the good fortune to own Ch. Dryad's Candy's Duchess, ROM, a top producing bitch of the sixties, and Dryad's Naval Prince.

Tranquilus produced such notables as Ch. Franco Cassandra and Ch. Dryad's Anthony Penelope, ROM, two of the foundation bitches of Halirock Kennels. Also among the Bellowses' standard bearers were Ch. Tranquilus Neptune; Am., Can. Ch. Tranquilus Tempting Tidbit; Ch. Tranquilus Betty of Subira, National Specialty Best of Breed winner: Ch. Tranquilus Semy Gold

Am., Can. Ch. Edenglen's Banner, ROM (Ch. Dryad's Sea Rover, ROM, ex Ch. Dryad's Christine of Glenora, ROM), bred by Edenglen Kennels of Helena and Bill Linn and owned by Mae S. Freeland of Bandom Acres. Banner won Best of Breed at two National Specialties and was a multiple all-breed Best in Show winner.

Ch. Edenglen's Beau Geste, ROM (Ch. Dryad's Sea Rover, ROM, ex Ch. Dryad's Nancy of Glenora, ROM), a top winning and producing Newfoundland from the late 1960s, owned by Robert and Frances Dibble of California. Beau produced 25 champions, eight working titlists and two ROMs.

Ch. Edenglen's Oscar, ROM (Ch. Dryad's George, ROM, ex Edenglen's Eleanor), bred by Edenglen Kennels. Oscar was another well-known top winning and producing dog owned by Robert and Frances Dibble. He did much to influence the breed in the early 1970s, by passing on his massive head and bone. Oscar was also the first multi-regional Specialty winner.

Vulcan, ROM; Ch. Tranquilus Banner Duch Baby, ROM; Ch. Tranquilus Taffy, ROM; Ch. Tranquilus Honey Bear, ROM.

For many years the Dryad and Little Bear bloodlines were seldom bred to one another. It was as if there was some unwritten law that you either bred from Little Bear bloodlines or Dryad, but you didn't mix the two. Perhaps it was because the each kennel produced a different type.

The Little Bear dogs usually were smaller overall, were shorter in body length, and because of that had stronger toplines and shorter hocks with more rear angulation. Some of the heads appeared flat.

The Dryad Newfoundlands were usually larger throughout, had more bone and larger heads with more dome and more depth of muzzle. They also tended to be longer backed and straighter in the rear.

The Little Bear dogs were better balanced, but the Dryad dogs were typier.

Am., Can., Bah., Ber. Ch. Newton, ROM (Topsail's Captain Bob Bartlett ex Merry of Sperry), bred by the Hon. Harold MacPherson of Westerland Kennels in Newfoundland, Canada, and owned by Melvin Sokolsky. Shown with his handler, Alan Levine, Newton held the record as the all-time top winning Newfoundland for many years with fifteen Bests in Show, 199 Bests of Breed and eight Specialties, including two National Specialties.

3

Current U.S. Kennels

O VER THE YEARS the Newfoundland breed has been fortunate to have had the loyalty of so many truly dedicated breeders. Many of these fanciers have devoted major efforts to the development of the Newfoundland. Some breeds never have truly great kennels as Newfoundlands have enjoyed in the past fifty years.

The Newfoundland breed has made great strides in the past couple of decades, demonstrating that beautiful dogs possessing the working purpose that the breed was developed for are eminently possible. The record attests to the fact that show dogs can and do indeed work. Gone are the days of thinking that working Newfoundlands are the small, untypical dogs that can't make it in a show ring.

While we have done much to promote the qualities of the breed, there is still much that needs to be done to continue to ensure the Newfoundland its proper place in the dog world in the years to come.

It is through the devotion of some of the breeders whose kennels are listed in this chapter that we have achieved ever higher ideals. Some kennels may be small in size, but have impacted the breed in a very positive manner. The American kennels have certainly earned their place in Newfoundland history by producing some of the finest dogs in the world.

Allison Acres

Connie Allison's Allison Acres Kennel, of Lunenbarf, Massachusetts, was home to Ch. Sampson of Allison Acres, the very handsome Ch. Sam's Son of

Allison Acres, and, most recently, the brown dog Ch. Allison Acres Willie Wonka.

Amity

Tom and Diane Broderick, of Franklin Lakes, New Jersey, purchased their first Newfoundland in 1974 and began the Amity breeding program in 1977. Since that time, the Brodericks have emphasized both beauty and brains in their Newfoundlands. Their first dog was Newton Ark's Pax of Pouch Cove, CD, WD, and their first bitch was Ch. Nerissa of Pouch Cove, UD, WRD.

Showing and training typey Newfoundlands has become a way of life at Amity since the early days. This is best illustrated by Tom's accomplishment of completing the requirements necessary for a Versatility title on two of the Amity Newfoundlands in one day (VN Ch. Amity's Applause of Pouch Cove, WRD, DD, and VN Ch. Amity's Storm Tide Sensation UD, WRD, DD). Indeed, to date Tom's training, persistence and gentle manner with the Newfoundlands has resulted in four UDs, five WRDs, three CDs and three WDs.

While Tom pursues the training and handling dogs to conformation and working titles, it is Diane who manages the breeding program at Amity. Though Diane and Tom have bred many attractive dogs, their most successful combination resulted when Ch. Pouch Cove Gref of Newton Ark bred the lovely Amity's Daydream of Pouch Cove, CD. This breeding produced Ch. Amity's Bearfoot of Pouch Cove, ROM, Ch. Amity's Osborne of Pouch Cove and Ch. Amity's Pipedream of Pouch Cove, in addition to several working titlists. Bearfoot left Amity at three months of age, though after his new owners were unable to keep him, he was eventually returned and went to live with David and Peggy Helming at Pouch Cove, Peggy being Bearfoot's co-breeder. The rest is truly Newfoundland history, and good history at that! Similar in style to his grandfather Rego, Bearfoot produced type as consistently as did his sire Gref, siring thirty-six champions, ten obedience titlists and two ROM recipients as of this writing. Pouch Cove breeding and the Bearfoot influence in particular live on at Amity today through Bearfoot's daughter Ch. Amity's Panache of Pouch Cove and his granddaughter, the Group-placing Ch. Amity Abracadabra Pouch Cove.

Aotea

Based on the Tuckamore and Dryad lines and located in Honeoye Falls, New York, Gillian McArthur's Aotea Kennel is the home and/or birthplace of Ch. Aotea Nicklaas of Tuckamore, Ch. Aotea's Bonavista Beauty, Ch. Aotea's Saint Sebastian Bay, Ch. Aotea's Lady Marlo and Ch. Aotea's Blue Chip Bruin among others.

Apogee

Using the Nashau Auke Benhil and Pouch Cove lines, Jerry and Betty Zarger's Apogee Kennel in Connecticut, is home to many working titlists and

Amity's Causin' A Commotion, DD (Am., Can. Ch. Benhil's Stillwater Gulliver ex Ch. Amity's Abracadabra Pouch Cove), bred and owned by Diane and Tom Broderick of Amity Newfoundlands. *Tatham*

Ch. Oprasus of the Good Shepherd, ROM (Ch. Good Shepherd's Joel, CD, ex Ch. Good Shepherd's Tamar). Bred by Jane Hogh Strasser and owned by Paul and Betty Ramey of Bethward Kennels. "J.R." was the top winning Newfoundland in 1980.

champions, including Ch. Cherokee Harold De Nashau Auke, Ch. Pouch Cove's Mailorder Bride, Apogee's Top Hat 'N Tails, CD, and the homebred Ch. Apogee's Windsurfer.

Apollo

Richard and Susan Beres, of Painesville, Ohio, were owners of the multiple Group winners Ch. Benhil's Lucan De Nashau Auke, Ch. Benham Knoll's Mighty Tonka and Ch. Spillway's Michael. Additional Apollo winners include Ch. Apollo's Lady Ebony and Ch. Sir Nicholas of Apollo.

Barharber

Using Tar Baby and Pouch Cove stock, David and Donna Barber, of London derry, New Hampshire, are the breeders of many champions, including Ch. Barharber's Wilbur Right, ROM, Ch. Barharber's Zebony Angel, Ch. Barharber's Puddnhead Wilson, Ch. Barharber's Just Right, Ch. Barharber's Orville Wright, Ch. Barharber's Just Claudia, Ch. Barharber's Sweet William and Ch. Barharber's Chloe. Barharber is also home to the very handsome Best of Breed winner at the 1988 National Specialty, Ch. Barharber's Rosco Pouch Cove. Additionally, Frank and Carol Winnert are the proud owners of VN Ch. Barharber's Tessa Ranchero, CD, WRD, DD, and VN Ch. Barharber's Just Right, CD, WRD, DD. Tessa is the dam of the lovely bitch Ranchero's Tara of Barharber, Winners Bitch at the 1992 National Specialty and co-owned by Carol Winnert and Micket Fickett, and the male VN Ch. Ranchero's Kingscote, CDX, WRD, DD.

Bearwood

Located near Buffalo, New York, is Carl and Laura Durr's Bearwood Kennel. Breeding on the Edenglen and Newton Ark lines, Bearwood is home to Ch. Bearwood's Sir Ruggles, Ch. Bearwood's Lumberjack, Ch. Bearwood's Star Struck and Ch. Bearwood's Willow.

Benhil

Joan Bendure, of Fairview, Pennsylvania, purchased her first Newfoundland in 1970 from Mae Freeland's Bandom Acres Kennel. Mrs. Freeland was the owner of the two-time National Specialty Best of Breed winner Ch. Edenglen's Banner, ROM, and the great majority of her stock was of Dryad and Edenglen breeding. Joan's first champion was Ch. Bandom's Puff the Magic Newf, and the beginning of a line of champion males that continues today. Puff's son was the typey Ch. Benhil's Shenanigans. A successful producer, Shenanigans sired Ch. Benhil's Trebor, who in turn sired Ch. Benhil's Squire Benson, Ch. Benhil's Black Prince, CD, Ch. Benhil's Shana of Harmonia and Ch. Benhil's Honey Bear to name a few. Joan is the co-owner of a Ch. Benhil's Black Prince son, Ch. Benhil's Man About Town.

At this writing (1993), Benhil's top stud dog is the multiple-Group-winning Ch. Benhil's Stillwater Gulliver, who was Best Puppy in Sweepstakes at the 1986 National Specialty. Another Benhil dog, Ch. Stillwater's Private Party, was awarded Select Bitch at that same National. In the 1980s Benhil branched out into Landseers with the acquisition of Ch. Topmast's Starbright, ROM. When bred to Ch. Moonlite's Sea Czar, "Brighty" produced Ch. Nashau Auke Benhil Scrimshaw, Ch. Nashau Auke Benhil Megan and the Group-winning Landseer Ch. Nashau Auke's Charlie Two Shirts, CD, WRD.

Though the Benhil breeding program is restricted to only one or two litters per year, it has nevertheless resulted in an honor roll that includes over thirty conformation champions, several Group placers and winners, and working titlists. The Benhil line has been incorporated into several other lines, including Amity, Bonnie Bay, Darbydale, Nashau Auke, Springtide, Stillwater and Teddy Tug.

Bethward

Perhaps the most well known Newfoundland fanciers in the Midwest are Paul and Betty Ramey of Lemont, Illinois, who began Bethward Kennels in 1961. The Rameys have bred and/or owned several Group-placing and top winning Newfs, including Ch. Carr's Black Sam of Bethward, ROM, and his grandson Ch. Oprasus of the Good Shepherd, ROM ("J.R."). Sam was the #1 Newfoundland in the United States in both 1968 and 1969, a time when Newfoundlands held more popularity in the East than in the Midwest. Following in his grandfather's footsteps, J.R. was America's top Newfoundland in 1980, received Select Dog honors at the 1981 National Specialty, all while being exclusively owner-handled throughout his show career. Though the Rameys breed few litters, Bethward has produced several champions. More importantly, Sam and J.R. produced many Specialty winners, Group winners and Obedience titlists for both the Rameys and many other Newfoundland enthusiasts.

Boradaile

Helen Mancuso, of Sand Lake, New York, has owned and bred Newfoundlands for many years under the Boradaile prefix. Well-known Boradaile champions include Ch. Boradaile's Billie H, Ch. Boradaile's Beau Son and Ch. Boradaile's HMS Essex.

Bonnie Bay

Karen Cole, of Camino, California, obtained her first Newfoundland in 1970. That particular puppy was a pet, but Karen's next dog, Ch. Shayna's Bonnie Bell, ROM, turned out to be a notable show dog and a producer of many champions and Specialty winners. Shayna took Best of Winners at the 1975 National Specialty and Best of Breed at a Regional Specialty the next year. When bred to Ch. Pooh Bear's Stormalong, ROM, Shayna produced such notables as

Ch. Bonnie Bay's Ursa (Best of Winners at the 1980 National Specialty, Regional Specialty Best of Breed winner), the multiple Group-winning Ch. Bonnie Bay's Brigus, ROM, Ch. Bonnie Bay's Sailing Free (Regional Specialty Best of Breed winner), Ch. Bonnie Bay's Secret Brew and Ch. Bonnie Bay's Cotton. Ursa went on to produce Ch. Bonnie Bay's Baloo of Benhil, ROM, who, when linebred to Ch. Bonnie Bay's Brigus, produced two of Karen's favorites, Ch. Bonnie Bay's Misty Morning and the all-breed Best in Show dog Ch. Bonnie Bay's Nicholas Jasam. One of the most successful kennels in the West, Bonnie Bay has clearly done much to promote the breed on the Pacific Coast.

Briny Deep

A very active Newfoundland breeder during the 1970s and 1980s, Claire Ives's Briny Deep Kennels, of North Troy, Vermont, produced such notables as Ch. Briny Deep's Outrigger, Ch. Briny Deep's Bull Winkle, Ch. Briny Deep's Trail's End, Ch. Briny Deep's Celtic Arran, Ch. Nonesuch's BD's Abby, Ch. House of Churchill BD's Erin, the very nice gray dog Ch. Briny Deep's Captain Grayson and Sally Grasse's Ch. Briny Deep's Captain Midnight in addition to many others.

Briny Deep's foundation bitch was from Little Bear Kennels, and Claire incorporated several Nashau Auke studs into the Briny Deep breeding program.

Britannia

Britannia Kennels, of Mount Shasta, California, has been a major force in Newfoundlands on the West Coast for nearly two decades. The breeder and/or owner of fifty champions, Ms. Shirley's Newfoundlands have also won many Regional and National Specialties, Working Groups and one Bermudian Best in Show.

Breeding predominantly from Dryad and Edenglen lines, a few of the more well known Britannia champions include Ch. Britannia's Union Jack, Bermudian BIS winner, Ch. Britannia's Hurricane Jack, winner of seven all breed Bests in Show, nine Group 1s, Best of Breed at the 1981 National Specialty and Select Dog at the 1982 National Specialty; Ch. Britannia's Morgan, CD, a multiple Group winner and placer and Best of Breed winner at three Regional Specialties; and the multiple Group placers Ch. Britannia's Brigantine Rig, Ch. Britannia's Joshua Slocum, CD, Ch. Britannia's Free Spirit, Ch. Britannia's Rescue at Sea and Ch. Britannia's Tabu of Pouch Cove. Recent Britannia champions include Ch. Britannia's Bery of Pouch Cove, Ch. Britannia's Aja of Pouch Cove, Ch. Britannia's Bear of Pouch Cove, Ch. Britannia's Blis of Pouch Cove and Ch. Britannia Baron of Pouch Cove, all out of Ch. Mooncusser Sail of Pouch Cove, ROM.

Burningstar

Beginning with litter sisters, Ch. Darbydale Burningstar Becky and Ch. Darbydale Burningstar Beri, and breeding them to Catherine and Clyde Dunphy's

Ch. Bonnie Bay's Nicholas Jasam (Ch. Bonnie Bay's Brigus, ROM, ex Ch. Bonnie Bay's Baloo of Benhil, ROM). Multiple Group and Best in Show winner. Bred and owned by Karen Cole. Co-breeder: Joan Bendure. *Fox & Cook*

Ch. Bonnie Bay's Baloo of Benhil, ROM (Mountain Magic Sea Shadow ex Ch. Bonnie Bay's Ursa), bred and owned by Karen Cole of Bonnie Bay Newfoundlands. Co-owned with Joan Bendure. *Fox & Cook*

Int. Ch. Britannia's Hurricane Jack, multiple all-breed Best in Show winner, National Specialty Best of Breed and select multiple Regional Specialty breed winner. Bred and owned by Alana Manzer Shirley. *Søren Wesseltoft*

Ch. Viking's IOU Harley, CD, WD, DD, Becky Black's Burningstar Kennels, of Duquoin, Illinois, has produced several champions and Specialty winners, including Ch. Burningstar Cassiopeia, Ch. Burningstar Bodacious, Ch. Burningstar's Dark Continent and Burningstar Orion Black Star.

Callisto

Based on Topmast breeding and known for quality Landseers Susie Purvis's Callisto Kennels, located in Corrales, New Mexico, is home to and/or the producer of Ch. Topmast Magpie, ROM; Ch. Callisto Graniteledge Panda; Ch. Callisto's Bonnie Bay Burrito; Ch. Callisto's Sam; Ch. Callisto's Little Wizard; Ch. Callisto's Herschel; Ch Callisto's Amazing Grace, CD; and VN Ch. Callisto's Calamity Jane, CD, WRD, DD.

Carillon

Mark and Joanne Chilcoat's Ohio-based Carillon Kennels is home to Ch. Teddy Tug's Lady Gabrielle, the dam of Ch. Carillon's Upper Classman, a showy male who completed his championship in 1993 at the tender age of ten months. Dylan's sire is the handsome Ch. Crystal Bays English Butler, owned by Sue Wolfe's Springtide Kennels.

Carlo Newfoundlands

Mary Price, of Mount Horeb, Wisconsin, started with Newfoundlands from the Hugybear Kennel. Ch. Hugybear's Cameo of Carlo, bred to Ch. Hugybears James Joseph Ralee, produced Ch. Carlo High Born O'Muine Bheag. Although her breeding has been limited, Mary has devoted her time to the Newfoundland Club of America's national rescue program and has served the club as treasurer for many years.

Celtic

Based on the Briny Deep and Nashau Auke lines, Tom and Nancy McGill's Celtic champions include Ch. Briny Deeps Celtic Arran, Ch. Celtic's Tomasina For My Lord and Ch. Celtic's Benbecula in addition to others. From a base in Hendersonville, North Carolina, Tom has been actively involved in the Newfoundland Club of America, including serving as president.

Chadwick

John and Sally Adams' Chadwick Newfoundlands, of Lexington, Massachusetts, has been home to the pretty bitch Ch. Chadwick's Susan D Nashau Auke, the Landseer Ch. Nashau Auke Benhil Winter Hawk and his son Nashau Auke Chadwick's Timothy.

Companionway

Connie Holt's Companionway Kennels, based in Hope Valley, Rhode Island, experienced a great deal of success in the 1970s and early 1980s. Famous Companionway champions include the all-breed Best in Show bitch Ch. Companionway's Windjammer, her litter brother Ch. Companionway's Sir Walter, who won the Working Group at the Westminster Kennel Club Show in 1978, and Ch. Companionway's Wind Dodger. The Companionway Newfoundlands descend from the Shipshape and Indigo lines.

Dalken

Ken and Dallas Anderson, of Center, Colorado, have achieved much success in the Newfoundland world, through the combining of Shipshape, Graniteledge, Newton Ark, Pouch Cove and Shadybrook lines. Well-known Dalken champions include the foundation bitch Ch. Shipshape's Midnight Mist, ROM; Ch. Dalken Captain's Mate; Ch. Dalken Storm of Graniteledge, CD; Ch. Dalken's Windlass; Ch. Dalken's Fleetwing; Ch. Dalken's Grey Calm; Ch. Dalken's Afternoon Delight; Ch. Dalken's Sunrise Summer Breeze (top winning bitch in 1987); Ch. Dalken's Bo Derek, Ch. Dalken's La Rochelle (Best in Puppy Sweepstakes at the 1984 National Specialty); Ch. Dalken's Denver of Pouch Cove, ROM; the Group-winning Ch. Dalken's General Patton; Ch. Dalken's Summer Sail; and Ch. Dalken's Captain Englehorn (Select Dog at the 1989 National Specialty).

Darbydale

Carol Ann Bernard-Bergmann's Darbydale Newfoundlands, from Chelsea, Michigan, combine the Benhil, Thunder Bay and Pouch Cove lines. Carol bred her foundation Ch. Benhil's Honey Bear to Ch. Nordstrand Bjorn Newton Ark to produce Ch. Darbydale's Mystique and Ch. Darbydale's Sea Holly. When bred to Ch. Thunder Bay's Storm A Brewin, Holly produced Ch. Darbydale's Just Charles, Ch. Darbydale's Kinnebrew, Ch. Darbydale Burningstar Becky, Ch. Darbydale Burningstar Beri and Ch. Darbydale She's Like the Wind. Darbydale is also home to the multiple Group placer and Specialty Best of Breed winner Ch. Pouch Cove's Darbydale Booker, sire of Ch. Darbydale's Weiser Boy.

De Lorene

Beginning with the foundation bitch Ch. Bellisima De Lorene and using such males as Ch. Topsail Cruisin at Kimtale and Ch. Sealcove's First Mate, Henry and Lorraine Rossi, of Clarkston, Michigan, have bred several champions, including the multiple Group and Select Dog winners Ch. Delorene's Top of Black Sea and Ch. De Lorene's Enrico. Additional De Lorene champions include

Ch. De Lorene's Avanti, Ch. De Lorene's Contessa, Ch. De Lorene's Giovana and Ch. Delorene's Pendragon's Pride.

Bob & Fran Dibble

Though Bob and Fran Dibble didn't breed Newfoundlands to any extent, they may well have had a bigger impact on the breed than any West Coast kennel. Based in Thousand Oaks, California, the Dibbles owned four of the winningest and best producing Newfoundlands of their time for the area, including Ch. Little Bear's Night Train; Ch. Edenglen's Beau Geste, ROM; Ch. Edenglen's Oscar, ROM; and Ch. Kilyka's Jupiter Rex.

Night Train was acquired in 1964 from Little Bear, and was a multiple Group winner and placer. Beau Geste was acquired one year later from Edenglen, and he too was a multiple Group placer. Oscar left Edenglen and headed west in 1970. A top sire, Oscar was also the Best of Breed winner at three Regional Specialties. Jupiter took up residence with the Dibbles in 1972 after winning Best of Breed at the 1971 National Specialty and a Group placement at the Westminster Kennel Club.

Beyond making the "gang of four" available at stud to West Coast breeders, the Dibbles really did quite a lot to promote Newfoundlands in the West. Indeed, their regular attendance at dog shows throughout the area, at a time when Newfoundlands were not well known, caught the attention of many and the interest and dedication of an important few. Fran was actively involved with the Newfoundland Club of America, which she served as secretary for a number of years. Fran and Bob also devoted considerable time to the Newfoundland Club of Southern California.

Ebonewf

On a trip abroad Roy and Louise Esiason, of Granville, New York, encountered and fell in love with Newfoundlands. Newfoundland owners since the early 1960s, Roy and Louise have devoted more time to promoting Newfoundlands through their participation in the Newfoundland Club of America than to breeding or showing. However, they have owned and bred several champions, including the foundation bitch Ch. Thunder's Karla, Ch. Ebonewf's Tamara Karla, Ch. Ebonewf's Rhett Butler, Ch. Ebonewf's Brown Bomber and more recently Ch. Topmast's Sasquatch among others. As nice as these dogs were or are, none are probably as well known as Ebonewf's Charlie Bear and Ebonewf's Raider Bear, both owned by Roy and Louise's renowned nephew, Cincinnati Bengals' quarterback Boomer Esiason! Louise served as president of the Newfoundland Club of America.

Ebontide

Ebontide, owned by Peter Anderson and Janice Kiseskey, was founded on stock from Riptide Kennels, and included Ch. Riptide's Kamikazi Kid. Since

Ch. Dryad's Flagship, ROM (Ch. Pooh Bear's Stormalong, ROM, ex Ch. Dryad's Brigantine, CD, ROM). Best in Show winner; bred and owned by Mary Dewey of Dryad Kennels. Co-breeders: Dave and Katy Sturtz. *John Ashbey*

Ebonewf's Carla Bear (Ch. Halirock's Bjorn Bear ex Ebonewf's Chantilly) being shown by breeder/owner Louise Esiason of Ebonewf Kennels. *Phoebe*

the early days, Peter and Janice have incorporated both the Britannia and Kendian lines in their breeding, resulting in such champions as Ch. Ebontides Andrea Doria, Ch. Ebontides Causin a Commotion, Ch. Ebontides Micah O'Kekai, Ch. Ebontides Harmony O'Kekai, Ch. Ebontide Black Tie Affair and Ch. Kendian's Rare Bear Ebontide. The Ebontide Newfoundlands are from Bakersfield, California.

Ebunyzar

Quite active within both conformation and working pursuits is Hannah Hayman, of Cazenovia, New York, and her Ebunyzar Newfoundlands. Hannah is the breeder of many champions, including Ch. Ebunyzar's Water Witch; Witch's Group winning son, Ch. Ebunyzar's Salty Tang; Ch. Ebunyzar's Bogey D'Wunderland; Ch. Eb's Denali Rocky of Novella, VN Ch. Ebunyzar's Ditto, CDX, WRD, DD; and VN Ch. Ebunyzar's Raven Beauty CD, WRD, DD.

Far Hills

Based primarily on the Nashau Auke lines is John and Marcia White's Far Hills Kennels, of Gardner, Massachusetts. A few of the many Far Hills champions include Ch. Far Hill's Flying Cloud; Ch. Far Hill's Drummer Boy, CD; Ch. Far Hill's Black Eyed Suzy; Ch. Far Hill's Blaze of Glory; and Ch. Far Hills Mizz T Sioux.

Flying Cloud

Vic Nebeker's Flying Cloud Newfoundlands, located in Colorado, descend from the Nashau Auke line. Though the Nebekers owned Newfoundlands for many years, it was their acquisition of Ch. Benham Knoll's Amy that really set the kennel on the path to success. When bred to Ch. Canoochee de Nashau Auke, Amy produced several champions, including Ch. Flying Cloud's Far Hill, ROM ("Billy"), Ch. Flying Cloud's Silver Streak and Ch. Flying Cloud's Leading Lady. Billy proved to be a producer of lovely type; his offspring including Ch. Flying Cloud's Sir Beauregard, CD; Ch. Flying Cloud's Pooh Bear; Ch. Flying Cloud's Drifter; Ch. Flying Cloud's Square Rigger; Ch. Flying Cloud's Sunrise Sable; Ch. Flying Cloud's Nordic Mist; the top producing Ch. Highland Bear of Pouch Cove, ROM; and the Best in Show bitch Ch. Flying Cloud's Yankee Spirit.

Halcyon

Roberta Jarel's Halcyon Kennels, located in Oakland, Minnesota, is home to such Newfoundlands as the Group-placing Ch. Halcyon's Bjorn Free and Ch. Halcyon's Magnum Tinn Lizzy (top producing bitch in 1989). When bred together, Bjorn and Lizzy produced Ch. Minnemato's Halcyon Firebird, Ch. Halcyon's Gangway It's Rigel, Ch. Halcyon's Oprah and Ch. Halcyon's Mark of A Gentleman.

Halirock

Roger and Joan Foster, of Vermont, and their children (for whom the Kennel is named) have owned and bred quality Newfoundlands for some thirty years, breeding their foundation bitches Ch. Little Bear's Chulavista and the little sisters Ch. Dryad's Anthony's Penelope, ROM, and Ch. Franco Cassandra to such males as Dryad's Bounty, ROM; Ch. Edenglen's Beau Geste, ROM; and Ch. Edenglen's Oscar, ROM. Offspring from those breedings were then bred to the Foster's own males in addition to Ch. Dacody De Nashau Auke, ROM, and Ch. Mogen of Newton Ark, ROM, resulting in nearly fifty Halirock champions and fifteen working titlists.

A few of Halirock's honor roll members include Ch. Halirock's Avalanche, Ch. Halirock's Boulder (Best of Winners at the 1971 National Specialty); Ch. Halirock's Chatty Kathy; Ch. Halirock's Ulysses Odyssey, ROM; Ch. Halirock's Advantage In, ROM; Ch. Halirock's Gundabear, ROM; Ch. Halirock's Ebony Anne, CD, DD, WD; Ch. Halirock's Great Expectation, CD, DD; and Ch. Halirock's Knight of Thunder, WD, CD. Ch. Halirock's Tyche served as the foundation dog for Tyche Kennels, and Ch. Halirock's Icebreaker WD, WRD, resides with Judy and Janeane Cappara at Icebreaker Kennels.

Haven Hills

Joyce Hieber's Haven Hills Newfoundlands, of Illinois, descend from the Barbara Allen, Moonlite and Bethward lines. There are many Haven Hills champions and working titlists including Ch. Havenhill's Sinbad The Sailor; Haven Hill's Painted Pony, CD, WRD; Haven Hill's Biscuit Eater, CD, WD; Ch. Haven Hill's Tigger Lilly (top producing dam in 1988); VN Ch. Haven Hill's Ima Tigger Too CD, WRD, DD; Ch. Haven Hill's Irish Knight; Ch. Haven Hill's Midnight Triumph, CD; Ch. Haven Hill's Teddy; Ch. Haven Hill's Stormy Girl; and VN Ch. Haven Hill Sea Raven, CDX, TDX, WRD, DD. Joyce has been an avid promoter of the working Newfoundland.

Holiday

Ron and Erma Pemberton of Howell, Michigan, have been breeding Newfoundlands under the Holiday prefix for many years. Using predominantly Edenglen lines, Holiday has produced a long list of champions, including Ch. Holiday's Sea Witch, ROM; Ch. Holiday's Dreadnought Ensign, CDX, WRD; Ch. Holiday's Dear Gideon; Ch. Holiday's Hy Crown Prince; Ch. Holiday's Mayflower; Ch. Holiday's Pacesetter, CD; Ch. Holiday's Abigail Adams; and Ch. Holiday's Uriah. Ron has served on the Newfoundland Club of America's

Roger (upper left) and Joan (upper right) Foster, of Halirock Kennels, with their children and dogs.

VN Ch. Kilyka's Aphrodite Pouch Cove, UD, WRD, DD, ROM (Ch. Schooner Yosef of Newton-Ark, ROM, ex Ch. Tis' The Season of Pouch Cove, ROM), bred by Peggy Helming and owned by Betty McDonnell of Kilyka Kennels.

board several terms and is an AKC licensed judge of Newfoundlands and all Sporting breeds.

Hugybear & Windrift

Long time breeders of both blacks and Landseers, Rou and Joyce Woody's Hugybear Kennels of Winchester, Wisconsin, and Susan and Susie Woody's Windrift Kennels of University City, Missouri, have produced such champions as Ch. Hugybear's Inside Track, Ch. Hugybear's Gorgeous George, Ch. Hugybear's Chicory Chip, Ch. Hugybear's Sweet Magnolia, Ch. Windrift's Gentle Ben and Ch. Windrift's Major Motion. The Woodys' association with Richard Lee and his Ralee Kennels resulted in Ch. Ralee's First Mate of Hugybear, Ch. Ralee's Windwalker, Ch. Hugybear's Pay the Piper and Ch. Ralee Pay the Piper Piperette.

A top junior handler at the time of this writing, Susie Woody continues to successfully pilot the Hugybear and Windrift Newfoundlands.

Jolly Roger

Using foundation stock from Outtrail Kennels is Roger and Barbara Frey's Jolly Roger Kennel in Alden, New York. A few of the Jolly Roger champions include Ch. The Hostage of Jolly Roger, Ch. Jolly Roger's Dark Victory, Ch. Jolly Roger's Flash Dance and the Group placers Ch. Jolly Roger's Broadway Ruby, Ch. Jolly Roger's Tazmanian Chief and Ch. Jolly Roger's Perlie Gate. Jolly Roger Landseers include the lovely bitch Ch. Sunberry's Ramblin's Rose and the young dog Jolly Roger's Beau Maverick.

Donna Jorgensen

Best known for Landseers, Donna Jorgensen's Newfoundlands, based in Longmont, Colorado, descend from the Canadian Topmast and Hornblower Kennels. Some of the Jorgensen champions include Ch. Jorgensen's Polly Checkers, Ch. Jorgensen's Snow Mass, Ch. Jorgensen's Commander Quasar, Ch. Jorgensen's Snowy Kesha and Ch. Jorgensen's Ranger Radar.

Kendian

Though Ken and Diane Price maintain a small kennel in Los Gatos, California, they certainly have enjoyed a great deal of success in the show ring. Concentrating mostly on males, the Prices' dogs include the Group placers Ch. Pooh Bear's Chimo, CD, and Ch. Bonnie Bay's Brigus, ROM.

However, it is the brown Brigus son Ch. Kendian's Cadbury that is most famous, having been the number one Newfoundland in 1986, a multiple Specialty winner and a winner of two all-breed Bests in Show. During his show career,

Cadbury became the top-winning brown Newfoundland in the history of the breed.

Later Kendian champions include Ch. Kendian's Rare Bear Ebontide, Ch. Kendian's Just Too Much and Ch. Springhaven's Kava Of Kendian.

Kilyka

Betty McDonnell, of Mahwah, New Jersey, began breeding Newfoundlands under the Kilyka prefix in 1966. Betty's foundation stock was essentially Dryad-bred dogs, the two best-known being Ch. Dryad's Lord Nelson, UDT, ROM, and Ch. Shipshape's Sybil, UDT, ROM. Sybil (not to be confused with her modern-day namesake, VN Ch. Kilyka's Sybil, UD, WRD, DD, ROM), the top producing bitch of all time is the dam of fourteen champions and ten working titlists, including Ch. Kilyka's Black Bart, Ch. Kilyka's Jupiter Rex and the Pouch Cove foundation bitches Ch. Kilyka's Jessica of Pouch Cove, CD, ROM, and Ch. Kilyka's Becky Jo of Pouch Cove, ROM.

Betty has clearly experienced a good deal of success, having bred approximately sixty champions and fifty-six working titlists. However, those numbers do not tell the whole story. Of those champions, two were National Specialty Best of Breed winners (Ch. Kilyka's Jupiter Rex and Ch. Kilyka's Black Bart); two were National Specialty Best of Opposite Sex winners (Ch. Kilyka's Jessica of Pouch Cove, CD, ROM, and VN Ch. Kilyka's Sybil, UD, WRD, DD, ROM); three have been chosen as Selects at National Specialties (Ch. Kilyka's Remarkable Rufus, Ch. Kilyka's Riverwatch Hudson Spy, Ch. Kilyka's Lady Burgundy); five have earned a total of ten High in Trial awards at National Specialties (Ch. Dryad's Lord Nelson UDT, ROM; Ch. Kilyka's She Shell, UD, WD, DD; VN Ch. Kilyka's Pollyanna, UD, WRD, DD; VN Ch. Kilyka's Sybil, UD, WRD, DD, ROM; VN Ch. Kilyka's Saving Grace, UD, WD, DD); one is an all breed Best in Show winner (Ch. Kilyka's Black Bart); two are multiple all-breed High in Trial awardees (VN Ch. Kilyka's Sybil, UD, WRD, DD, ROM, and VN Ch. Kilyka's Saving Grace UD, WD, DD); and eight have earned the distinction of being awarded the Versatility Newfoundland title (VN Ch. Kilyka's Collosus, UD, WRD, DD; VN Ch. Kilyka's Calypso, UDTX, WRD, DD; VN Ch. Kilyka's Pollyanna, UD, WRD, DD; VN Ch. Kilyka's Aphrodite of Pouch Cove, UD, WRD, DD, ROM; VN Ch. Kilyka's Sibyl, UD, WRD, DD, ROM; VN Ch. Kilyka's Mariah, CD, WRD, DD; VN Ch. Kilyka's Saving Grace, UD, WD, DD; and VN Ch. Kilyka's Merry Blackberry, CD, WRD, DD).

As the aforementioned accolades indicate, Betty McDonnell emphasizes the Newfoundland's working ability in addition to breeding very pretty dogs. Betty's Nelson and original Sybil were the first Newfoundlands to earn both championships and UDTs. These many years of experience have paid off, and it is indeed a pleasure to watch Betty and her well-trained Newfies work through their routines at Obedience Trials, draft tests and Water Trials. As the competition well realizes, more often than not the Kilyka team is a force to be reckoned with.

Manitouloa

Carrying on the Castaway and Thunder Bay lines, John and Kathy Shelden's Manitouloa Kennel of South Lyon, Michigan, has owned and/or bred several champions, including Ch. Manitouloa's Cruisin the Farm, Ch. Manitouloa's Snow on Manitoba and Ch. Wee Lovett's Island of Manitou. Without question the Sheldens' best-known homebred is the brown dog Ch. Manitouloa's My Bear Kodiak. This multiple Specialty winner was Best of Breed at the 1992 National Specialty, and is multiple all-breed Best in Show winner. Co-owned with William and Patricia Connolly, Kodiak is handled in the show ring by Kathy.

Mastway

A long-established prefix, Ann Parson's Mastway Newfoundlands of New Hampshire was originally based on the Indigo and Shipshape lines, and has since incorporated the multiple Best in Show dog Ch. Hornblower's Long John Silver and Ch. Moonlight's Sea Czar into its Landseer line, and several Pouch Cove males into its line of quality blacks. Well-known Mastway Newfoundlands include the lovely bitch Ch. Mastway's Big Plans Ahead and her two sons, the Best in Show dog Ch. Mastway's Rockbottom Ripship (Best in Puppy Sweepstakes at the 1983 National Specialty) and Ch. Mastway Marcus Me First (Select Dog at the 1987 National Specialty).

Mooncusser

Suzanne Jones began breeding under the Mooncusser prefix from her base in Orleans, Massachusetts, in 1972. Her first homebred titlists Ch., Mooncusser Friendship Sloop (Bertha) was Best Puppy in Show at the 1976 National Specialty. Bertha began the very successful line of quality bitches that Mooncusser is well known for today. Linebreeding on the Shipshape lines produced Bertha's daughter Ch. Mooncusser's Dutch Treat ("Emma"), Best in Sweeps and Winners Bitch at the Niagara regional Specialty in 1978 at nine months of age. Emma bred to Ch. Pouch Cove Gref of Newton-Ark produced offspring that have had a dramatic impact on the breed. They include Ch. Mooncusser's Making Waves ("Martha"), Ch. Mooncusser's Reef of Pouch Cove ("Wimpy") and Ch. Mooncusser's Pieces of Eight. Martha was a Select Bitch at two National Specialties, the top producing dam for 1987, the dam of eleven champions, two ROM titlists and one Obedience titlist, and the dam of the top producing bitch of 1990, Ch. Mooncusser Sail of Pouch Cove. Wimpy, sire of twenty-nine champions and seven Obedience titlists, was the top-producing sire of 1990, Best of Breed at the 1989 National Specialty and the sire of twenty-nine champions and seven working titlists. Additional Mooncusser dogs worthy of special mention include Ch. Mooncusser's Starking Sagamore, ROM; Ch. Mooncusser's Clean Pair O'Heels; Ch. Mooncusser's RSVP of Pouch Cove; and the girls at Tracy Warncke's Evenkeel Kennels, Ch. Mooncusser's Making A Splash, Ch. Mooncusser's In Full Sail and Ch. Mooncusser Splish Splash, CD.

It is quite clear that Sue has had a good deal of success in crossing her Mooncusser bitches with Pouch Cove males. That trend has continued into later generations, as evidenced by Mooncusser's rising count of stars including Ch. Mooncusser's In Full Sail, sired by Ch. John's Big Ben of Pouch Cove, the two-time Best in Sweeps winner Mooncusser Maid to Order, sired by Ch. Pouch Cove's Favorite Son, and Mooncusser's Aye Aye, sired by Ch. Mooncusser's Reef of Pouch Cove. In total, there are over forty Mooncusser champions, twelve working titlists, one Versatility title, five ROMs and numerous specialty winners at this writing. Such a proud record also points to the many hours of work and thought that Sue Jones has dedicated to the Newfoundland dog.

Moonlite

Nancy Moon's Moonlite Newfoundlands of Laconia, New Hampshire, is best known for quality Landseers. There have many Moonlite champions, including Ch. Moonlite's Alpha Centauri, Ch. Moonlite's Colossal Comet, Ch. Moonlite Quasar and her beautiful son Ch. Moonlite's Sea Czar.

Moonshadow

Mickey Fickett's Moonshadow Kennels, located in Charlestown, Rhode Island, is the home of Ch. Moonshadow of Newton-Ark, CD, and Am., Can. Ch. Thundrn Thumpr of Newton-Ark, CD, DD, and co-owner of the lovely Ranchero's Tara of Barharber, Winners Bitch at the 1992 National Specialty.

Mountain Lore and Bearington

Jean Bridge and her daughter Tami Palomba of Tolland, Connecticut, own Mountain Lore and Bearington Newfoundlands respectively. The majority of their stock results from a cross of the Mooncusser and Ebunyzar lines. Tami's Ch. Mooncusser Bruno Bear is the sire of Ch. Mountain Lores Minuit, Ch. Mountain Lores Toby Bearington and Ch. Mountain Lores Ted E. Bearington, who in turn sired Mountainview Lore Dakota Bearington. However, Jean also breeds Landseers such as Ch. Jeanne's Jacob of Mountain Lore.

Muddy Creek

Breeders of both blacks and Landseers, Rick and Brenda Santiago's Muddy Creek Kennels of Pearl River, New York, is largely based on Pouch Cove and Topmast lines. Some of the Muddy Creek champions include Ch. Muddy Creek Michael Angelo; Ch. Muddy Creek's Take A Gander; Ch. Muddy Creek's Keely; Ch. Muddy Creek's Savannah, CD; Ch. Pouch Cove Muddy Creek's Tess; and Ch. Topmast's Muddy Creek Crocker.

Ch. Mooncusser's Reef of Pouch Cove, ROM (Ch. Pouch Cove's Gref of Newton-Ark, ROM, ex Ch. Mooncusser's Dutch Treat, ROM), a National Specialty Best of Breed winner, bred by Suzanne Jones and Donna Dodge and owned by Margaret and David Helming.

Ch. Mooncusser Widow's Walk (Ch. Pouch Cove's Favorite Son, ROM, ex Ch. Mooncusser Clean Pair of Heels), bred and owned by Suzanne Jones of Mooncusser Kennels.

Helen Munday

Helen Munday, of South Salem, New York, has bred and/or owned several well-known Newfoundlands, including Ch. Munday's Old Post Road, Ch. Munday's Misty Morn, Ch. Munday's Stormy Weather and the all-breed Best in Show winners Ch. Dryad's Flagship and Ch. Tuckamore's Boomerang, who was also Best of Breed at the 1987 National Specialty.

Nanwick

Located in Medina, Ohio, is Nancy Wick's Nanwick Kennel. A breeder of both blacks and Landseers, the Nanwick champions list includes Ch. Nanwick's Sheza Tuffy, Ch. Nanwick's Kodiak Lost at Sea, Ch. Nanwick's Randee of Waterlord, Ch. Nanwick's Lady of Sandy Cove and Ch. Nanwick's Sam the Sham.

Nashau-Auke

As previously indicated, until the mid-1960s three kennels dominated the Newfoundland breeding and show scene, those being Little Bear, Dryad and Edenglen. Though Wilma Lister (Shipshape) began to cross these lines, it was Jane and Ron Thibault, of Ashford, Connecticut, who took aim at combining Little Bear structure with Dryad type. The results were, in many cases, even better than expected, propelling Nashau-Auke (pronounced Nasha-Nook) to the pinnacle of success in the Newfoundland world.

Indeed, Nashau-Auke's long-lasting breeding and show program has resulted in worldwide renown. More importantly, Nashau-Auke is largely responsible for providing the foundation stud dogs and brood bitches to many of today's most prominent kennels.

However, before getting to that, a bit of history is in order.

The foundation stock at Nashau-Auke included the two bitches Ch. Shipshape Nana of Nashau-Auke (Dryad bred) and Ch. Little Bear's Cutty Hunk, and the male Ch. Little Bear's Dauntless. When bred to Dauntless, Nana produced Ch. Koki de Nashau Auke, who went on to sire twenty-seven champions and eight working titlists. And when bred quite differently to Ch. Indigo's Fritzacker, Nana produced Ch. Canoochee De Nashau-Auke, an all-breed Best in Show winner, Best of Breed at the 1974 National Specialty and sire of twenty-five champions and six working titlists. Nana was clearly the type of foundation bitch most breeders only dream of, going on to produce other notables such as Ch. Ki Nun Ka De Nashau-Auke, ROM, Ch. Yanoo De Nashau-Auke, Ch. Volcana de Nashau-Auke and Ch. De Koryak De Nashau-Auke, CD.

Carrying on the Little Bear line, Cutty Hunk produced many wonderful puppies, including the lovely Ch. Keema De Nashau-Auke out of Ch. DaCody De Nashau-Auke, ROM, a multiple all-breed Best in Show winner, Best of Breed winner at the 1977 National Specialty and the sire of sixteen champions and two working titlists. Cutty Hunk produced Ch. Tanda De Nashau-Auke, Ch. Tasha

Am., Can. Ch. DaCody De Nashau-Auke, ROM (Ch. Kilyka's Black Bart ex Ch. Keema De Nashau-Auke), National Specialty Best of Breed winner and multiple Best in Show winner, bred and owned by Jane Thibault of Nashau-Auke Kennels.

Ch. Canoochee De Nashau-Auke, ROM (Ch. Indigo's Fritzacker, ROM, ex Ch. Shipshape Nana of Nashau-Auke, ROM), bred and owned by Jane and Ron Thibault of Nashau-Auke Kennels. A multiple all-breed Best in Show winner and National Specialty Best of Breed. Shown here winning an all-breed BIS under Kitty Drury from the Veterans Class at a regional Specialty. The handler is Gerlinde V. Hockla. *Graham*

of Nashau-Auke, and Ch. Koki Winota De Nashau-Auke, who herself went on to produce many champions, including Ch. Revelation De Nashau-Auke, Ch. Mamacoke De Nashau-Auke, CD, and Ch. Minowe De Nashau-Auke. Further crossing of Little Bear and Dryad breeding and more recent incorporation of other lines through such dogs as the English import Ch. Littlecreek Sea Cutter, Ch. Seaward's Blackbeard, ROM, and Ch. John's Big Ben of Pouch Cove, ROM, has resulted in an honor roll that includes well over one hundred champions and working titlists. Recent Nashau-Auke winners include Ch. Nashau-Auke's Pipedream; Ch. Nashau-Auke's Hatchet Jack; Ch. Nashau-Auke Arapaho (Select Dog at the 1990 National Specialty); VN Ch. Nashau-Auke's Timber, UD, WRD, TDD; and Ch. Nashau-Auke Nicholas Nickabee (Winners Dog and Best of Winners at the 1985 National Specialty) and breeder of the multiple all-breed BIS and Specialty-Winning bitch Ch. Flying Cloud's Yankee Spirit.

Nashau-Auke's goal of breeding quality Landseers has also paid off, as evidenced by Ch. Nashau-Auke Benhil Scrimshaw, Ch. Nashau-Auke Benhil Winterhawk, Ch. Nashau-Auke Benhil Kittyhawk, Ch. Nashau-Auke Benhil Megan and the Group winner Ch. Nashau-Auke's Charlie Two Shirts, CD, WRD.

As previously noted, it would be difficult to find a contemporary Newfoundland that has not been influenced by the Nashau-Auke line. Nearly every prominent Newfoundland kennel in existence today has used at least one (and usually more) of Nashau-Auke's best-known studs—Koki, Canoochee and Da-Cody. The long-term benefits to the breed are obvious.

Newfport

May and Jack Bernhard, of Putnam Valley, New York, acquired their first Newfoundland in 1968. Like many new people destined to impact the breed, their second Newfoundland pup had the show potential the first one lacked. That bitch grew up to be the beautiful Ch. Hidden Lakes's Cassiopeia, and what a start the Bernhards were off to. Cassie's first litter was sired by the National Specialty winner Ch. Indigo's Fritzacker, producing several Group placers, including the multiple Group winner Ch. Newfport's Fleet Commander and his sisters Ch. Newfport's Mae West and Ch. Newfport's Megean. Fleet Commander sired the Group winner Ch. Newfport's Noah's Ark, and when later bred to Fritzacker's brother Ch. Indigo's Bozo the Clown, Cassie produced Ch. Newfport's Belle Bottom. Having fulfilled her whelping box obligation in a very big way, Cassie turned the reins over to daughter Megean. When bred to Ch. Samson VII, Megean produced the Group-winning Ch. Newfport's Maximillian in addition to the Bernhard's best-known homebred, Ch. Newfport's Outward Bound ("Byron"). A top Newfoundland in the early and mid 1980s, Byron was a multiple Group winner, received Select Dog honors at two National Specialties and won the stud dog class at two National Specialties. Byron's get include the Best in Show dog Ch. Tarbell's Jethro, Ch. Newfport's Thunder Bay, Ch. Newfport's Top Gun and Ch. Newfport's Winslow Homer.

Newfport senior citizens—at the time of this picture all dogs were over ten years of age. Left to right: Ch. Newfport's Fleet Commander, Ch. Newfport's Belle Bottom, Ch. Newfport's Megean, Newfport's S.O.S. and Graniteledge Cali of Newton-Ark. All are owned by May and Jack Bernhard.

Ch. Pouch Cove's Favorite Son, ROM (Ch. Schooner Yosef of Newton-Ark, ROM, ex Souvenir Of Pouch Cove), bred by Margaret Helming and Phyllis Welch and owned by Margaret and David Helming. "Jacob" is an all-breed Best in Show winner and National Specialty Best of Breed winner.

Numa

Diane Keyser's Numa Newfoundlands, located in Middleville, New Jersey, is based predominantly on Tar Baby, Mooncusser, Pouch Cove and Newton-Ark breeding. Numa champions include Ch. Tarbaby's Mean Joe Green Numa, Ch. Senkara's Harriet of Numa and the lovely Select Bitch at the 1988 National Specialty Ch. Numa's Anticipation.

Paddlewheel

Mary W. Price's Paddlewheel Kennels from Edina, Minnesota, is seldom absent a top-winning and/or top-producing dog. Having owned Newfoundlands since the 1960s, Mary's best known dogs include Ch. Little Bear's Shipshape Rig, ROM; Ch. Topmast's Prairie Queen, a top show bitch in the late 1970s and early 1980s and Best of Opposite Sex at the 1980 National Specialty; and Am., Can., Bda., Mex., Col. and FCI Int. Ch. Topmast's Show Boat, ROM (''Billy''), a multiple Specialty and all-breed Best in Show winner. Additional Paddlewheel champions include Ch. Paddlewheel's Penelore, ROM, Ch. Paddlewheel's Jesse Benton, Ch. Paddlewheel's Alice Dean, CD, Ch. Paddlewheel's One Over Par, Ch. Paddlewheel Belmire Sunrise, Ch. Paddlewheel's Showboat Annie and Ch. Paddlewheel's Joe Montana. Mary Price has been very active in the Newfoundland Club America, serving as membership chairperson and AKC delegate.

Pooh Bear

Shelby Guelich, from California, has bred Newfoundlands for many years under the Pooh Bear prefix. There are many well-known Pooh Bear Newfoundlands on the West Coast, including Ch. Pooh Bear's Stormalong, Best of Breed winner at the 1980 National Specialty and the sire of thirty-four champions and seven working titlists. Pooh Bear's most famous Newfoundland from the distaff side is the multiple Specialty winner, Ch. Pooh Bear's Katie.

Pouch Cove

Few would dispute the assertion that David and Peggy Helming, of Flemington, New Jersey, and their Pouch Cove breeding program have been the major influence on Newfoundlands in recent years. Hardly the average hobby kennel, Pouch Cove's unprecedented success results from the Helmings' unwavering dedication to the breed, a professional staff (and dedicated Newfoundland fancier Peggy's sister Chris LaMuraglia), state-of-the-art kennel facilities, a prime geographic location, a large dose of perseverance and, most importantly, a well-reasoned breeding and show program that has culminated in what today is known as the Pouch Cove type.

Acquiring their first Newfoundland in the late 1960s, the Helmings soon went on to expand their canine numbers, breeding and finishing Ch. Katrina of Pouch Cove, and Katrina's son Ch. Waldo of Pouch Cove, CD, ROM. However, the breedings that really struck gold for Pouch Cove were those which crossed and then linebred their Ch. Shipshape Sybil, UDT, ROM, daughters—Ch. Kilyka's Jessica of Pouch Cove, CD, ROM, and Ch. Kilyka's Becky Jo of Pouch Cove, ROM—with the litter brothers Ch. Kuhaia's Rego, ROM, Ch. The Sleeper of Newton-Ark, ROM, and Loki's Drummer of Newton-Ark, ROM, sons of Ch. Jack the Ripper, ROM, and Ch. Edenglen's Lady Rebecca, ROM. When bred to Sleeper, Jessica produced Ch. Pouch Cove Kasha of Newton-Ark, and Kasha bred to Rego then produced the top sire of all time Ch. Pouch Cove Gref of Newton-Ark, ROM.

A dog of tremendous type, Gref was the number one Newfoundland in 1979, Select Dog at the 1982 and 1983 National Specialties and winner of the stud dog class at the 1982 National Specialty. Fortunately for the breed, Gref stamped his signature head, substance, neck, topline, angulation, movement and coat on the vast majority of his get, resulting in forty-three conformation champions and twenty-six other titlists. More importantly, Gref was not a flash in the pan, as many of his offspring have also reached ROM status, literally producing hundreds of champions around the world. Though Gref died in 1984, his indelible type carries on in every Pouch Cove Newfoundland.

Throughout the years the Helmings have incorporated other lines into their breeding program, most notably the lovely bitches Ch. Mooncusser RSVP of Pouch Cove, ROM; Ch. Mooncusser Kayla of Pouch Cove; VN Ch. Mooncusser Ahoy of Pouch Cove, CDX, WRD, DD; and Ch. Mooncusser Sail of Pouch Cove, ROM, all bred by Suzanne Jones's Mooncusser Kennels. Additionally, Pouch Cove extensively used Phyllis Welch's handsome male Ch. Schooner Yosef of Newton-Ark, ROM, a dog also linebred on Ch. Jack the Ripper, ROM, and Ch. Edenglen's Lady Rebecca, ROM. Indeed, a few of Yosef's most famous Pouch Cove kids include but are not limited to Ch. Motion Carried of Pouch Cove, ROM; VN Ch. Kilyka's Aphrodite Pouch Cove, UD, WRD, DD, ROM; Ch. Never Grow Up of Pouch Cove, WRD, DD; Ch. Moon Shadow of Pouch Cove; Ch. Pouch Cove's Treasure Chest; and, most notably, the multiple Best in Show and National Specialty Best of Breed winner Ch. Pouch Cove's Favorite Son, ROM.

Though the Pouch Cove show record cannot be done justice in a few simple lines, some important statistics are worth noting. Pouch Cove has shattered nearly all Newfoundland kennel records, at this point in time having produced or owned over 120 champions, 30 Obedience titlists, several Best in Show winners and Specialty winners too numerous to list. In addition to Gref, Jessica (Best of Opposite at the 1976 National Specialty) and Becky Jo (Best of Winners at the 1976 National Specialty), other well-known Pouch Cove winners include Ch. Tuckamore's Dutch of Pouch Cove (all-breed Best in Show winner); Ch. Season's Autumn of Pouch Cove (all-breed Best in Show winner); Ch. Pouch Cove's Favorite Son, ROM (all-breed Best in Show winner, Best of Breed at the 1991 National Specialty, Winners Dog at the 1990 National Specialty); Ch. Motion Carried of Pouch Cove, ROM (Winners Bitch from the six-to nine-month puppy class at the 1982 National Specialty, Select Bitch at the 1985 and 1988 National Specialties); Ch. Mooncusser's RSVP of Pouch Cove, ROM (Best of Winners and Select Bitch at the 1983 National Specialty); Ch. Barharber's Rosco Pouch

Ch. Keepsake of Pouch Cove, CD, WD (Ch. Pouch Cove Gref of Newton-Ark ex Ch. Mooncusser RSVP of Pouch Cove, ROM), bred by David and Peggy Helming. Owned by Peggy Helming and Chris LaMuraglia, "Sage" was the top winning Newfoundland bitch in 1989. Best of Breed at the Niagara Frontier Newfoundland Specialty, she is shown with handler Robert Stebbins.

Ch. Riptide's Steamboat Willie (Ch. High Tide's Captain Crunch ex Brassibear's Schooner Bonney), multiple Group winner, bred by Ginger and Grant Hoag of Riptide Kennels and owned by Elizabeth and Christopher Hibler.

Cove (Best of Breed at the 1988 National Specialty); Ch. Mooncusser's Reef of Pouch Cove, ROM (Best of Breed at the 1989 National Specialty); Ch. Rocky Reef of Pouch Cove, CD (Winners Dog at the 1989 National Specialty); Ch. Never Grow Up of Pouch Cove, WRD, DD (Winners Bitch and Best of Winners at the 1988 National Specialty); Ch. Spillway's Devon of Pouch Cove (Best in Puppy Sweepstakes at the 1987 National Specialty); Ch. Amity's Bearfoot of Pouch Cove, ROM (#3 top producer in the history of the breed, Reserve Winners Dog at the 1984 National Specialty); Ch. Highland Bear of Pouch Cove, ROM (top producer in 1988); Ch. Keepsake of Pouch Cove, CD, ROM (Group winner and top winning Newfoundland bitch in 1989); Ch. Moon Shadow of Pouch Cove (top winning Newfoundland bitch in 1988); Ch. Pouch Cove's Jacks or Better (Best in Puppy Sweepstakes at the 1992 National Specialty); and Ch. Pouch Cove's On All Fours (Best of Opposite Sex at the 1992 National Specialty) to name just a few!

Though they have spent less time being shown and more time in the breeding program, one would be remiss not to call special attention to two Pouch Cove favorites, Ch. Ad Lib of Pouch Cove, ROM (dam of eleven champions and six working titlists), and her son Ch. John's Big Ben of Pouch Cove, ROM (top producing stud in 1991), who has influenced the breed in a very positive way, reproducing his near perfect head and substance. Indeed, the achievements of Pouch Cove are awesome, but the breeding program continues, vigorously yielding a host of new, young standard bearers—the headliners of the future.

Riptide

Grant and Ginger Hoag, of Northridge, California, purchased their first Newfoundland in 1964. However, it was their acquisition of Ch. Edenglen's Eloise that set Riptide on a course of breeding fine browns. When bred to Ch. Edenglen's Beau Geste, Eloise produced the first brown champion in California, Ch. Riptide's Cinnamon Bear. Bear was then bred to the Hoag's brown Ch. Old Mole's Malcolm of Riptide, to produce an all-brown litter.

The tradition of raising brown Newfoundlands continues in California today. Recent Riptide champions include VN Ch. Riptide's Brown Kodiak Bear, CD, WRD, DD (the canine star in the movie *Police Academy*, and who also saved the life of his owner Kathie Cullen—for real), and Ch. Riptide's Cinnamon Bear Too, owned by Jeff and Joan Givens' Springhaven Kennel, which has bred such notables as the Best in Show winner Ch. Kendian's Cadbury, Ch. Springhaven's Kopper Kelli, Ch. Springhaven's Captain Tug, Ch. Springhaven's Sir Winston and Ch. Springhaven's Kava of Kendian. Riptide was also campaigning the Group-winning brown Ch. Riptide's Steamboat Willie, owned by Elizabeth and Christopher Hibler, when this book went to press.

Seamen

Seamen Newfoundlands, owned by Al and Chris D'Orio, of Mullica Hill, New Jersey, descend from Nashau Auke, Newton-Ark and Tuckamore lines.

Ch. Seamen's Swashbuckler was Winners Dog at the 1978 National Specialty, and more recent Seamen titlists include Ch. Seamen's Case of Rum; Ch. Seamen's Joyful Noise; Ch. Tuckamore's Abigail of Seamen; Seamen's Emily the Dickens, CD, WRD, DD; and Ch. Seamen's A Cut Above, owned by Dana and Terry Phillips.

Seaplay

Deborah Craig's Seaplay Kennels, located in Snow Hill, Maryland, has for the most part utilized the Mooncusser, Newton-Ark and Pouch Cove lines. Seaplay champions include Ch. Seaplay Shady of Newton-Ark; Ch. Seaplay Sunrise of Pouch Cove, Ch. Seaplay Eclipses Moses, CD; Ch. Seaplay Tyree Lady Jessica; Ch. Seaplay Casabianca, CD; Ch. Seaplay's Max A Million Bear, CD, DD; Seaplay Ruff'N Ready, CD, and Seaplay Rusty Rigging, CD.

Seaward

Though no longer active, Seaward, owned by Elinor Ayers, of Vermont, was until recently the oldest ongoing Newfoundland kennel in North America, having begun operations in the early 1930s.

Concentrating mostly on Landseers, Seaward produced many champions and working titlists. However, Seaward's success in blacks was largely a result of Ch. Dryad's Strong Sea Pirate, ROM, who was bred by Ed Wilson and owned by Elinor Ayers. Pirate produced such Seaward champions as Ch. Seaward's Yankee Ranger, Ch. Seaward's Barbary Pirate, Ch. Seaward's Satin Finish, CDX, Ch. Seaward's Zenith, CD, and Ch. Seaward's Jolly Roger Beaupre, who in turn sired the all-time top-winning Newfoundland Ch. Seaward's Blackbeard ("Adam"). Adam, handled by Gerlinde Hockla, won an amazing thirty-one all-breed Bests in Show, including Best in Show at the Westminster Kennel Club in 1984, and many Specialties, including Best of Breed at both the 1982 and 1984 Nationals.

Seawied

Betsy Wiederhold, of New Hampshire, and her daughter Nancy Wiederhold-Talgo, of Ashford, Connecticut, have the Seawied Newfoundlands, which are based on the Nashau Auke, Pouch Cove and Tuckamore lines. The list of Seawied champions includes Ch. Seawied's Tame, Best of Opposite Sex winner at the 1987 National Specialty; Ch. Seawied's Luv Boat; Ch. Seawied's Island Buoy; and the Regional Specialty Best of Breed winner and multiple Group placer Ch. Seawied's Bunker's Cove Boomer.

Shadybrook

Beginning with Edenglen lines, Richard and Jeri Krokum have developed their Hillsboro, Oregon-based Shadybrook Newfoundlands into one of America's

Ch. Shadybrook's Late Arrival, ROM (Ch. Shadybrook's Try For An Oscar, CD, WRD, ROM, ex Reaching Breeze of Pouch Cove), was Best of Opposite Sex at the National Specialty, Best of Breed at three regional Specialties and is a Group winner. Breeders/owners: Richard and Jeri Krokum. *Lindemaier*

Ch. Shadybrook's Keebear (Ch. Pouch Cove Gref of Newton-Ark, ROM, ex Ch. Shadybrook's Summer Breeze), Best of Winners and holder of three Selects at National Specialties, multiple regional Specialty Bests winner, twice NCA Show Dog of the Year and an all-breed Best in Show. Breeders/owners: Richard and Jeri Krokum. *Ross*

premier breeding and show kennels, producing many champions and Specialty winners since the mid-1970s. When bred to Ch. Edenglen's Oscar, the Shadybrook foundation bitch Ch. Edenglen's Prudence produced Ch. Shadybrook's Mama Bear, WRD, and the well-known Ch. Shadybrook's Try For An Oscar, CD, WRD, ROM ("Josh"). When bred to Reaching Breeze of Pouch Cove, Josh produced Ch. Shadybrook's Summer Breeze and Ch. Shadybrook's Late Arrival, ROM (Beau). The Best of Opposite Sex winner at the 1985 National Specialty and Best of Breed at three regional Specialties, Beau is also a producer of fine show dogs, as indicated by his ROM status.

However, it was Beau's sister, Summer, bred to Ch. Pouch Cove Gref of Newton-Ark, ROM, that produced Shadybrook's most famous dog, the handsome Ch. Shadybrook's Keebear. Kee's record includes Best of Winners at the 1986 National Specialty, three Select Dog honors at National Specialities, two NCA Show Dog of the Year awards (1989 and 1990), two-time Kal Kan Pedigree Award winner, eleven Regional Specialty Bests of Breed, seventeen Group firsts and an all-breed Best in Show. And the great majority of these wins, including the BIS, were made owner-handled.

Very much to their credit, the Krokums have established and maintained this very successful breeding program with only a relatively small number of dogs. And that tradition continues today with more Shadybrook winners on the horizon, some sired by the Krokums' latest special and a Beau son, Ch. Dalken's General Patton.

Shadow Bear

Using both the Benhil and Ebunyzar lines, Jim and Sue Miller's Shadow Bear Kennels, of Clay, New York, is home to Ch. Benhil's Squire Benson, CD, Ch. Ebunyzar's Mr. J of Shadow Bear and the homebred Ch. Shadow Bear's Admiral Dokken, WRD, DD.

Shadowwood

Mike and Sarah Boyko's Shadowwood Newfoundlands, of Warrenton, Virginia, combine the Shadybrook and Pouch Cove lines. Shadowwood champions include Ch. Shadowwood's Charming Charlie, CDX, Ch. Shadowwood's Special Edition, Ch. Dalken's Echo of Shaddowwood, Ch. Shadowwood's Sailor Boy and Ch. Shadowwood's April Storm.

Skimeister

Basing their breeding predominantly on the Newton Ark, Pouch Cove and Spillway lines, Dwight and Debbie Summers have bred many champions at their Skimeister establishment in Shrewsbury, Pennsylvania. These include the Best in Show bitch Ch. Skimeister's Best Kept Secret, Ch. Skimeister's Coral Reef (Best of Winners at the 1989 National Specialty), Ch. Skimeister's Keep the

Faith, Ch. Skimeister's Holly Berry, Ch. Skimeister's Murphy's Law, Ch. Skimeister's Caritas. Other Skimeister Newfies of note include Ch. Finders Keepers of Pouch Cove, Ch. Skimeister's Meg of Pouch Cove, Ch. SKI's Legacy from Pouch Cove and Ch. SKI's Amendment by Pouch Cove.

Skipjack

Skipjack Kennels, owned by Christine Griffith and located in Sylmar, California, is home to many champions and several Specialty, Group and Best in Show winners. Beginning in the early 1970s with the foundation bitch Hali-rock's Gay Abandon, ROM, Skipjack went on to breed such notables as Ch. Skipjack's Dinah Mite, ROM; Ch. Skipjack's Morocan Moonshine, ROM; Ch. Skipjack's Double Dare, ROM; Ch. Skipjack's Mobandy; Ch. Skipjack's JB of Gladshire; Ch. Skipjack's Go For the Gusto; Ch. Skipjack's Executive; and Ch. Skipjack's Bulkhead. However, the best-known Skipjack champions are the father and son all-breed Best in Show winners Ch. Skipjack's Moby and Ch. Skipjack's Buddha of Fathom, the first brown Newfoundland to win a Group 1st or Best in Show. The multiple Group winner Ch. Skipjack's Magnum was being campaigned when this book was submitted to the publisher.

Spillway

Phyllis Welch and her daughter Jamie, of Blanchard, Pennsylvania, began breeding Newfoundlands in the late 1970s. Spillway's foundation bitches included two Ch. Old Mole's Lucas, ROM, offspring—Ch. Schooner Thelma Lou and Schooner's Maggie Mae, ROM, both bred by Dail Corl, Lucas's owner. However, it was Dail Corl's other male that was to influence not only the Spillway breeding program, but the breeding programs of many other kennels as well. That very handsome male was Ch. Schooner Yosef of Newton Ark, ROM, by Ch. Kuhaia's Yankee of Newton Ark out of Ch. Ferryland's Abby of Newton Ark, ROM. Phyllis was fortunate enough to obtain Yosef when Dail retired from dogs, since Dail believed that Spillway was just the right home for Yosef. It was a dream come true for Phyllis, as up to that point she would make weekly pilgrimages to Dail's home in order to visit Yosef. This is totally understandable to anyone who knew Yosef, as he was clearly a beautiful Newfoundland.

Needing one point to finish his championship, Yosef was entered in the open dog class at the 1981 NCA Specialty. Groomed by Peggy Helming and handled by Dave, Yosef won his class, Winners Dog, and Best of Winners to finish. Not bad for Phyllis and Jamie's first National Specialty! To make the weekend even more exciting, Yosef's daughter Ch. Spillway's Mixed-M-Ocean, ROM, out of his first litter (and the first litter bred at Spillway) won the nine-to-twelve-month puppy bitch class. Spillway was off to an excellent start.

From that point on it was smooth sailing for Yosef. Used on a number of bitches (especially those at Spillway and Pouch Cove), Yosef has thus far produced thirty champions, eight working titlists and three ROM titlists. Yosef's

Ch. Skipjack's Magnum (Ch. Skipjack's Double Dare, ROM, ex Harbour Watch of Skipjack), bred, owned and handled by Christine Griffith. Magnum is a multiple Group winner. *Missy Yuhl*

Ch. Schooner Yosef of Newton-Ark, ROM (Ch. Kuhaia's Yankee of Newton-Ark ex Ch. Ferry-land's Abby of Newton-Ark, ROM), Winners Dog at the National Specialty and sire of many top winning and producing dogs. Bred by Robin Seaman and Janet Levine and owned by Jamie and Phyllis Welch.
Tatham

best-known offspring include Ch. Spillway's Mixed-M-Ocean; Ch. Spillway Devon of Pouch Cove; Ch. Motion Carried of Pouch Cove; VN Ch. Kilyka's Aphrodite of Pouch Cove, UD, WRD, DD, ROM; Ch. Never Grow Up of Pouch Cove WRD, DD; Ch. Moon Shadow of Pouch Cove; Ch. Pouch Cove's Treasure Chest; and the multiple Best in Show and National Specialty winner Ch. Pouch Cove's Favorite Son, ROM.

In total, Spillway has produced approximately thirty-five champions, including many Specialty winners. An impressive record for a kennel that has been breeding for just over a decade, and proving that there is no better way to start than with dogs of the greatest possible quality.

Spring Harbor

Ralph and Mary Averill's Spring Harbor Kennel, in Holly, Michigan, is home to Ch. Roosevelt of Thunder Bay, ROM, sire of many champions throughout the Midwest. Some of Roosevelt's Spring Harbor champions include Ch. Spring Harbor Root to Outport, Ch. Spring Harbor Comanche Bear, Ch. Spring Harbor Storm A Bruin, Ch. Spring Harbor's Black Orchid, Ch. Spring Harbor's Mauna Loa Isle, Ch. Spring Harbor's Sir Benjamin, Ch. Spring Harbor's Vi of Winlow, Ch. Spring Harbor Rebel of Outport and Ch. Thunder Bay's Storm A Brewin, CD, WD, ROM.

Starr King

Originally based on Nashau-Auke and Indigo lines is Marcia Davidson's Starr King Kennels, located in Needham, Massachusetts. Starr King champions include the Group-placing Ch. Starr King's Summit Flag, Ch. Starr King Meg of Nashau-Auke, Ch. Starr King's Buster Black, Ch. Mooncusser Starking Sagamore, ROM, and Ch. Numa's George of Starr King.

Stillwater

Milan Lint, of Columbus, Ohio, owner of Stillwater Kennels, has bred and/or owned such Newfoundlands as Ch. Haven's Garden Party; Ch. Stillwater's Private Party, who was a Select Bitch at the 1986, 1987 and 1990 National Specialties; the multiple Group-winning Ch. Benhil's Stillwater Gulliver; and Ch. Benhil's Stillwater Maxwell.

Storm Tide

Bill and Sue Reiher's Storm Tide Kennel in Annandale, New Jersey, is based on the Pouch Cove bloodline and is home to the multiple Group placer and #1 bitch in 1988 Ch. Moon Shadow of Pouch Cove. Additional Storm Tide champions include Ch. Amity's Storm Tide Sensation, Ch. Storm Tide's Bailin' Out and Ch. Amity's Storm Tide Enticer.

Sunrise

Tom and Sheila Gast's Sunrise Newfoundlands descend from the Dalken, Flying Cloud and Pouch Cove lines. Sunrise, based in Loveland, Colorado, has owned and/or produced many champions, including Ch. Dalken Sunrise Summer Breeze (top winning bitch in 1987), Ch. Sunrise Tommyknocker, Ch. Sunrise Rustic Charm, Ch. Paddlewheel's Belmire Sunrise, Ch. Sunrise Emerald Princess, Ch. Sunrise Riverhouse Potshots, Ch. Sunrise Jetta's Ebony, Ch. Sunrise Diablo, Ch. Sunrise Midnite Satin, Ch. Sunrise Sam's Song and Ch. Sunrise Doc Holiday.

Sun Valley

Breeding both blacks and Landseers, Mike and Lou Ann Lenner, of Sunbury, Pennsylvania, have concentrated on the Bearbrook and more recently Pouch Cove lines. When bred to Ch. Dalken's Denver of Pouch Cove, the Lenners' typey Landseer, Ch. Sun Valley's Solitaire, produced Ch. Sun Valley's Shiver Me Timbers and Ch. Sun Valley's Silhouette, Winners Bitch at a Regional Specialty en route to her title.

Sweetbay

Located in Sherwood, Oregon, the Adlers' Sweetbay Newfoundlands are known all over North America as top working dogs. Indeed, Sweetbay holds the record for the greatest number of Newfoundland obedience, tracking, water and draft titles earned, in addition to producing several dozen conformation champions. Beginning in 1972 with Barbara Allen's Grey October, TD, WD, ROM, Sweetbay incorporated the Shipway, Nine Mile, Topmast and Halirock lines into its breeding. Continually stressing the working instincts and intelligence of the Newfoundland has resulted in over four hundred working and conformation titles on Sweetbay dogs. Notable examples include OTCH Sweetbay's Gretl, TD; VN Ch. Sweetbay's Harmony, UDT, Can. CDX, Can. TD, WRD, DD; VN Ch. Sweetbay's Romney, Am., Can. CD, WRD, TDD; VN Ch. Sweetbay's Brigadier, CD, WRD, TDD; and VN Ch. Sweetbay's Karisma, CD, WRD, DD.

Tabu

Mike and Lou Lomax began providing direction to the Tabu breeding program, originally owned by Pres and Mary Hollander, in the early 1980s. Since that time Salinas, California-based produced dozens of champions, including several Specialty winners and Group placers. A favorite is Ch. Tabu's Mr. Otis Regrets ("Otis"), ROM, sire of Ch. Tabu's Ms. Otis Regrets, Ch. Tabu's Arrabella Respons, Ch. Tabu's Mr. Thorin Oakenshield, Ch. Tabu's Gem of Antares.

However, Otis's most prominent offspring is Ch. Tabu's Pooh Bearabella,

Ch. Haven's Garden Party (Ch. Kuhaia's Rego ex Ch. Haven's Dawn of Pouch Cove), foundation bitch for Milan Lint's Stillwater Kennel, bred by Julie Heyward and owned by Milan Lint and Joan Bendure.

Am., Can. Ch. Tarbell's Boaz (Ch. Mogen of Newton-Ark ex Ch. Kuhaia's Tarbell of Newton-Ark), all-breed Best in Show and National Specialty Best of Breed winner. Bred by Ruth March and Janet Levine and owned by Ruth March of Tarbell Kennels. *Fox & Cook*

the Best of Opposite Sex winner at both the 1990 and 1991 National Specialties, a multiple Specialty winner and the top winning bitch in 1991. Belle is owned by Kathy Griffin, Shelby Guelich and Lou and Mike, and as this is written is producing beautiful puppies at Kathy's Seabrook Kennel, home of Ch. Black Tie Optional at Tabu.

Tarbell

Ruth March, of Livingston Manor, New York, has owned Newfoundlands since 1973, obtaining her first from Little Bear Kennels. However, the Tarbell breeding program has predominantly been based on the Newton-Ark, Newfport and Pouch Cove lines. The breeder of many champions, Group placers and Best in Show winners, Tarbell males include Ch. Tarbell's Asa, the all-breed Best in Show Ch. Tarbell's Jethro, and the all-breed Best in Show and 1986 National Specialty Best of Breed winner Ch. Tarbell's Boaz. Tarbell's distaff side includes the typey bitches Ch. Jerusha of Newton-Ark, Ch. Tarbell's Tamar of Newton-Ark and Ch. Tarbell's Hagar. When this book went to press, Ms. March was watching the progress of two hopefuls—Kilyka's Tarbell of Riverwatch and Pouch Cove's Salome O Tarbell.

Teddy Tug

Using foundation stock from Benhil Kennels is Cheryl and Joe Cettomai's Teddy Tug Newfoundlands, located in Rootstown, Ohio. Teddy Tug champions include Ch. Benhil's Stillwater Maxwell, Ch. Benhil's Man About Town, Ch. Benhil's Uptown Girl and the homebreds Ch. Teddy Tug's Hot Gossip, Ch. Teddy Tug's Talk of the Town, Ch. Teddy Tug's Lady Gabriel, Teddy Tug's Bellweather, WD, and the Group-placing Ch. Benhil's Klein Bruder, CD. Jack and Aura Dean are owners of the young dog Teddy Tug's Marcus Tulius, WD, and Denise Fickey owns Ch. Teddy Tug's Jammin' Jamie.

Thunder Bay

A long-time breeder and exhibitor and AKC licensed judge of Newfoundlands, Norm Belanger's Thunder Bay honor roll includes Ch. Roosevelt of Thunder Bay, ROM; Ch. Thunder Bay's High Roller; Ch. Thunder Bay's Tawa Sun; Ch. Thunder Bay's Tugboat Annie; Ch. Thunder Bay's Midnight Vamp and many others. They make their home in Southfields, Michigan.

Tidalwave

Bob and Jean Quandt, of Libertyville, Illinois, have owned and trained several Edenglen dogs to their championships and Tracking titles, including Edenglen's Chocolate Chip, CD, TD; Edenglen's Titanic, CD, TD; Ch. Edenglen's Mister Christian, CD, TD; and Ch. Edenglen's Robinson Crusoe, CD,

TD. The Quandts also own the imported bitch, Bjornebanden's Nifty Nan, CD, TD.

Triton

John and Patty Tekus's Triton Kennels, located in Medina, Ohio, is home to Ch. Nanwick's American Maid and Ch. Kilyka's Goodness Gracious. The Tekuses are also the breeders of Ch. Triton's Gen. W T Sherman.

Tuckamore

Barbara Finch's Newman, Georgia-based Tuckamore Kennels has bred and/or owned over thirty champions, including the Best of Opposite Sex winner at the 1981 National Specialty Ch. Tuckamore's Ely of Pouch Cove, the Best in Show winner Ch. Tuckamore's Dutch of Pouch Cove, the Best of Breed winner at the 1985 National Specialty Ch. Tuckamore's Julie and the multiple Best in Show and Best of Breed winner at the 1987 National Specialty Ch. Tuckamore's Boomerang.

Tyche

Chris Plum and Maureen Cavanaugh are from Buffalo, Minnesota. Their foundation stock was from Halirock Kennels, and included Ch. Halirock's Tyche, CD. In recent years Tyche has incorporated the Pouch Cove line, breeding to such dogs as Ch. Pouch Cove's Favorite Son, ROM, and Ch. Mooncusser's Reef of Pouch Cove, ROM ("Wimpy"). It was the breeding between Ch. Tyche's Aurora Borealis, CD, and Wimpy that produced Ch. Tyche's Deus Ex Machina, Winners Dog at the 1991 National Specialty. Additional Tyche champions include Ch. Tyche's Demeter, Ch. Tyche's Classic Kodiak and Larry and Leita Cirjak's Ch. Tyche's Achates, CD. Ch. Halirock's Tyche is also the sire of Marilyn Fischbein-Byers's Ch. Itasca Annie O'Northwind, the top winning Newfoundland bitch in 1990 and Tyche's own Ch. Itasca Maya's Shadow Dancer.

Viking

Viking Kennels is owned by Flip Bowser Young of Chillicothe, Ohio. Based on the Shipshape, Kilyka and Pouch Cove lines, Viking is home to Ch. Kilyka's Yogi Bowser Too, CD, Ch. Hearthaven Deliverance, Ch. Viking's Greffa Garbo and the Group-winning Ch. Viking Gnoble Gnewf. Flip is a dedicated Newfoundland Club of America board member that maintains the computer data base at the time of this writing.

Watchbear

Based on Dryad and Topmast breeding is Jeanne and Terry Fashempour's Watchbear Newfoundlands of Medina, Ohio. Watchbear is home to such champions as Ch. Watchbear's Briana, Ch. Watchbear's Butch Cassidy, Ch. Watchbear's Annie Oakley, Ch. Watchbear's Judge Roy Beane and Ch. Watchbear's Lone Ranger. The very pretty Landseer Ch. Watchbear's Willo Hill Jolson is owned by Kathy Wertenberger's Willo Hill Kennels.

Waterlord

Tim Zeitz is the owner of the Ohio-based Waterlord Kennels, and breeder of several champions including Ch. Waterlord's Yankee Rose, Ch. Waterlord's Nautical Nanny and Ch. Waterlord's Miss Stoneybrook. Kathy Stowe's Majestic Bay Kennels is home to Ch. Waterlord's Majestic Princess and Maggie's typey son Majestic Bay First and Goal.

Wee Lovett

Though several of the Wee Lovett Newfoundlands, of Ada, Michigan, have finished their championships, Mike and Sandee Lovett are best known for their dogs' working accomplishments. Avid draft, obedience and water workers, a few of the Lovett's dogs include VN Ch. Spindrift Wee Lovett Alcor, CD, WRD, TDD; Ch. Wee Lovett's Chocolate Mousse; Wee Lovett's Sweet Siera, DD; Wee Lovett Alioth of Callisto, DD; Wee Lovett Windwalker, CD; Wee Lovett Jacobus DeBruyne, CD, WRD, TDD; Ch. Wee Lovett's Island of Manitou; Wee Lovett's Maritime Megrez, CD, WRD, TDD; and Wee Lovett's Star of Andromeda, WRD. Mike and Sandee travel all over the United States conducting working dog seminars and judging. Sandee has also served on the Newfoundland Club of America board.

Welcove

Candy Welch's Welcove Newfoundlands, of Columbia, South Carolina, predominantly descend from the Kuhaia and Newton Ark lines. A breeder of many champions, Welcove is well-known in the South for quality Newfoundlands. A few of the Welcove champions include Ch. Welcove's Lady Margaret, Ch. Welcove's Yogi Bear, Ch. Welcove's Once in a Blue Moon and Ch. Welcove's Rosan Rosanna Dana.

Windwagon

Marget Johnson's and Bill Matlock's Windwagon Newfoundlands, from Tipp City, Ohio, are predominantly a combination of the Mooncusser and Pouch Cove lines. Windwagon notables include Ch. Mooncusser Windwagon Kate; Ch. Pouch Cove's Jacks or Better, who was Best in Puppy Sweepstakes at the 1992 National Specialty; Ch. Jamboree of Pouch Cove; and Bill's favorite Kilyka's Windwagon Smith, CD. Marget has actively served on the Newfoundland Club of America's board.

Ch. Benhil's Uptown Girl, ROM (Ch. Benhil's Black Prince, CD, ex Nashau-Auke's Ashli of Benhil), was Select Bitch at a National Specialty. Bred by Joan Bendure and Jane Thibault, she is the foundation bitch for owner Cheryl Cettomai of Teddy Tug Kennels.

Ch. Teddy Tug's Hot Gossip (Ch. Benhil's Stillwater Gulliver ex Ch. Benhil's Uptown Girl, ROM), bred and owned by Cheryl Cettomai of Teddy Tug Kennels.

Eng. Ch. Kelligrews Terre-Neuve With Seaquaybear, Best of Breed at the Newfoundland Club's Championship show in 1990. Owned by Mr. and Mrs. S. Woolmore and Mr. and Mrs. R. Scothern.

E. T. Gascoigne LMPA

Sealcove Crystal, a lovely bitch bred and owned by Mr. and Mrs. A. Sussam, on her way to her championship with two Challenge Certificates and several Reserves.

4

The Newfoundland
in England and Canada

ANY SERIOUS STUDY of the Newfoundland breed must include the extremely important contribution of breeders on the other side of the Atlantic—especially the English. They were not only the first to popularize the breed outside its native land, starting back in the eighteenth century, they have also ensured its survival during periods when this invaluable breed was on the verge of extinction.

By the latter half of the 1700s, Newfoundlands were being imported to Britain in significant numbers. The port cities of Bristol, Hull and Poole were the major points of importation. Although some dogs were brought over on commission, a great number were sold at dockside or taken to London or other major cities. The fact that these dogs endured the harsh conditions of crossing the North Atlantic, but still maintained their gentle dispositions and adapted readily to their new owners, is eloquent testimony to the legendary strength of the breed's character.

During the first half of the nineteenth century, Newfoundlands were employed, to some extent, as draft animals, pulling carts along England's south coast, particularly in the city of Poole. The streets of many of these coastal cites were extremely narrow and crooked. A dog cart could negotiate these lanes much more easily than a horse-drawn wagon. This means of haulage was popular until the government outlawed it in 1850.

The Newfoundland's size, swimming ability, hardiness, intelligence, physical beauty and excellent temperament made it popular with the more affluent and the rural gentry. In addition to being something of a status symbol, New-foundlands were also employed as canine nannies and personal companions, and saw great popularity as gun dogs. There is even a story from the last century of a husband trading his wife for a Newfoundland dog!

The latter half of the nineteenth century saw the Newfoundland decline in popularity as a gun dog, but it was still used for crossbreeding with other varieties because of its unsurpassed water sense. It went on to assume what has become its major role to this very day, as a family pet, guardian and show dog.

The early English breeders were particularly concerned with preserving the Newfoundland's water-working characteristics and gentle temperament, as well as refining and stabilizing the breed type. The dog that we know as the present-day Newfoundland is the result of their careful breeding programs (unfortunately, few records survive) and through the particular efforts of J. C. Knight Bruce, who had a major influence in setting the breed Standard.

Bruce believed that a Newfoundland needed to have certain physical characteristics to enable it to swim properly. He thought that a true water dog would need certain physical characteristics similar to those of other mammals that spend a lot of their time in the water—otters, for example. He maintained that the Newfoundland's body should be relatively long in relation to its legs, which should not be long but short to medium length and muscular. He further noted that dogs of this build should have a characteristic "rolling gait" when moving about on land.

The shape of the head was another subject of Bruce's attention, as well as that of Henry Farquharson, one of the most prominent nineteenth-century English Newfoundland breeders. Both insisted that the heads of the dogs of the 1880s were too narrow and lacked a projecting eyebrow, which would make them more suitable for spending long periods in the water, especially in rough conditions.

The latter half of the nineteenth century could be considered the heyday of Newfoundland breeding in England and there was a large number of prolific breeders. A discussion of some of the more prominent ones will prove of interest.

Farquharson deserves some further mention at this point. Although his name first appears in show catalogs after 1870, he started his kennel in the 1830s with an imported dog from Newfoundland. He continued to import dogs, and a number became successful show animals.

Heenan I, owned by a Mr. Milvan and bred sometime around 1860, is reputed to have been one of the early contributors to the gene pool of a long line of English champions, including the Reverend S. Atkinson's Cato.

This dog further distinguished himself by rescuing a drowning woman, along with his master. Cato was also a prolific stud who had considerable influence on succeeding generations of show dogs.

Dr. Gordon Stables was an influential breeder whose personality departed from the rather eccentric but stuffy stereotype of the wealthy, nineteenth-century English dog breeder. In addition to being a popular author, he was also something of a traveling showman. He toured England in his Romany caravan (the British equivalent of an American circus wagon) with a large collection of dogs of various breeds. He wrote numerous literate but easily read articles on dog breeding and was the first author to describe the black-and-white Newfoundland as a "Landseer." (It seems reasonable to presume that he chose this term as the result of seeing a poplar portrait of a black-and-white Newfoundland by the famous English artist, Sir Edwin Landseer, who painted many.) Stables imported Theodore Nero from Newfoundland, who went on to become a champion. According to *The Newfoundland*, published by the English Newfoundland Club and edited by Carol Cooper, "he was probably the last quality import to this country."

The first Newfoundland champion was Ch. Dick, a Landseer, owned by a Mr. Evans. An engraving portrays him "as having a black head with white blaze, perfect saddle, black rump, and heavy white tail."

In the late 1870s T. E. Mansfield founded a kennel housing up to forty dogs, many of whom successfully competed and whose offspring also included a significant number of champions. Mansfield later became a highly respected judge of the breed and did much to ensure the preservation of soundness and type. (At that time some breeders were sacrificing type in order to produce larger dogs.) Among his champions were Ch. The Black Prince, Ch. Gunville, Ch. Coutier and Ch. Lady Mayoress.

E. Nichol, owner of Ch. Nelson I, was another prominent and influential breeder. Ch. Nelson sired many successful competitors including Mansfield's Ch. Lady Mayoress.

The 1860s saw the entry of the Newfoundland into English show rings. In 1860 a Newfoundland bitch won first prize at the Birmingham show. At an exhibition in 1862 the number of Newfoundland entries jumped to forty-one, and two of these dogs took first and second place in their classes. In 1864 Cabot, owned by the Prince of Wales, won a first place.

The number of Newfoundland show entries reached its maximum in 1892 at the Preston show, where 128 dogs competed.

The breed remained strong during the first decade of this century due largely to the efforts and expertise of breeders like Sheldon, Fern, Horsefield and Goodall. Of these, Miss Goodall deserves particular mention.

Although her kennel was named Starbeck, her dogs carried the "Gipsy" prefix with their names. Her kennel produced a number of champions, the most famous of whom was Ch. Gipsy Duke, who had won twenty-two Challenge Certificates by 1910. This record remained unbeaten until 1986. Goodall was also the owner of Ch. Shelton King, the sire of Ch. Siki, who was arguably one of the most important Newfoundland sires of this century.

The harsh conditions brought about by World War I, such as mandatory food rationing, almost extinguished the breed. By 1923 the number of registered dogs had plummeted to twenty-two, and it was only through Herculean efforts and very sound breeding practices (the gene pool was severely limited at that time) of Goodall and a few others that the breed survived and subsequently flourished.

Ch. Siki, owned by a Mr. Bland, has what almost amounts to a legendary reputation among knowledgeable fanciers of this breed. Even though he was not particularly outstanding in appearance, he was a prolific stud who consistently produced offspring of exceptionally high quality. It was the Siki offspring that were responsible for improving the breed in the United States.

In the period between the two world wars the Harligen kennel, owned by May van Oppen, and Fairwater, owned by the Handleys, were among the most prominent of the English kennels. These two kennels produced numerous champions, and the English Newfoundland Club's *The Newfoundland* offers an excellent, detailed account of their accomplishments.

World War II saw another episode of near-extinction in Britain. The War brought breeding nearly to a halt, and those dogs surviving at its end were too old to be bred.

It was largely through the generosity and help of American breeders that English Newfoundland bloodlines were revived. Interestingly, it was through dogs who traced their pedigrees back to Ch. Siki, sent to England from America, that the breed was restored. (A number of animals came from the Waseeka and Dryad kennels.) This effort was augmented by quality imports from Europe as well.

THE NEWFOUNDLAND IN ENGLAND TODAY

In the 1950s Perryhow Kennels, owned by Mona Bennett, became a major influence on the English breeding scene. Bennett imported a number of dogs from both the United States and the Continent and had an important influence into the 1960s.

From the 1950s up to the present, English breeding stock for both blacks and Landseers has been ocassionally mated to imports from Europe, the United States and Canada. *The Newfoundland* provides a detailed description of contemporary kennels and the more important dogs, but it is also worthwhile to briefly mention some of them here.

The Esmeduna Kennel, owned by the Whittakers, was very prominent in the 1960s and source of breeding stock for the following: Mapleopals, owned by the Ludlows; Orovales, owned by a Miss Yeoward; and Hambledown, owned by the Pratts. The Esmeduna Kennel has produced ten champions in all.

Sigroc Kennels, owned by Miss Davies, has done much to improve the breed. One of her dogs, Ch. Sigroc Sail by the Stars, was the top Newfoundland of 1979.

The Adeys, owners of Shermead Kennels, have been the first to breed and show brown Newfoundlands since World War II. They have done much to popularize the browns in Great Britain.

Stormsail Kennels, owned by the Orianis, has produced a number of champions. One of their first dogs, although purchased from another kennel, won the water trials in 1969 and 1971.

From what I can tell, it seems that English breeders are seriously committed to preserving and improving the type and temperament of the breed. They are

Mrs. Phylis Colgan, many times the "Top Breeder" in Newfoundlands, with Eng. Ch. Karazan Jemima Beam.

Challenge Certificate winners at The National Working Breeds Championship Show, 1992. Left: (Bitch C.C.) Eng. Ch. Stormsail Tokachi of Kubear (JW), bred by Mr. and Mrs. P. Oriani and owned by Mr. and Mrs. D. Munday. Right: (Dog C.C. and B.O.B.) Eng. Ch. Kelligrews Eagle at Tidesoak (JW), bred by Mr. and Mrs. S. Woolmore and now residing in the United States with his owners, Mr. and Mrs. R. Tyler.

particularly careful to use not only their intuition and experience, but also take advantage of the latest veterinary technology, in breeding their dogs.

THE BRITISH SHOW SYSTEM

The British show system is, to put it mildy, "complex." Its structure and rules can be confusing. And, rather than confuse the reader by describing it in my own words, I'll quote an excerpt from a letter sent to me by Maggie Tyler, who is originally from England but is currently residing in the States:

Essentially there are six levels of dog shows run under the auspices of The Kennel Club, but the most commonly seen are Exemption, Open and Championship shows. Exemption shows are fun meetings often held to raise money for charity. All manner of dogs, pure-bred, mongrel, registered and unregistered may enter—and classes are often HUGE! (Classes are separate for pure-bred, registered dogs and "novelty" classes such as dogs with the waggiest tail!!)

Open shows come further "up the ladder," and many people stop at this level as the standard of dogs can be very high indeed. These shows are usually all-breed shows and are for registered dogs only. An average Open show will have ten or so Newfs entered and a total entry of some 1,500 to 2,500 dogs. Many Champions will be found at Open shows, looking for Group and BIS wins. No wins at Open level count toward that elusive Title [sic]. (These look *very* similar to your shows both in number and quality.)

Now it starts getting interesting . . . The only place you can make up a Champion is at a Championship Show, logical, hey? I will write every last little detail, take from it what you will.

There are about 30 Championship Shows in Britain offering Challenge Certificate to Newfoundlands (annually). Each Show has pair, one for the dog, one for the bitch. These Challenge Certificates are also known as CCs or "Tickets." To earn that most esteemed of titles in Britain, a dog must win three Tickets under three different judges and at least one must be won after the dog is one year old.

In order to award Tickets, a judge will have proven his knowledge of the breed by judging an inordinate number of classes at Open level and have judged the breed for a minimum of five years. In practice a very much longer "apprenticeship" is usual.

All our Championship shows are benched and are very large affairs, averaging 11,000–14,000 dogs over two or three days! (Every weekend from April thru to October! You will see why I miss my regular showing here.)

There are many possible classifications but by far the most common are:

1)	Minor Puppy	(6–9 months)
2)	Puppy	(6–12 months)
3)	Junior	(6–18 months)
4)	Novice	(Dog not to have won four or more 1sts at Open or Champ. shows.)
5)	Post Graduate	(Dog not to have won a CC or five or more 1sts at Champ. shows at this class level or above.)
6)	Limit	(Dog not to have won three CCs or more 1sts at Champ. shows at this level or above.)

| 7) Open | (Open to any registered dog of the breed of any age and allowable colour. This is where Champions are shown and, of course, any other dogs that exhibit the necessary maturity and quality to fight it out with the "Big Guns"! |

Dogs and bitches have their own classes and a dog can be entered in as many classes as the owner wants.

Males are judged first and prize cards awarded 1st (red), 2nd (blue), 3rd (yellow), Reserve (green), and Very Highly Commended (or Very Humble Canine!!!) (white). When all the males are judged through the classes, all unbeaten males come back into the ring to challenge for the Ticket. The judge awards his Dog Challenge Certificate (amid great roars of excitement!) and then his Reserve Challenge Certificate. The dog who came second to the Ticket winner may challenge for the Reserve. The Reserve is very important because if, for any reason, the Ticket winner is disqualified the Reserve holder is deemed to have won the Ticket. Therefore the wording on the two cards is very similar. "[The dog] is of such outstanding merit as to be worthy of the title of Champion."

The judge has the right to withhold Tickets, but rarely does.

The bitches are judged in the same way, then the Best Dog (Ticket winner) and the Best Bitch (also a Ticket winner) come together for BOB. There is also a challenge for Best Puppy, and this award is very hotly contested!

There are two major things that make the finishing of a British Champion nigh on impossible. Firstly, once "made up" the Champions stay in the competition for those CCs, [and] not drop out into the BOB class. Therefore it is quite possible to have a particularly good dog "block" many other worthy dogs from gaining their Titles purely because the owner is keen to see how many titles the dog can win. (This is happening a lot at the moment.) The second problem for your beloved Newf is the sheer size of entries at these Championship shows. Rarely is the Newf entry less than 100 (yes, every week!), with the increasing popularity of the Newf as a show dog, entries are very often over 130. That's a lot of dogs to beat!!! That is the reason why, when asked how we make up Champions in Britain, I reply, "Imagine having to go BOB or BOS at three Regional Specialties here in America!!" There are some 1,000 or so Newfs registered annually, of those on average four to ten earn their title each year. That's it! You will see, now, why I am so very proud to have brought a British Champion over to the States with me! (Even if most people don't recognise the significance of the Title in Britain.)

An interesting point is that ALL dogs are owner handled.

An obstacle that stands between your BOB and a Group first is that there are 45 breeds in the British Working Group! Still, occasionally a Newf does make it and, even more rarely, a Newf will go BIS having beaten upwards of 11,000 dogs. (It was a good year for Newfs this year and we have had two Newf BIS with two different dogs.)

There is another award that is available to young dogs and this is the Junior Warrant. To gain this award a dog needs to amass twenty-five points between the ages of one year and eighteen months. A dog wins one point for winning a class at an Open show and three points for doing the same at a Championship show. If a dog holds this award you will see (JW) after its name. (Yes, Chief has this too!!)

One thing I miss here is critiques. In Britain judge at an Open and a Championship show is expected to critique the dogs they placed 1st and 2nd. Some of the critiques

Wooddales Louise of Wellfont, dam of seven Challenge Certificate winners, four of which are champions. Bred by Mr. Nielson and imported to the United Kingdom by Mr. and Mrs. Birch. Later owned by Mr. and Mrs. Richards, who bred the above winners from her, she was the top brood bitch in Great Britain in the early 1990s.

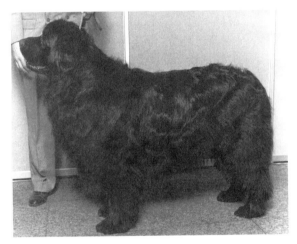

Eng., Ir. Ch. Sheridel Crawford, bred by Mr. and Mrs. Richards. Top winning Newfoundland dog in the United Kingdom at the time of writing, he is strongly bred on Danish bloodlines. Owned by Mr. and Mrs. John Evans.
Dave Freeman

Am., Can. Ch. Arval's Ocean Splendor (Ch. Little Bear's H.M.S. Challenger ex Ch. Arval's Satin Doll), bred by Arne Berg and owned by Margaret Brown of Littlecreek Kennels.

run to the same old formula . . . "nice head, good topline, well angulated and moved well," but some are very enlightening indeed. These critiques appear weekly in the two major canine newspapers, *Dog World* and *Our Dogs*. I have whole scrapbooks full of photos and critiques of Chief and his puppies.

As I think you can see, the English take their dogs and competitive showing very seriously.

In other correspondence, Carol Cooper notes that while the Kennel Club, England's equivalent of the American Kennel Club, does not formally recognize "draught" and water competitions, there is growing interest in convincing the Kennel Club to license judges and offer formal qualifications.

And, unlike the United States, England has only two breed clubs. "The senior one [was] established in 1886 and the Northern one, in 1986. These groups are relatively small."

Newfoundlands compete in Obedience trials but, so far, none have earned a championship. It is obviously more difficult to gain any of the English titles than it is in the States or Canada.

The April 1992 edition of the *Kennel Gazette* has a number of enlightening articles about Newfoundlands. In a particularly interesting one, "The Judge's Choice," a number of judges render their opinions as to which Newfoundland they consider the all-time greatest. There is also another one on Newfoundland "collectables" and has some excellent color plate illustrations of the breed's portrayal on postage stamps from various nations. It is quite obvious from the article and the pictures from Di Sellers of her wonderful collection of Newfoundland memorabilia that includes prints, paintings, statues and banks that the English have enjoyed a long and profound love affair with the Newfoundland breed.

The Newfoundland Club of England publishes one of the most wonderful books available on the breed. *The Newfoundland* is superbly done, includes many color pictures and is written by Club members and edited by Carol Cooper. *The Newfoundland* can be purchased directly from the English Club, with details available through the NCA secretary.

All Newfoundland people owe a debt of gratitude to the English fanciers of the breed. Their generosity kept the Newfoundland breed alive and well in America. Their continued enthusiasm for excellence augurs well that our favorite breed has a secure future both here and in the British Isles.

THE NEWFOUNDLAND IN CANADA

Newfoundland, the land from which the breed takes its name, is Canada's easternmost province. It is also home of the legendary Hon. Harold MacPherson, who owned Westerland Kennels and was the key figure in the restoration of the Newfoundland dog in his native land. MacPherson also served on the board of the Newfoundland Club of America.

Prominent kennels over the years include Montague Wallace's Drummond Kennels, the Gibsons' Perivale Kennels, the Topsail Kennels (owned by the

Pages), Black Ledge Kennels (owned by the Hockridges), Edric Emmet's Laurel Brea Kennels, and the Shelton Kennels of D. R. Oliver, and the Harbourbeem Kennels of Mr. and Mrs. Robert Nutbeem. The following Canadian fanciers currently maintain active breeding programs: Kimtale Kennels of Joyce Mac Kenzie, Bearbrook Kennels of Hilda Deslauriers, Jackie Petrie's Kennel in St. John's (Newfoundland), Moonfleet Kennel of Ray and Donna Overman, Hannibal Kennels of Peter and Maribeth Maniate, Castanewf Kennels of Denise Castonguay, Dorlin Kennels of the Linkletters and Blackgold Kennel of Terry Lambert.

Although Canada is the Newfoundland dog's country of origin, the Newfoundland Dog Club of Canada was not formed until 1963. Mrs. S. J. Navin (owner of Shipmate's Kennels) was the founder along with fourteen charter members. The Club also publishes *Newf News,* which contains articles, Club activities and other items of interest.

The first independent Specialty of the NDC of Canada was held in 1972 in Windsor, Ontario.

The Club's Working Dog Committee was set up in 1981. In 1982 it sent the proposed rules for Draft Dog, Draft Dog Excellent, Water Dog and Water Dog Excellent trials out to the members for comment. The rules were then sent to the Canadian Kennel Club's Versatility Committee. In March 1986 the Canadian Kennel Club approved the rules for Draft and Water Dog titles.

To earn a championship in Canada a dog must earn a total of ten points. A dog can earn up to five points in one show. Points are based on the number of dogs defeated. Canada also selects a best puppy in each breed that goes on to compete for Best Puppy in Show.

Dogs whelped and registered in Canada must have a tattoo or be nose printed by the breeder for registration.

Littlecreek Kennels

Hugh and Margaret Brown's Littlecreek Kennels was started in 1971. Their first stud dog was Ch. Little Bear's HMS Challenger, who made a impact on the Canadian and American bloodlines. Challenger was the sire of their foundation bitch, Can., Am. Ch. Arval's Ocean Splendor. The Browns have owned and bred many champions, Obedience titlists and numerous Specialty winners, Group and Best in Show dogs. Canada's top Newfoundland for 1990 and 1991 was BIS, BISS, Ch. Littlecreek's Feller O'Fortune. Some of the Brownses' other notable dogs are Can., Am. Ch. Littlecreek's Dazzling Opal; Ch. Littlecreek's Grace Darling, BIS; Ch. Littlecreek's Buccaneer; and Ch. Sterncastle's Comic Relief.

Bayside Kennels

Jim and Diane Bricknell's foundation bitch for their Bayside Kennels was Ch. Arval's Bayside Tarah, who was the top brood bitch in Canada for three

Can. Ch. Littlecreek's Feller O'Fortune (Am., Can. Ch. Thunder Bay's Storm A Brewin ex Littlecreek's Ocean Clipper). A Canadian all-breed Best in Show and Specialty winner, he was bred by Margaret Brown, handled by Ann Forth and owned by Jim Cartwright.

Alex Smith

Am., Can. Ch. Littlecreek's Dazzling Opal (Am., Can. Ch. Evangeline's Cochise ex Can. Ch. Littlecreek's Grace Darling) was Best of Winners at the Newfoundland Club of America National Specialty in 1987 under Kitty Drury. Shown by her breeder and owner at that time, Margaret Brown, Opal was later sold to Inge Artsøe of Denmark. *Phoebe*

Can. Ch. Bayside's Smoke "N" Joe (Am. Ch. Springharbour's Storm "A" Bruin ex Can. Ch. Bayside's Jasmin) is a Best Puppy in Show winner. He is shown here with his breeder/owner Jim Bricknell.

Am., Can. Ch. Bayside's Second-In-Command shown going Best of Winners at a Newfoundland Club of America regional Specialty. He is owned by Jim Bricknell.

The Landseer is Am., Can. Ch. Topmast's Pied Piper, ROM (Can. Ch. Napanewf's Angus of Kimtale ex Calli's Shade of Black, ROM), and the black is Am., Can. Ch. Outtrail's Kojak of Topmast, ROM (Can. Ch. Ebonewf's Hilarion, Am., Can. CD, TD, ex Can. Ch. Little Bear's Hope Ten Guns), owned by Margaret Willmott of Topmast Kennels.

consecutive years. Some other champions include Ch. Bayside's Ishtar, Ch. Bayside's Brazen Beauty, Ch. Bayside's Black Beauty, Ch. Bayside's Smoke "N" Joe, Ch. Bayside's Jasmin, Ch. Bayside's Running Bear, Ch. Bayside's Black Ember, Ch. Bayside's Lightning and the beautiful Ch. Bayside's Royal Commander.

Arval Kennels

Val DeGaust's Arval Kennel has produced well over a hundred champions and provided the foundation stock for many of the Canadian Kennels breeding and showing today.

Topmast Kennel

The Topmast Kennels of Margaret and John Willmott has been responsible for the resurgence and quality of Landseer Newfoundlands. Although raising beautiful Landseers was not Marg's goal, it just kind of happened with the birth of "Piper." His pedigree shows mostly black dogs, but obviously carries the Landseer recessive. Topmast also produces typey blacks.

Can., Am. Ch. Topmast's Pied Piper, ROM, won Best of Breed at the 1976 Newfoundland Club of America's National Specialty.

Landseers were not popular at the time of Piper's win, but he certainly had the crowd behind him that day. Up until that time the Landseers were very lacking in type, but everyone was in awe of Piper. Breeders that had no desire to own a Landseer were quickly converted.

Piper's achievements between Canada and the States include twenty-five Bests in Show and four Specialty Bests of Breeds. Marg's theory for producing typey Landseers and blacks is to only breed typey dogs. If one selects for markings over type, type will be lost. She notes that some of the prettiest-marked Landseers have in their background the Continental Landseer from Europe. These dogs were bred with pattern as of the utmost importance; as a result type suffered greatly. That those Landseers were not bred with typey blacks when typey Landseers were not available also contributed to the problem. Type must always come first, and it is better to breed from poor-patterned, typey Landseers than from beautifully-marked off-type animals. Eventually, both type and correct pattern will result. Landseer Newfoundlands should be no different in type or temperament than any other Newfoundland—regardless of color.

Some of the dogs on Topmast's honor roll include Topmast's Blackberry Blossom, multi-Specialty and Best in Show winner and two times Danish gold cup winner; Am. Ch. Topmast's Starbright, ROM; Can., Am. Ch. Topmast's Bartleby; Topmast's Sarah Jane, ROM; Can., Am. Ch. Topmast's Duncan Mac-Iver, ROM; Ch. Topmast's Orange Blossom Special; Can. Am. Ch. Topmast's Jack Frost; Ch. Topmast's Belvedere; Ch. Topmast's John Houston; and many more.

Am., Can. Ch. Topmast's John Houston (Ch. Topmast's John Henry ex Abbey Acres Topmast Sophie Tucker), bred and owned by Margaret Willmott and co-owned with Heather Brady. *Mikron*

Can. Ch. Topmast's Checkers (Topmast's Fiddler ex Topmast's Cheers), bred and owned by Margaret Willmott.

Am., Can Ch. Greer's Shogun, ROM, Am., Can. CD (Nanicoth Peter Pan Evergreer, Can. CD ex Am., Can. Ch. Nanicoth Peter Pan Victoria, ROM, NCA, DD), bred and owned by Fay and Robert Greer. *Mikron*

Can. Ch. Greer's Lucky Oreo Dream (Am., Can. Ch. Greer's Mighty Blocker ex Am., Can. Ch. Greer's Lonesome Charlie), bred and owned by Fay and Robert Greer. *Mikron*

Greer Newfoundlands

Robert and Fay Greer have consistently produced large-type Newfoundlands. Perhaps their most outstanding dog is Can., Am. Ch. Greer's Shogun, Am., Can. CD, ROM ("Gunner"). Gunner was only bred three times and produced sixteen puppies, so to have achieved ROM status is quite a feat. Fay knew the quality of this wonderful dog, but she couldn't stand to have him away from home to be campaigned, so home he stayed, hidden in the northern woods of Canada. But he had a special job, keeping the bears out of the backyard!

At this writing, Fay has recently imported a dog from the Culnor Kennel in England and is waiting for a puppy bitch from the Aarozeen Kennel in England. She hopes these outcrosses will enable her to progress in her breeding program.

Some of the more notable dogs from the Greer Kennel include Am., Can. Ch. Greer's Tyler of Blackgold, owned and handled by Terry Lambert of Blackgold Kennels; Am., Can. Ch. Greer's Special Export, #3 Newf in the United States in 1991, shown by Sandy and Richard Donnay. Others include Am., and Can. Ch. Greer's Block Buster, Am., Can. CD, DD; Ch. Greer's Mighty Block Buster; Am., Can. Ch. Greer's Velveteen Newf; Can. Ch Greer's Lovelee Lacee; Can. Ch. Greer's Oreo Dream; Am., Can. Ch. Greer's Mighty Blocker, Am., Can. Ch. Greer's Lonesome Charlie; and Am., Can. Ch. Greer's Great Heart Carebear.

Canadian breeders have produced a considerable number of champions and made invaluable contributions to the breed in an important variety of ways. In addition to this, there has been a high degree of cooperation with breeders in the United States and Great Britain, to the benefit of all.

Ch. John's Big Ben of Pouch Cove, ROM (Ch. Highland Bear of Pouch Cove, ROM, ex Ch. Ad Lib of Pouch Cove, ROM), is an outstanding example of the correct, massive male Newfoundland head. Ben is bred and owned by Peggy and Dave Helming's Pouch Cove Kennels.

Søren Wesseltoft

5

Official Standards
of the Newfoundland

$\mathbf{T}$HE STANDARD of any breed is the blueprint that describes the ideal type, movement and temperament of that breed. It is the written criteria by which a dog of a particular breed is to be judged while stationary and in action. It is what breeders should go by in selecting dogs for breeding and describes to judges what characteristics a particular breed should possess.

Included are the Standards of the American Kennel Club, the Canadian Kennel Club and the The Kennel Club (England). The breeding of Newfoundlands from these three countries has gone full circle from imports and exports to each other in the past century.

I think you will find that most of the European Standards are similar to that of The Kennel Club (England).

The Newfoundland breed Standard is written by the Newfoundland Club of America, Inc., and approved by the American Kennel Club, Inc. All breeds of dogs that are AKC registered must have their Standards approved by the AKC. The Newfoundland Club of America is recogized by the AKC as the parent club for Newfoundlands in the United States.

CURRENT AKC-APPROVED STANDARD

General Appearance

The Newfoundland is a sweet-dispositioned dog that acts neither dull nor ill-tempered. He is a devoted companion. A multipurpose dog, at home on land

and in the water, the Newfoundland is capable of draft work and possesses natural lifesaving abilities.

The Newfoundland is a large, heavily coated, well balanced dog that is deep bodied, heavily boned, muscular and strong. A good specimen of the breed has dignity and proud head carriage.

The following description is that of the ideal Newfoundland. Any deviation from this ideal is to be penalized to the extent of the deviation. Structural and movement faults common to all working breeds are as undesirable in the Newfoundland as in any other breed, even though they are not specifically mentioned herein.

Size, Proportion, Substance

Average height for adult dogs is 28 inches, for adult bitches, 26 inches. Approximate weight of adult dogs ranges from 130 to 150 pounds, adult bitches from 100 to 120 pounds. The dog's appearance is more massive throughout than the bitch's. Large size is desirable but never at the expense of balance, structure and correct gait. The Newfoundland is slightly longer than tall when measured from the point of shoulder to the point of buttocks and from withers to ground. He is a dog of considerable substance, which is determined by spring of rib, strong muscle, and heavy bone.

Head

The head is massive, with a broad **skull**, slightly arched crown and strongly developed occipital bone. Cheeks are well developed. **Eyes** are dark brown. (Browns and grays may have lighter eyes and should be penalized only to the extent that color affects the expression.) They are relatively small, deep-set, and spaced wide apart. Eyelids fit closely with no inversion. **Ears** are relatively small and triangular with rounded tips. They are set on the skull level with, or slightly above, the brow and lie close to the head. When the ear is brought forward, it reaches to the inner corner of the eye on the same side. **Expression** is soft and reflects the characteristics of the breed: benevolence, intelligence, and dignity.

Forehead and face are smooth and free of wrinkles. Slope of the stop is moderate but, because of the well developed brow, it may appear abrupt in profile. The **muzzle** is clean cut, broad throughout its length, and deep. Depth and length are approximately equal, the length from tip of nose to stop being less than that from stop to occiput. The top of the muzzle is rounded, and the bridge, in profile, is straight or only slightly arched. Teeth meet in a scissors or level **bite**. Dropped lower incisors, in an otherwise normal bite, are not indicative of a skeletal malocclusion and should be considered only a minor deviation.

Neck, Topline, Body

The **neck** is strong and well set on the shoulders and is long enough for proud head carriage. The **back** is strong, broad, and muscular and is level from

Ch. Mooncusser's Making Waves, ROM, shows a lovely feminine head with soft expression (Ch. Pouch Cove Gref of Newton-Ark ex Ch. Mooncusser's Dutch Treat, ROM), bred and owned by Suzanne Jones, Mooncusser Kennels.

Ch. Benhil's Shenanigans, shows correct proportion of muzzle to back skull (Ch. Bandom's Puff the Magic Newf ex Sunbeam's Poehken by Moonglow), owned by Joan Bendure. *Hardman*

Ch. Crystal Bay's English Butler (Ch. Benhil's Trebor ex BB's Sheena of Pouch Cove) shows a beautiful head, with proper length of neck and level topline. Bred by Dawn and Jeff Beathard and owned by Susan Wolfe. *Tatham*

just behind the withers to the croup. The chest is full and deep with the brisket reaching at least down to the elbows. Ribs are well sprung, with the anterior third of the rib cage tapered to allow elbow clearance. The flank is deep. The croup is broad and slopes slightly. **Tail** set follows the natural line of the croup. The tail is broad at the base and strong. It has no kinks, and the distal bone reaches to the hock. When the dog is standing relaxed, its tail hangs straight or with a slight curve at the end. When the dog is in motion or excited, the tail is carried out, but it does not curl over the back.

Forequarters

Shoulders are muscular and well laid back. Elbows lie directly below the highest point of the withers. Forelegs are muscular, heavily boned, straight, and parallel to each other, and the elbows point directly to the rear. The distance from elbow to ground equals about half the dog's height. Pasterns are strong and slightly sloping. Feet are proportionate to the body in size, webbed, and cat foot in shape. Dewclaws may be removed.

Hindquarters

The rear assembly is powerful, muscular, and heavily boned. Viewed from the rear, the legs are straight and parallel. Viewed from the side, the thighs are broad and fairly long. Stifles and hocks are well bent and the line from the hock to ground is perpendicular. Hocks are well let down. Hind feet are similar to the front feet. Dewclaws should be removed.

Coat

The adult Newfoundland has a flat, water-resistant, double coat that tends to fall back into place when rubbed against the nap. The outer coat is coarse, moderately long, and full, either straight or with a wave. The undercoat is soft and dense, although it is often less dense during the summer months or in warmer climates. Hair on the face and muzzle is short and fine. The backs of the legs are feathered all the way down. The tail is covered with long dense hair.

Excess hair may be trimmed for neatness. Whiskers need not be trimmed.

Color

Color is secondary to type, structure and soundness. Recognized Newfoundland colors are black, brown, gray, and white and black.

Solid Colors—Blacks, Browns and Grays may appear as solid colors or solid colors with white at any, some, or all, of the following locations: chin, chest, toes, and tip of tail. Any amount of white found at these locations is typical and is not penalized. Also typical are a tinge of bronze on a black or gray coat and lighter furnishings on a brown or gray coat.

Ch. Stillwater's Private Party (Can. Ch. Bearbrook's Sargeant Pepper ex Ch. Haven's Garden Party), showing a typey bitch with proper angulation and leg to body length. Three-time Select at National Specialties. Shown with her breeder/owner Milan Lint. Co-owner: Joan Bendure.

Ch. Mooncusser Friendship Sloop (Shipshape's Sea Master ex Mooncusser's Quahog), a well-balanced bitch in a natural stance. Breeder/owner: Suzanne Jones of Mooncusser Kennels.

Landseer—White base coat with black markings. Typically, the head is solid black, or black with white on the muzzle, with or without a blaze. There is a separate black saddle and black on the rump extending onto a white tail.

Markings, on either solid colors or Landseers, might deviate considerably from those described and should be penalized only to the extent of the deviation. Clear white or white with minimal ticking is preferred.

Beauty of markings should be considered only when comparing dogs of otherwise comparable quality and never at the expense of type, structure and soundness.

Disqualifications—Any colors or combinations of colors not specifically described are disqualified.

Gait

The Newfoundland in motion has good reach, strong drive, and gives the impression of effortless power. His gait is smooth and rhythmic, covering the maximum amount of ground with the minimum number of steps. Forelegs and hind legs travel straight forward. As the dog's speed increases, the legs tend toward single tracking. When moving a slight roll of the skin is characteristic of the breed. Essential to good movement is the balance of correct front and rear assemblies.

Temperament

Sweetness of temperament is the hallmark of the Newfoundland; this is the most important single characteristic of the breed.

Disqualifications

Any colors or combinations of colors not specifically described are disqualified.

Approved May 8, 1990
Effective June 28, 1990

CURRENT CKC APPROVED STANDARD

General Appearance

Massive, deep bodied, well muscled, co-ordinated, projecting dignity in stance and head carriage. Appearance is square in that the length of the dog, from top of withers to base of tail, is equal to distance from top of withers to ground. Distance from top of withers to underside of chest is greater than distance from underside of chest to ground. Body of bitch may be slightly longer, and is less massive than that of the dog. A mature dog should never appear leggy or lacking substance. Free moving with a slight roll perceptible. Substantial webbing of toes is always present. Large size is desirable but never at the expense of gait, symmetry and balance. Fine bone is faulted.

Temperament

Soft and reflects the character of the breed—benevolent, intelligent, dignified but capable of fun. Known for his sterling gentleness and serenity. Any show of ill temper or timidity to be severely faulted.

Size

Average height for adult dogs, 28 in. (71 cm), for adult bitches, 26 in. (66 cm). Average weight for adult dogs, 150 lb. (68 kg), for adult bitches, 120 lb. (54 kg). Large size is desirable but not favoured over correct gait, symmetry, soundness and structure.

Coat and Colour

Water resistant double coat. Outer coat moderately long, straight with no curl. Slight wave is permissible. When rubbed the wrong way, coat tends to fall back into place.

Undercoat soft, dense, less dense during summer months, but always found to some extent on rump and chest. Completely open coat to be faulted. Hair on head, muzzle, ears short, fine. Front and rear legs are feathered. Tail completely covered with long dense hair, but does not form a flag. Traditional colour is black. Sunburned black is permissible. The Landseer Newfoundland is white with black markings, and is of historical significance to the breed. Preferred pattern of markings for the Landseer is black head with white blaze extending onto muzzle, black saddle and black rump and upper tail. All remaining parts to be white with minimum of ticking. Symmetry of markings and beauty of pattern characterize the best marked Landseers. Landseers are to be shown in the same class as blacks unless special classes are provided.

Head

Massive with a broad **skull**, slightly arched crown and strongly developed occipital bone. Forehead and face smooth and free from wrinkles. Stop is not abrupt. **Muzzle** clean-cut, covered with short fine hair. Rather square, deep, moderately short. Nostrils well developed. Bitch's head follows the same general conformation, but is feminine and less massive. Narrow head, snipey or long muzzle to be faulted. Pronounced flews not desirable. **Eyes** dark brown, relatively small and deep set. Spaced wide apart and show no haw. Round, protruding or yellow eyes are objectionable. **Ears** relatively small, triangular with rounded tips. Set well back on side of head and lie close. When ear of the dog is brought forward, it reaches to inner corner of eye on same side. **Teeth** meet in a scissors or level bite.

Neck

Strong, muscular, well set on shoulders. Long enough to permit dignified head carriage, should not show surplus dewlap.

Forequarters

When the dog is not in motion, forelegs are straight and parallel, with elbows close to chest. Shoulders well muscled and well laid back at an angle approaching 45 degrees. Pasterns are slightly sloping. Down in pasterns to be faulted. Feet proportionate to body in size, well rounded and tight, with compact toes (cat-foot type). Splayed toes are a fault. Toeing in or out undesirable.

Body

Chest broad, full and deep, with brisket reaching to elbows. Back broad, with good spread of rib, and topline is level from withers to croup, never roached, slack, or swayed. Loins strong and well muscled, and croup is broad. Pelvis slopes at an angle of about 30 degrees. Viewed from the side, body is deep, showing no discernible tuck-up. Bone structure is massive throughout but does not give sluggish appearance.

Hindquarters

Because driving power for swimming, pulling loads or covering ground efficiently is largely dependent upon the hindquarters, the rear structure is of prime importance. Hip assembly is broad, strong, well developed. Upper thighs wide, muscular. Lower thighs strong, fairly long. Stifles well bent, but not so as to give a crouching appearance. Hocks well let down, well apart and parallel to each other. They turn neither in nor out. Feet firm, tight. Dewclaws, if present, should have been removed. Straight stifles, cowhocks, barrel legs, and pigeon toes to be faulted.

Tail

Tail acts as a rudder when the Newfoundland is swimming; therefore it is strong and broad at base. When the dog is standing, tail hangs straight down, possibly a little curve at tip, reaching to or slightly below hocks; when in motion or excited, tail is carried straight out or with slight upward curve but never curled over back nor curved inward between legs. A tail with a kink or curled at the end is very objectionable.

Gait

Good reach and strong drive, giving impression of effortless power. In motion legs move straight forward, parallel to line of travel. A slight roll is present. As speed increases, the dog tends to single track, with topline remaining level. Mincing, shuffling, crabbing, too close moving, weaving, crossing over in front, toeing out or distinctly toeing-in in front, hackney action and pacing are all faults.

Disqualifications

Bad temperament, short flat-coat (Labrador Retriever type), markings of any other colour than white on a black dog, any colours other than the traditional black, or Landseer (white and black).

THE KENNEL CLUB (ENGLAND) STANDARD FOR THE NEWFOUNDLAND

General Appearance

Well balanced, impressive with strength and great activity.
Massive bone throughout, but not giving heavy inactive appearance. Noble, majestic and powerful.

Characteristics

Large draught and water dog, with natural life-saving instinct, and devoted companion.

Temperament

Exceptionally gentle, docile nature.

Head and Skull

Head broad and massive, occipital bone well developed, no decided stop, muzzle short, clean cut and rather square, covered with short fine hair.

Eyes

Small, dark brown, rather deeply set, not showing haw, set rather wide apart.

Ears

Small, set well back, square with skull, lying close to the head, covered with short hair without fringe.

Mouth

Soft and well covered by lips. Scissor bite preferred, i.e., upper teeth closely overlapping the lower teeth and set square in the jaws, but pincer tolerated.

Neck

Strong, set well onto shoulders.

Forequarters

Leg perfectly straight, well muscled, elbows fitting close to sides, well let down.

Body

Well ribbed, back broad with level topline, strong muscular loins. Chest deep, fairly broad.

Hindquarters

Very well built and strong. Slackness of loins and cowhocks most undesirable. Dewclaws should be removed.

Feet

Large, webbed and well shaped. Splayed or turned out feet most undesirable.

Gait/Movement

Free, slight rolling gait. When in motion, slight toeing in at front acceptable.

Tail

Moderate length, reaching a little below hock. Fair thickness well covered with hair, but not forming a flag. When standing hangs downwards with slight curve at end; when moving, carried slightly up, and when excited, straight out with only a slight curve at end. Tails with a kink or curved over back are most undesirable.

Coat

Double, flat and dense, of a coarse nature, water resistant. When brushed wrong way it falls back into place naturally. Forelegs well feathered. Body well covered but chest hair not forming a frill. Hindlegs slightly feathered.

Colour

Only permitted colours are:

Black

Dull jet black may be tinged with bronze. Splash of white on chest, toes and tip of tail acceptable.

Brown

Can be chocolate or bronze. In all other respects follow black except for colour. Splash of white on chest, toes and tip of tail acceptable.

Landseer

White with black markings only. For preference black head with narrow blaze, evenly marked saddle, black rump extending to tail. Beauty in markings to be taken greatly into consideration. Ticking is undesirable.

Size

Average height at shoulder: Dogs 71 cms (28 inches); Bitches 66 cms (26 inches). Average weight: Dogs 64–69kgs (140–150 pounds); Bitches 50–54 kgs (110–120 pounds).

Faults

Any departure from the foregoing points should be considered a fault and the seriousness with which the fault should be regarded in exact proportion to its degree.

Note

Male animals should have two apparently normal testicles fully descended into the scrotum.

(Courtesy of The Kennel Club)

The only significant difference among the three Standards is in the color. The United States accepts browns and grays in addition to the traditional black and Landseer. Canada, the native land of the Newfoundland dog, allows only the black and Landseer and disqualifies both brown and gray. While England accepts the brown in addition to the black and Landseer, it does not recognize gray.

All three Standards specify the traditional Landseer markings, but Canada makes no mention of white on the feet, chest or tip of tail in blacks. England allows the blacks and the browns to have the minimal amount of white in the specified areas. While the American Standard specifies the ideal marking of a Landseer, it goes on to state that the white markings on solid colors or Landseers "might deviate considerably from those described and should be penalized only to the extent of deviation."

6

The Newfoundland
Standard Explained
and Illustrated

THE AKC NEWFOUNDLAND STANDARD DEFINED

General Appearance

Our standard is a description of a large, strong, working dog that should have the physical capabilities for doing draft/pack work and be a strong swimmer, possessing the natural life-saving instincts. These are traits for which the breed has been renowned for centuries.

The Newfoundland is an all-around working dog and devoted companion to both adults and children. *More important than any other feature of the Newfoundland is its outstanding good nature and temperament.*

Size, Proportion, Substance

While the Newfoundland is a large breed, the important thing to remember here is that the dog must also possess substance and balance in relation to height. Substance is having heavy bone, and well-developed amounts of muscle. Balance is how all the parts or features of a particular dog fit together in relation to each other. The width and mass of a dog must be in proportion to height and length.

Because of the Newfoundland's heavy coat, it is important to feel the dog to judge bone and substance. Don't misinterpret fat for substance. A dog in good condition will have only a light covering of flesh over the ribs.

The average height for male Newfoundlands is 28 inches and the weight for a dog that size should range from 130 to 150 pounds. A male Newfoundland that is 26 inches at the shoulder and weighs only 110 pounds would be considered small. In the same sense, a male that is 32 inches at the shoulder and weighs only 130 pounds would be lacking in substance.

You will hear the term "bitchy dog." It refers to a male that is too slight or refined and looks more like a female than a male. It is a very serious fault. It should be immediately obvious upon looking at a dog whether it is a male or female. Conversely there are some bitches that are considered "doggy bitches." This means that they are extremely masculine, to the point they resemble a male more than a female. While it too is a serious fault, and some of those types are never able to reproduce, it appears to be more acceptable to have a "doggy bitch" than a "bitchy dog." This is probably because the Newfoundland is a large breed and large size is more desirable than small.

Head

Generally the most distinguishing characteristic of a breed is the head.

The Newfoundland Standard calls for a massive head with a broad skull and a well-developed occipital bone. The occipital bone is the pointed bone located at the top and back of the skull. The skull should be domed or round, never square or flat. The cheeks are prominent and well developed.

The Newfoundland appears to have an abrupt stop, particularly when viewed from the side. This is due to the well-developed superciliary arches or ridges, the rounded bone in the front of the skull that form the brows. If you feel between the eyes you will find that the stop itself feels like a furrow between these ridges. It is not steep but moderately sloped.

Muzzle

The muzzle is deep and broad throughout its length. The muzzle is squarish when comparing depth to length. It should never be pointed, excessively long or refined or shallow. The muzzle, as seen from the top, should be broad and round. The bridge of the muzzle in profile is straight or only slightly arched. The muzzle should not curve downward from the stop to the nose. The base of the muzzle should be approximately level with the inside corner of the eye. When the base of the muzzle starts from high above the inside corner of the eye it gives the dog a "houndy-looking face."

The muzzle and forehead should be free of wrinkles. A properly shaped muzzle comes from the bone structure of the upper jaw and a well-developed underjaw, never from excessive depth of the flews (upper lip). Pendulous lower flews/lips that turn down are not desirable. This will allow the saliva to run out of the mouth, instead of being channeled down the throat. When the dog is hot or exercising this will cause excessive drooling.

Profile of a bitch (female) on the left and a dog (male) on the right. Note that they should appear the same, except that the dog should be larger throughout. Bitches will appear feminine compared with males, which should always appear masculine. Upon first glance, gender should be immediately obvious. *D. Vitale*

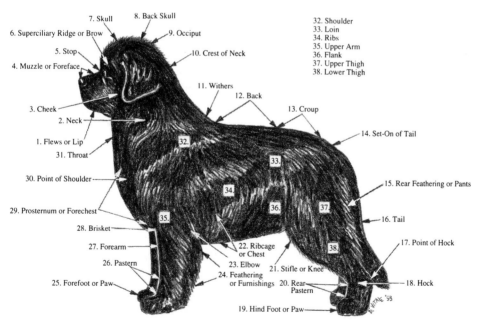

7. Skull
8. Back Skull
6. Superciliary Ridge or Brow
9. Occiput
5. Stop
10. Crest of Neck
4. Muzzle or Foreface
11. Withers
12. Back
3. Cheek
13. Croup
2. Neck
14. Set-On of Tail
1. Flews or Lip
32.
31. Throat
33.
30. Point of Shoulder
15. Rear Feathering or Pants
29. Prosternum or Forechest
34.
28. Brisket
36.
37.
16. Tail
35.
27. Forearm
22. Ribcage or Chest
38.
17. Point of Hock
26. Pastern
23. Elbow
21. Stifle or Knee
25. Forefoot or Paw
24. Feathering or Furnishings
20. Rear Pastern
18. Hock
19. Hind Foot or Paw

32. Shoulder
33. Loin
34. Ribs
35. Upper Arm
36. Flank
37. Upper Thigh
38. Lower Thigh

Parts of the dog.

D. Vitale

101

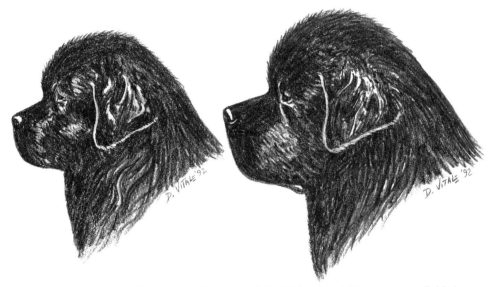

Profile of a bitch's (female) head on left and a dog's (male) head on right.   *D. Vitale*

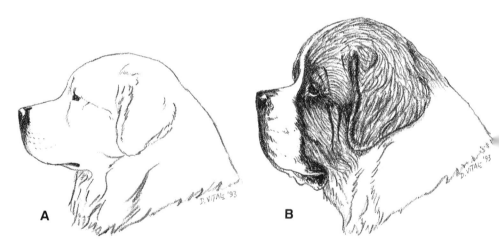

A. Great Pyrenees head—Incorrect for a Newfoundland, with an elongated muzzle and lacking a well-domed topskull for a Newfoundland. **B.** Saint Bernard head—incorrect for a Newfoundland. Head is too chiseled and muzzle too short for a Newfoundland.   *D. Vitale*

Ch. Kuhaia's Rego, ROM (Ch. Jack the Ripper, ROM, ex Ch. Edenglen's Lady Rebecca, ROM), owned by Ronni Farkas. Rego shows the proper well-developed brows, or superciliary arches/ridges, that give the Newfoundland the appearance of an abrupt stop. Note the furrow between the eyes, which is moderate, not steep.

Beautiful Newfoundland heads, male on left and female on right, depicting the desired massiveness but showing the sweet, benevolent Newfoundland expression. The male is Ch. John's Big Ben of Pouch Cove, owned and bred by Peggy and David Helming. The bitch is Ch. Stillwater's Private Party, bred by Milan D. Lint and owned by Joan C. Bendure and Milan D. Lint.   *D. Vitale*

103

Ears

The ears are relatively small and triangular with rounded tips. Long ears give a Newfoundland a sad or houndy look. If the length of the ear is in correct proportion to the head, the tip will just reach to the inner corner of the eye on the same side. The base of the ear will be level with, or only slightly above, the brow.

The actual leather of the ear should be thick, not thin.

In repose the ears will lie flat against the skull. When the dog is alert the ears will be raised, the back edge of the ears will be brought forward away from the head and the front edge of the ear will stay close against the cheek. When the dog is being submissive, the ears will be held low and back.

Eyes

The eyes are basically small, deep set and spaced widely apart. A small arch in the upper lid gives the eye a slightly triangular shape. The eye rims should be reasonably tight-fitting with no inversion or gaps. A gap in the lower lid is seen most often in dogs with excessively loose skin. This is not desirable, as it does not protect the eye from dust particles or water. This can cause excessive tearing or chronic conjunctivitis. Inversions in the eye rim will eventually cause scarring of the cornea. The haw or inner eyelid should not be visible.

Correct eye color is dark brown. Browns and grays may have lighter eyes that follow the coat color. Eye color should be penalized only to the extent that it affects the expression.

No matter how well shaped the head is, round, protruding or yellow eyes will ruin the sweet Newfoundland expression.

Bite

Both the level or scissors bite are equally correct. In both the level or scissors bite it is very common to find the two center, lower incisor teeth dropped below the normal arrangement in the jaw. Most Newfoundlands will exhibit this by age three. This is a dentition fault, not a malformation of the jaw.

The parts of the head blend smoothly together to give the soft, benevolent Newfoundland expression. The head should never be chiseled or squared as in the Saint Bernard, nor should it be flat or tapered as in the Great Pyrenees.

Neck

The Newfoundland should have a strong, powerfully muscled neck. The muscling should not be so massive that the neck is excessively thick. A Newfoundland needs to have a neck that is long enough to give proud head carriage. This will also aid the dog in performing the tasks it was meant to perform. The neck should be well set on and blend smoothly into well-laid-back shoulders. Necks that are too short are more commonly seen than necks that are too long.

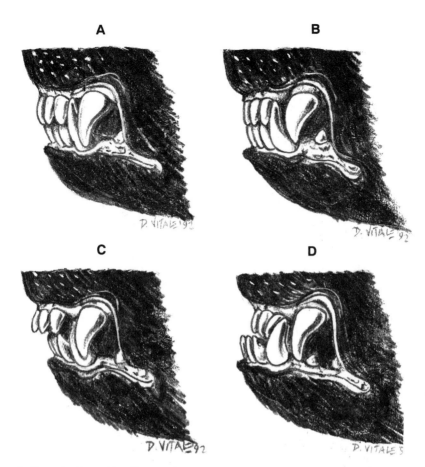

A. Correct scissors bite. Outer surface of the lower teeth just touch the inner surface of the upper teeth when the mouth is closed. In Newfoundlands it is common to see the two center lower incisors set lower in the jaw than those on either side. **B.** Correct level bite. Edges of both the lower and upper incisor teeth meet edge to edge when the mouth is closed. Again, it is common to see the two center lower incisors dropped slightly below the incisors on either side. **C.** Incorrect overshot bite. Lower jaw is shorter in length than upper jaw. Upper and lower incisor teeth do not make contact with one another. **D.** Incorrect undershot bite. Lower jaw is decidedly longer than upper jaw, with lower incisors protruding beyond the upper incisors. Upper and lower incisor teeth do not make contact with one another. *D. Vitale*

Misaligned incisors. Newfoundlands frequently have the two center lower incisors set lower than the incisors on either side by three years of age. If moderate, it does not cause a problem, but if the two center incisors are decidedly lower, it allows the other incisors to move from their correct position. This in turn can cause the lower incisors to interfere with the upper incisors causing them also to be misaligned. This is a dentition fault, not an incorrect bite. Breeders need to guard against this becoming prevalent in the breed. *D. Vitale*

Dogs with too-short necks usually have straight, upright shoulders and short front legs.

Newfoundlands due to their massiveness will have a certain amount of dewlap, the loose folds of skin on the throat. The dewlap should not be so extreme that it swings excessively when the dog is in motion. Dogs that have too much dewlap will also have excessive skin on the lower jaw, which again will contribute to excess drooling.

Back

The Newfoundland's back is broad, strong and well muscled.

The body is only slightly longer than the dog is tall; a measurement is taken from the point of shoulder to the point of buttocks, and from the withers to the ground. The back of the Newfoundland is only a part of this length.

The back should not be excessively long, as this will cause the back to be weak, and the dog will tire quickly. Too short a back will cause the rear feet to overreach and interfere with correct movement. Newfoundlands have a greater tendency to be too long in back than too short. The back should never be swayed or roached. Correct back length is important in a working dog. In recent years there has been great improvement in both back length and movement.

The loin, the area that extends from the end of the rib cage to the start of the pelvis or croup, should be just long enough to allow for ease of maneuvering. A dog that is too long in the loin will lose the driving power that is generated from the rear. A dog with too short a loin will not be able to maneuver or turn easily.

The croup, the area from the hip joints to the buttocks, is broad and slopes only slightly. The croup should never be flat or steep. If the croup is too flat the tail set will be too high. If the croup is too steep the hindquarters will be set too far under the dog, making the dog look out of balance when standing. A steep croup will also cause loss of power and drive from the rear.

The junction of the croup and the tail is known as the tail-set. The base of the tail should be broad and strong. The last bone in the tip of the tail reaches to the hock. The shape of the Newfoundland tail is like a brush, the hair about the same length on the top, bottom and sides. The Newfoundland tail should never form a flag. There should be no kinks in the tail.

When the dog is standing in repose, the tail will hang straight down or may have a slight curve at the tip. When the dog is moving or excited, the tail will be carried straight out or only slightly above the level of the back. The tail should never curl over the back.

Body

The chest is deep and should reach at least down to the elbows. It is important in evaluating a Newfoundland to feel how deep the chest is, as the heavy coat of hair can make a shallow chest appear deep. The chest of a Newfoundland is its keel for swimming. The anterior (front) portion of the ribs tapers

106

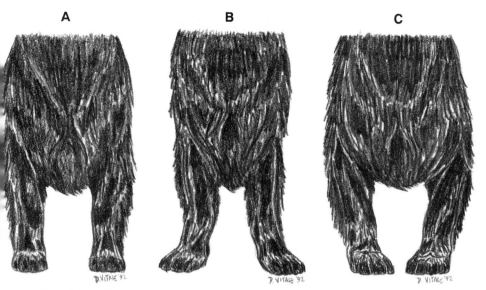

A. Correct front. **B.** Incorrect, east-west front—narrow front with elbows pinched in. **C.** Incorrect, barrel-legged front, too wide and out at the elbows, pigeon-toed.   *D. Vitale*

A. Correct cat foot—round, compact, with well-arched toes—side and front views. **B.** Incorrect—splayed, weak foot, with toes spread rather far apart, and weak pastern—side and front views.

D. Vitale

C. Incorrect, hare foot. Center toes are decidedly longer than outer toes. Toes are not well arched. Down in pastern.   *D. Vitale*

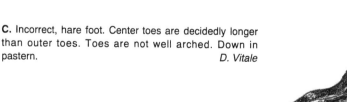

107

slightly to allow for elbow clearance. The deep, well-developed chest and well-sprung ribs are necessary for greater heart and lung capacity.

The flank should be deep in the adult dog and never excessively tucked up in the abdomen.

Forequarters

The Standard calls for a muscular, well-laid-back shoulder. The shoulders are connected to the chest or body by muscle, ligaments and tendons.

As there are no bones connecting the shoulders to the chest, it is imperative to have strong muscular development in this area. Correct shoulder formation and muscling is essential for proper movement and to enable the dog to work efficiently and tirelessly.

"Laid back" refers to the angle or slope of the shoulder blade. The shoulder blade slopes upward and toward the rear. The highest part of the shoulder is the withers.

Front angulation refers to the angle at which the shoulder blade (scapula) and the upper arm (humerus) meet. The shoulder blade and upper arm should be the same length.

The elbows should lie directly below the highest point of the withers. Properly angulated forequarters will place the front well under the body.

The forelegs are muscular, straight and parallel to each other. The measurement from the elbow to the ground should be about half a Newfoundland's height.

Newfoundlands are to be heavily boned. It is important to feel for bone size, as the heavy coat can make the bone appear heavier than it really is. Dogs with fine bone should be faulted. A Newfoundland is never penalized for having too much bone. To judge the amount of bone, grasp the leg on the forearm, just above the pastern. The amount of bone should be in proportion to the size of the dog.

The pasterns should be strong and slightly sloping. Newfoundlands are always born with front dewclaws, which do not need to be removed.

The feet are shaped like a cat's foot. Toes are rounded and well knuckled, and fit close together. The toes should never be splayed or spread apart. The two center toes are only slightly longer than the outer toes. The toe and foot pads are thick and well padded, never flat.

The webbing between the toes should be strong, well developed and complete, as befits a water dog.

Fronts that are barrel legged, east and west, out at the elbows or pinched in or too narrow are all faults in the Newfoundland.

Hindquarters

The rear assembly of the Newfoundland is powerful, muscular and heavily boned.

Again, to properly assess the amount of bone, one must feel the area

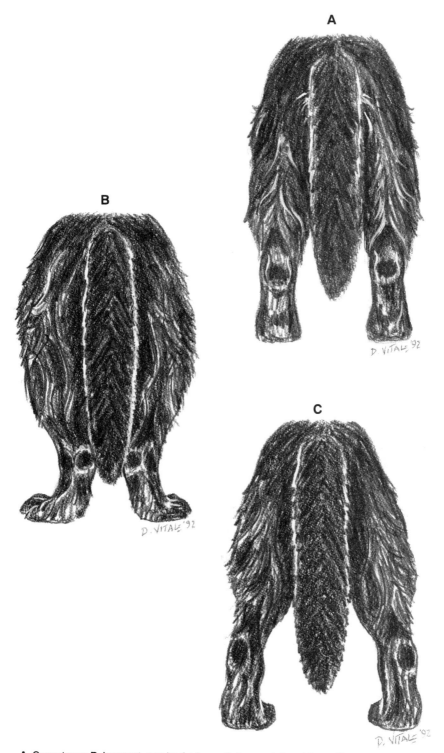

A. Correct rear. **B.** Incorrect, cow-hocked rear. **C.** Incorrect, barrel-legged/hocked. *D. Vitale*

between the foot and the point of hock. Some Newfoundlands will have heavy bone in front but an inadequate amount of bone in the rear. I have never seen a Newfoundland with heavy rear bone to lack bone in front.

The rear legs are straight and parallel to each other when viewed from behind.

Cow hocks (hocks turned in), barrel legs (outward-turning hocks) and pigeon toes are all signs of weakness in the rear.

The dog must be viewed from the side to evaluate rear angulation, thigh length, muscling and hocks.

The thighs are fairly long and broad. Stifles—the joint of the hind leg where the upper and lower thighs meet—and hocks are well bent. Well-bent hocks have the correct amount of rear angulation.

The hock is properly perpendicular to the ground. It is well let down or short and close to the ground.

A correctly balanced Newfoundland will stand with its rear legs out behind it.

Rears that are straight in stifle, sickle hocked, toeing in behind or too narrow are undesirable.

The hind feet are shaped like the front feet.

It is extremely rare for a Newfoundland to be born with rear dewclaws. If present at birth, they should be removed.

Correct structure of the hindquarters and forequarters is important for the Newfoundland to efficiently be able to jump from a dock or boat, perform draft work or move correctly.

Coat

The Newfoundland is a double-coated breed, the coat consisting of both an outer coat and a undercoat.

The outer coat is coarse, of moderate length and full. It is either straight or has a slight wave. The coat should lie flat. When brushed or rubbed against the nap, it should fall back into place. An open coat, hair that stands out from the body, is incorrect.

The undercoat consists of softer, finer hair than the outer coat. The undercoat is dense, but will be less so during the summer or in warmer climates.

The backs of the front and rear legs are feathered all the way down.

The hair on the face and muzzle is short and fine.

The density of the coat is very important. The Newfoundland coat afforded the dog the protection necessary to survive the harsh winters and icy cold waters of its native land. Hair that is wiry, silky, kinky, curly or woolly is undesirable.

Excess hair should be trimmed for neatness, but it is not necessary to trim the whiskers, not even for the purpose of showing.

Color

Recognized Newfoundland colors under the American Standard are black, brown, gray and Landseer (white with black).

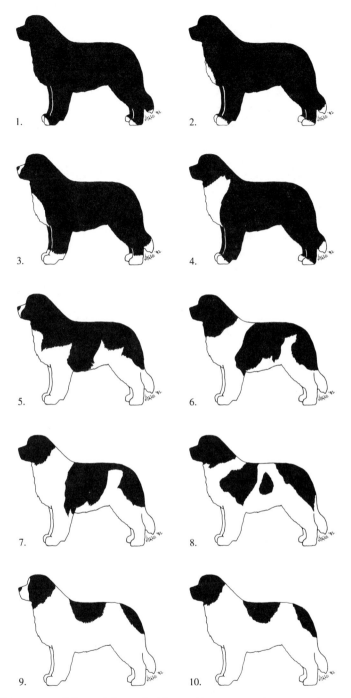

This shows some of the variations of white markings commonly seen on Newfoundlands. White markings can vary considerably from those illustrated. Landseers are white dogs with black markings. Examples 9 and 10 are ideal Landseer markings. Ticking is not desired. Brown and white, and gray and white are not acceptable in Landseers. All-white dogs are disqualified. *D. Vitale*

All recognized colors have equal status when being judged.

Blacks, browns or grays may be solid in color; or they may have white on the chin, chest, toes or tip of tail. Any amount of white at these locations is typical and should not be penalized.

A tinge of bronze on a black or gray coat and lighter furnishings on a brown or gray coat is not uncommon. This is usually caused from weathering or sun bleaching and should not be penalized.

A Landseer is a white dog with black markings. The head can be solid black; or black with white on the muzzle, with or without a blaze between the eyes. There is a separate black saddle or patch on the back. There is another black patch on the rump extending onto a white tail. There should be a definite break of white between the black on the back and rump.

Markings on black, browns, grays or Landseer may differ significantly from those described. They should be penalized only to the extent of the difference.

Beauty of markings should only be considered when all else is equal, as type, structure and soundness of body and mind are always of the utmost importance,

Ticking is not desirable. The white should be pure white. If ticking is present, it should be minimal. Heavy amounts of ticking detract from the beauty of markings. A minimum amount of ticking is a few spots on the front of the legs. Or, if the face has white, it will sometimes be located there also. You will also find ticking on the white body coat of dogs with excessive ticking.

Acceptable colors and markings are:

Solid black
Black with white
White with black
Solid brown or gray

If a brown or gray has white, it may not be so excessive that the brown or gray cannot be identified as the base coat.

See illustrations for the acceptable amounts of white allowed.

The black-and-white, or white-and-black Newfoundland can have markings so different from the patterns illustrated that it will be difficult to determine if it is a black or Landseer. Such dogs may be exhibited in either the Black class or the Any Other Color class. They would not be disqualified because any combination of black with white, or white with black, is acceptable.

Any colors or combinations of colors not specified in the standard are disqualified.

Disqualifying colors:

Brown or gray with excessive white
Black and tan; all white; roan; brindle; merle; cream; beige; honey; tan; buff; blond; yellow; or any pale shade of brown
Black, brown or gray base coat with other than white markings
Any other color or combinations of colors not listed as a recognized Newfoundland color

Int. Ch. Topmast's Blackberry Blossom (Am., Can. Ch. Topmast's Pied Piper, ROM, ex Topmast's Blackberry) shows beautiful Landseer markings and type. Bred by Margaret Willmott of Canada and owned by Manlio Massa of Italy. *Søren Wesseltoft*

This shows two beautiful, typey male Newfoundlands. The Landseer is Can. Ch. Abby Acres Tobias (Am., Can. Ch. Topmast's Pied Piper ex Can. Ch. Abigail Adams), bred and owned by Lori-Ann Miller of Canada. The black is Ch. Amity's Bearfoot of Pouch Cove, ROM (Ch. Pouch Cove Gref of Newton-Ark ex Amity's Daydream of Pouch Cove), bred by Diane Broderick and Margaret Helming and owned by Margaret Helming.

Søren Wesseltoft

113

A beautiful brown Newfoundland that attained multiple all-breed Best in Show wins, multiple NCA Regional Specialty Bests, the top winning Newfoundland of 1986, Ch. Kendian's Cadbury (Ch. Bonnie Bay's Brigus, ROM, ex Ch. Riptide's Cinnamon Bear Too). Bred by Joanne and Jeff Givens and owned by Diane and Ken Price. *Callea*

The lovely gray bitch Newfield's Martha Gray (Ch. Nashau-Auke's Boo Boo Bear, C.D., ex Ralaur's Pure Joy of Newfield), bred and owned by Polly Loring. *John Ashbey*

Gait

The Newfoundland should be exhibited at a moderate trot. Its gait should be smooth and rhythmic. It should have good reach and strong drive and give the impression of effortless movement. It should cover the ground with a minimum number of steps. As the dog's speed increases, the feet will move toward the centerline of the body. This action is commonly referred to as single tracking.

The topline should remain level when the dog is moving.

Some dogs with good fronts will toe in slightly.

Dogs that cross over in the front or are out in the elbows should be faulted.

No matter how correct a dog is when standing, the true test will come when the dog is gaited. Good movement is a sign of proper physical construction.

Temperament

Sweetness of temperament is the hallmark of the Newfoundland; this is the most important single characteristic of the breed.

Newfoundlands should be friendly, outgoing dogs. They are always happy and eager to greet people.

They should never be shy, fearful or exhibit any signs of a suspicious or aggressive nature toward people or other animals.

No matter how perfect a Newfoundland dog may appear physically, if it does not have the sterling temperament for which the breed is known, it is not a good specimen of the breed.

Black-and-tan Newfoundlands. Black and tan is a disqualified color in the conformation ring, but such dogs can still be entered in the working events. The adult pictured is Niagara's Wizard Wiskers, CD, WRD (Echo Hill's Elmo Winthrop ex Echo Hill's Jill of Niagara), bred by Julie Wildenstein and shown with owner Leo Gorton. Four-month-old puppy is Native's Great Spirit (Ebunyzar's Beauregard Bear ex Niagara's Native Bramble Rose, CD, WD), bred and owned by Leo Gorton.

"Who says I'm not the real lifeguard?" VN Ch. Kilyka's Sibyl, UD, WRD, DD, ROM, sitting atop a lifeguard's chair. Bred and owned by Betty McDonnell, Sibyl is the sixth generation of ROM bitches in her family.

7

Newfoundland Characteristics and Health

CHARACTERISTICS

The characteristic that Newfoundlands are best known for is their sweet, docile disposition. They are also intelligent and eager to please.

These descriptions are a generalization of Newfoundland breed characteristics. The environment a dog is raised in has as much or more to do with personality and behavior as genetics does.

Newfoundlands love people and have a great desire to be with them. It is very seldom that a Newf wants to be independent and aloof from people.

They are very forgiving of ill treatment toward them, but not against their family. When reprimanded they may sulk for a short time, but they don't hold a grudge.

A Newfoundland is not a one-man dog but will sometimes pick a favorite member of the family, generally the person who spends the most time with it. These dogs always seem attracted to children, even if they have not been raised with them.

While they do bond with their family, they will easily accept another family as theirs. They are very adaptable.

Newfoundlands can also be very stubborn. But to a greater or lesser degree, that may be true of any breed of dog. Sometimes they will make up their mind that they just don't want to do something, and it can take a lot of convincing to persuade them otherwise.

Instead of becoming nasty when the owner is trying to make it do something it doesn't want to do, a Newf will usually sit down, refusing to move or just lie down and go limp.

In their desire to be close to people, they will jump up or sit on anyone if not properly trained. When standing or sitting by a favorite person, they all tend to want to lean against the object of their affection. Indeed, they can sometimes be obnoxious in trying to gain a person's attention and affections.

They are a fun working breed, capable of performing many useful tasks. They can be used for drafting or giving children cart rides. They can also be a fun dog in the water that can be trained to be a lifeguard. They are not runners. If not confined by a fence they will wander, to find companionship.

The biggest drawbacks of the breed are their occasional drooling, shedding and large size.

Yes, Newfoundlands sometimes drool. The more massive the dog, the more inclined it is to drool. Newfoundlands do not walk around with drool—or, as it seems now popular to call it, "slime"—running out of their mouth at all times. They drool when they are hot. It is how a dog's body works to cool itself. Dogs do not perspire through their skin as people do. When a dog gets excessively hot from physical activity or weather conditions, it will start to pant. Panting is how a dog cools itself, through the evaporation of water from the tongue and mouth. Of course when dogs pant, they also drool.

They will also sometimes drool when they become excited, like when they are waiting for their food.

Some Newfs can be very messy when getting a drink of water. Such a dog will often submerge its whole muzzle into the water and then lift its head, allowing the last slurp to run out of its mouth and down onto its chest.

Or, right after getting a drink, a Newf may decide it is a good time to shake, and water will fly in all directions. Or maybe your big wet friend wants to be affectionate and lays its head in your lap, at the same time wiping the excess water off its chin.

Newfoundlands shed profusely twice a year, and lose some hair all year long. They do require regular brushing.

Due to their large size, the cost of upkeep is naturally higher than for a smaller breed of dog.

Because they are not an overly active breed, Newfoundlands do not consume the great amount of food that one might think for such a large breed. The food intake is highest in rapidly-growing older puppies. A Newfoundland will eat forty or fifty pounds of dry food a month, depending on the quality of the food and the dog's size and activity level.

A Newf is not the breed for you if you are meticulous about your home. Like any dog, they do make extra housework. Stray hairs will occasionally show up on your carpeting, funiture and clothing. Since they love to lean against their owner's leg, you will sometimes have hair or a temporary mark from drool on

"Anyone for a basket of teddy bears?" Ch. Spillway's Man of Pouch Cove, CD loves to carry everything. Bred by Dave and Peggy Helming and owned by Phyllis Welch and Peggy Helming.

your clothing. No, Newfoundland owners do not walk around with drool and hair on them as a "badge of honor," but it will happen from time to time.

The Newfoundland's easygoing, sweet disposition is usually what attracts people to wanting to own one. They have been held up on a pedestal because of it. And yes, I will go so far to say that their temperament is probably more tractable than that of most dogs of other breeds. But it must be remembered that the Newfoundland is still a dog, and as such needs to be properly trained.

Temperament testing on litters of Newfoundland pups reveals they will almost all test to be middle-of-the-road type dogs. Not aggressive and not shy.

Occasionally one will test dominant or independent. This is the exception and not the rule. Placed in the proper home, those dogs will not experience or present a behavior problem.

Good breeders who spend a lot of time with their litters will know, even without a test, each pup's individual personality.

Unfortunately, there have been cases of Newfoundlands exhibiting less than desirable temperament. Dogs that exhibit this type of behavior should never be considered for breeding lest we lose the Newfoundland's most desired characteristic. If a dog is properly bred, socialized and trained, temperament should never be a problem.

The Newfoundland has long been depicted as a guardian of children and protector of family and home. As for the Newfoundland being a family protector, fortunately I have never had the occasion arise for it to be necessary for any of my Newfs to react in this way. There have been many stories written through the history of the breed depicting it as reacting as a protector when the situation required.

The large size of the Newfoundland is generally all that is necessary to make any would-be thief or attacker have a change of mind. It is always interesting to watch a Newf stand between his family, particularly his children, when a stranger is approaching. I really do believe that they have an inner sense for judging people. If they are uncertain as to the person's intentions, they will generally just stand still and wait. For the most part they are always eager to greet most anyone approaching. Usually the size of a Newfoundland and the deep bark will deter anyone bent on harm.

When someone comes to the door, these dogs usually only lift their heads to size up whoever has come to visit. If it is someone that they sense will make a fuss over them, they sit next to them, collecting what they feel is due them. When the pats are done they go back to doing what every Newf does best— holding down the carpet!

As anyone who has ever been owned by a Newf can tell you, they all have the same determined penchant for getting people to pet them. The Newf will raise its great head, usually when you are about to take a sip of coffee and least expecting it, and shove it under your elbow, throwing your arm up, so the head will be under your hand when it comes down. I have seen other breeds do this but never with the determination of the Newf. It will continue to do this over

"Just let me know when it's my turn." Ch. Benhil's Stillwater Maxwell waiting patiently to eat his dinner. Breeders/owners Milan Lint and Joan Bendure. Co-owned by Joe and Cheryl Cettomai.

"Oh, what a Newfoundland must endure!" Lauren Harrington sharing her hat with Am., Can. Ch. Benhil's Stillwater Gulliver, bred and owned by Joan Bendure and Milan Lint.

and over until you finally speak to it very firmly. After having been rebuked, the dog will walk away, lie down to face you and give you that forlorn Newfie look and then the big sigh as the head goes down onto the paws.

A Newf is not a guard dog. Their size will make whoever is at your door step back when you open it. People who don't know the breed will normally give you a wide berth when you meet on a sidewalk.

But don't think your house is safe when you're not home. Newfies are usually not barkers, unless they are outside and want in with the family. They can be taught to bark when someone comes to the door. If you are looking for a dog that acts and sounds as if it'll tear an intruder apart, you had better find another breed. Newfs are bred to be placid, people-loving dogs—big, happy friends you can have a lot of fun with. But they are not attack dogs by any means. Newf owners all say the same thing: "If someone broke into the house when we weren't home, the dog would show them where we keep the silver."

Most Newfoundlands love the water. The breed is renowned for its swimming ability and natural lifesaving instincts. Puppies love to spill their water dish so they can lie in the water. Most Newfoundlands will have no qualms about lying down in a puddle of water.

Then there are some Newfs that just don't particularly care if they swim or not. Some dogs are fearful because they were not properly introduced to the water for the first time or were never taught how to swim correctly.

It is very important that your Newfoundland's first introduction to deep water and swimming be a pleasant experience.

Newfoundlands are not notorious for digging holes in the ground. Some will dig out of boredom, or for a cool spot to lie in.

A family we sold a male pup to got a kitten at that same time they got their pup. Raider and the kitten became great friends and could always be found in each other's company. One evening the family was taking a walk on its property, and of course ten-month-old Raider and the cat were with them. Suddenly the cat took off and ran across the road. Raider knew that he was not allowed near the road, but when he saw his friend cross the road he bolted after him. The dog crossed the road, scooped his friend up in his mouth and quickly turned to run back. When crossing the road to return, Raider was hit by a car and killed instantly. The cat survived with only minor abrasions.

Two of our favorite house dogs took up wandering the neighborhood. We live in a rural area with the houses well back from the road. We have acres of lawn, woods and pastures and a pond for the dogs to use and enjoy, and also kennels to confine them in. Imagine my surprise when I found out that my two "angels," Yankee and Chubby, were leaving the property. They would go through the woods and fields and come out on the road where the kids waited for the school bus. There they would beg treats from school lunches.

I called one of our neighbors to see if she had ever seen our dogs off our property. She told me that her house was only one of the stops they made—and

"This is a great kid! He's too young to know I'm supposed to be pulling him." Ch. Pooh Bear's Stormalong, ROM, National Specialty Best of Breed winner, getting a ride from Logan Gamble. Bred by Shelby Guelich and owned by "Doc" and Kathy Gamble.

"I just know these guys are going to try to steal my float." Ch. Benhil's Yankee De Nashau-Auke, breeder/owner Jane Thibault, co-owner Joan Bendure. Yankee liked to spend his summers floating around in the pool. Joe Cettomai is in the background and Paul Bendure on the right.

of course she would give them a treat. After that the two dogs were never allowed out to run loose on the property at the same time. This worked for a long time until Yankee took up visiting on his own. I would drive around the neighborhood until I found him and chastised him for leaving home, as if he really knew what he had done wrong. He would then be confined to a kennel run for a few weeks to serve his jail sentence. He always seemed to repent for a period of time, but then would take up his wandering ways again. He was never gone for very long. Actually, you could set your watch by him. If I didn't leave immediately to go look for him, he would be coming up the driveway at 7:20 A.M.

I never knew if he left for the treats, just to be sociable, or for the ride back home.

Chubby and Yankee were better mousers than any cat we ever owned. They would spend hours in the pasture catching mice. Of course they were always around the horse barn, scooping up the mice under the grain bins. If Chubby saw a mouse run under something in the barn, she would start pushing everything and anything out of her way. My husband would never allow her in his shop.

The only drawback to their mousing was that they ate their catch whole. They would grab the mouse in their mouths, with the tail usually hanging out, and swallow hard. The tail would be sucked in, like a kid with poor manners eating spaghetti.

Frogs were another favorite delicacy of Chubby's. She would stand stock-still in the pond for hours, waiting for a frog to jump. When it did, she would have it.

Cocoa was another very special Newf. Cocoa was fully grown when another Newfy breeder and I purchased her.

The night I brought her home it was raining, and not knowing her house manners I had put her in one of the kennel runs. Everyone had gone to bed and I was sitting up reading. I heard a noise at the sliding glass door. I opened the door and in bounded a soaking wet, muddy Cocoa. And I mean bounded—across the end table, down the length of the sofa, across the other end table and into the kitchen and over the snack bar. I could only watch in horror as everything in her path got covered with mud. All I could think of was that my husband would kill the two us if he saw what she was doing to the house.

In a panic I grabbed the paper towels, trying to wipe up the mess, while Cocoa was still delightfully streaking through the family room and kitchen. I finally got my wits about me and realized I needed to stop the dog or the mud would never get cleaned up.

I took Cocoa back to the kennel. She had dug under two chain-link fences to get out. I put her in a different run and went back to the job of cleaning up the mud. I now knew what her house manners were—none. I stayed up most of the night, afraid she would escape again. I kept checking to make sure she was still in her kennel.

"The next frog that jumps is lunch." Benhil's Hobie Cat, affectionately known as "Chubby," enjoying her favorite pastime, hunting frogs.

"Now where did I put that paddle?" Benhil's Nashau-Auke T.K.O. just drifting around the lake. Bred by Joan Bendure and Jane Thibault and owned by Carol Heinel.

"Hey—you cat, get away from that bird feeder." Dolly, owned by Fay and Bob Greer, looking out for her feathered friends.

First thing in the morning I went to the kennel to fill in her holes. By midmorning she was back at the door. This went on all day.

I finally called my breeder friend with whom I co-owned Cocoa. Cocoa had been at her kennel for two weeks prior to my bringing her home. I told her what had happened, and she said Cocoa had never tried to get out when she had her, but the original owner did say that they could not keep Cocoa and her sister in a fence.

I took Cocoa back down to her kennel until we could cement a run so she wouldn't dig out.

I brought her back home, put her in her newly cemented run and left the kennel, thinking I had won the battle. An hour later I was amazed to see Cocoa standing at the door.

I marched her back to the kennel. I found where she had dug out of the exercise area, but could find no way that she could have gotten out of her run— unless it was over the top. Well, that had to be impossible. Newfoundlands couldn't get over a six-foot chain-link fence.

I put her in her run and I went to the house to watch. She never tried to get out when I was standing there watching her.

She paced around her run and would stop and look up at the top of the fence. Sure enough, she went to the back of her kennel and made a running leap for the top rail. Once on the top, she would drop down on the other side, run for the hole she had dug and head for the house.

So Cocoa had won the battle—she became a housedog. Besides, what was one more full-time house Newf?

We had just had a two-story bank barn built for the horses when Cocoa came into season. Knowing she wouldn't stay in the kennel I put her in the top of the barn, with orders to the children not to let her out. Well, five minutes after I was in the house, Cocoa was at the door.

I accused the children of opening the door and letting her out. Of course, they all swore they hadn't. I went down to the barn to see for myself how she achieved this great feat. Well, she had gone through the glass in the window on the side that was two stories, and landed on the cement below. She didn't have a mark on her.

Cocoa always went everywhere with me, even if I was only driving down the driveway to get the mail.

One day I was at a shopping plaza and had left her in the station wagon. I had left the windows down just enough so that she would have plenty of air, but of course not enough for her to get out—or so I thought.

First I went to the card shop, then to the bank, the drug store and then to the variety store. I was in the back of the store when I heard a commotion in the front of the store by the door. I went to see what everyone was looking at. There was Cocoa, proudly sitting at the door, tail wagging, hoping someone would let her in. Talk about embarrassing.

Of course, everyone wanted to know what kind of dog she was, how much she weighed and all the usual questions people ask when they have never seen a Newf before.

As I was walking up the plaza with her they came out of every store I had been in and told me she had been there sniffing around by their door, and then went on down the line.

Shortly after we had got Cocoa, we spent a weekend camping at the lake with a large group of friends.

The first night around the campfire I was busy telling everyone all about the Newfoundland breed and what natural water dogs they were. I told them all about the heroic Newfoundlands being carried on ships and rescuing people.

The next day we all trekked down to the beach with the kids and the usual variety of nondescript mongrel dogs.

Of course I was proudly walking with my beautiful Newfoundland, which I knew was going to show the other dogs how it was done. Everyone was waiting in anticipation of seeing this great breed in action.

I became a little apprehensive when Cocoa didn't make the usual dash for the water. She just stood at my side staring up at me. In the meantime, the other dogs were in the water playing and retrieving sticks.

Not one to let my disappointment show, I proceeded to enter the water, praying after all my bragging the night before that Cocoa wouldn't embarrass me. Again.

Well, Cocoa didn't let me down. She dutifully entered the water with me.

Everything was fine until we hit swimming depth—suddenly her front feet were flailing the water and she was walking on her hind feet.

At the time I didn't know that all Newfs were not natural swimmers. And back then I didn't know how to properly introduce a dog to the water.

My husband came to the rescue. He would swim underneath Cocoa and hold up her rear; she would then calmly stroke the water with her front feet. She at least looked like she knew what she was doing.

For the rest of the weekend everyone made it a point to tell me how well their ''mutts'' could swim.

In the fall of the year that Cocoa was eleven, it was obvious that she was failing and just kind of wasting away. She slept all the time, as old dogs do. I was worried that she wouldn't be able to get around in the snow that winter. I discussed with the family that maybe we should think about putting her to sleep before winter. Of course no one would hear of it, and how could I even consider such a thing? She made it through that winter and into the spring, but there was not really much left to her. She could still get around without help, her appetite was good, but she looked as if a strong wind would blow her over.

I had made the decision that the time had come. I made arrangements for our vet to come and put Cocoa down when I was at the Newfoundland National Specialty. I just didn't think I could be there with her. I had always been there at the end for all of the other dogs. I thought maybe it would be easier on me if I wasn't there. The previous autumn I had held our seventeen-year-old Border Collie while he received the ultimate kindness.

The day before I was to leave I had my son, David, go down to the bottom of the pasture by the pond and dig Cocoa's grave. I was carrying the groceries in when I noticed that Cocoa wasn't in her usual sleeping place. I looked out the window and there was Cocoa, lying next to her grave just staring into the sunset. A chill ran through me. It was as if she knew.

Cocoa had not been in the pasture since many years before, when she had followed me down to feed the fish and one of the horses came out of the woods and attacked her. After that she would sit at the top of the hill and wait for me, with her chin resting on the rail fence, watching as I went down to the pond.

Not knowing if she could make it up the hill, I drove down to get her. What a surprise—she had been in the pond and was totally wet.

Late that night, when everyone was in bed, I was in the kitchen making a list of chores that would need to be done while I was gone. Cocoa came in from the mudroom. She stopped at the food and water bowls and ate a few pieces of dry food. She then smelled the water bowl and gave me the look that said she would need fresh water because another dog had taken a drink from the bowl. I gave her fresh water and sat down to continue my lists. Cocoa came over and laid her head in my lap. I sat there petting her head, crying, and reminiscing with her about all the good times we had together and apologizing for not being able to be with her in the end. She got up and went to the sliding glass door to go out. I let her out, and as soon as her rear legs cleared the door she fell dead on the deck. I was in total shock. I couldn't believe that she could be fine one minute and dead the next. I guess even in death Cocoa was going to have the last word.

Oliver and Molly were littermates that belonged to friends of ours.

One evening after dinner our friends were sitting in the family room watching the news when they heard something in the kitchen. The kitchen had been cleaned up except for a pan of mashed potatoes sitting in the sink. They peeked around the doorway to see Oliver, with his front feet up on the sink and his head in the pan, eating the potatoes. Molly was standing on the floor next to him, looking up. They watched in silence as Oliver got down from the sink and placed a mouthful of potatoes on the floor for Molly to eat. Then he got back up on the sink to get more for himself. This was repeated over and over until the pan was licked clean. Now, how could you scold a dog for stealing when he was nice enough to share with his sister?

HEALTH

The two most serious health problems in the Newfoundland breed are hip dysplasia and inherited heart problems, probably the most common being subaortic stenosis.

Canine Hip Dysplasia

Canine hip dysplasia is a developmental disease of the hip joint. Dysplasia means malformed or badly formed joint.

It can be either unilateral, affecting only one hip; or bilateral, affecting both hips. Hip dysplasia in dogs can vary from borderline to complete subluxation of the ball and socket.

In young dogs hip dysplasia starts as a loose joint. As the femur head moves around in the socket, wearing of the bone surfaces takes place, later causing osteoarthritis.

The veterinary community generally believes that hip dysplasia is a genetic problem. While an exact mode of inheritance has not been established, it is considered to be polygenic.

Polygenic relates to characters controlled by multiple genes, each of which have a little significance, but which have great significance combined together.

In recent years scientists have shown that, like many other diseases, environment is also a factor.

Hip dysplasia can appear in any breed but occurs more frequently in heavy, rapidly-growing pups of the large or giant breeds such as the Newfoundland. It is not congenital as the hip joints are normal at birth. It is rarely found in dogs maturing at under twenty-five pounds.

Orthopedic Foundation for Animals

The Orthopedic Foundation for Animals, commonly referred to as OFA, evaluates X-rays of dogs' hips and elbows for hip and elbow dysplasia. OFA was started in 1967 and was originally started for the evaluation of hips.

Dogs must be two years of age for OFA certification of both hips and elbows, but X-rays taken before two years can be sent to OFA for a preliminary evaluation. The X-ray will be read by three board-certified radiologists.

The following is the incidence of hip dysplasia reported by Corley and Hogan (1985) from OFA data from 1974–84.

OFA evaluated 2,190 Newoundland X-rays. Of these, 32.5 percent were dysplastic, 65.2 percent were normal and 2.2 percent were borderline.

Of course, you must take into consideration that X-rays of severely dysplastic dogs are not usually submitted by owners and veterinarians to OFA for an evaluation.

How to X-ray

All medium-sized and larger dogs should have their hips X-rayed at two years of age before being used for breeding. This can be done by your veterinarian, although not all veterinarians have X-ray equipment suitable for Newfoundlands and some veterinarians do a better job of positioning the dog for the X-ray. Proper positioning of the dog for X-raying is very important. Dogs generally need to be anesthetized or tranquilized so they can be properly positioned. The dog is X-rayed while lying on its back with the rear legs being pulled straight and turned in slightly.

The X-rays can then be submitted to the Orthopedic Foundation for Animals (OFA) for evaluation and certification.

If the hips show no signs of dysplasia, the dog will be issued a number, certifying that the hips are normal. The gradings are Fair, Good or Excellent. The grading will appear in a pedigree of a dog as: Ch. Benhil's Uptown Girl OFA NF-2949E31F. The NF stands for Newfoundland, the four-digit number is the dog's individual number assigned by OFA; E is the grading of Excellent. The number 31 is the age in months of the dog when the X-ray was taken, and F denotes that the dog is a female. OFA numbers are also listed on the AKC papers after the dog's name.

While OFA certification can show that an individual dog has good hips, this does not mean the dog cannot produce puppies with dysplasia, including severely dysplastic individuals. Dysplastic dogs can also produce normal off-spring.

Of course, with a background for good hips the chances of avoiding hip dysplasia are much improved. Ideally, all Newfoundlands used for breeding would be OFA certified. But unfortunately in dog breeding, as in life, not everything is always ideal.

Even more important than the hip status of an individual dog is the status of the family the dog is from. We call these familial traits. You need to look at the hip status of the parents and the littermates.

If the parents and most of the littermates had good hips, there is a stronger genetic base for breeding. I would rather have for breeding the only dysplastic dog from a large litter, compared to the only dog with good hips from an affected family. Dr. Kyle Onstott said it best: "Marry not the only good maid in the clan."

Dogs of exceptional quality that have near-normal or very mild dysplasia should be bred only to dogs with good hips.

Dogs with moderate or severe dysplasia should never be bred from. It is important that a stud dog have good hips because he can produce far more puppies than any bitch ever can.

The hip status should never be the single determining factor of whether or not a dog should be used for breeding. It is just one of the many aspects of the whole dog that needs to be considered. The dog must have many other desirable qualities. It would be of no value to produce sound dogs with undesirable temperaments, lacking the physical features of the breed or with inherited traits that can be fatal, such as bad hearts.

Some clinical signs of hip dysplasia are the tendency to use both rear legs as one when gaiting (bunny hopping), reluctance to get up from a sitting position, preferring sitting to standing and evidence of lameness.

Some severely dysplastic dogs will show no clinical signs of hip dysplasia and lead perfectly normal lives. Some dogs with mild dysplasia will be crippled. That is why it is imperative that a diagnosis be based on X-rays.

OTHER FACTORS

Since hip dysplasia was first discovered, the experts have suggested many different causes and conducted research, most often in nutrition, to find the real cause of hip dysplasia in dogs.

Nutrition

Some experts and breeders feel that feeding puppies of the large and giant breeds dog foods that are high in calcium, protein and calories promotes too much rapid growth. This will in turn increase problems involving bone growth. Breeders know how their lines of dogs grow and can recommend the best diet for proper growth.

Vitamin C

Dr. Wendell O. Belfield, in his book *How to Have a Healthier Dog*, explains his theory and use of sodium ascorbate, or Vitamin C, to prevent hip dysplasia.

Dr. Belfield believes that hip dysplasia is a form of subclinical scurvy.

Many breeders of the large and giant breeds give sodium ascorbate to their pregnant bitches and puppies. They also recommend that their puppy buyers add it to their puppies' diet.

The scientific colony, and the geneticists and orthopedic veterinarians and radiologists, refer to this as artifically altering the phenotype of a dog, and that the dogs are still genetically dysplastic.

Hormones

Some of these theories include an imbalance in the estrogen hormone. It is known that bitches should not be X-rayed during oestrus because the hip joint will show more laxity than when not in season.

Others contend that hip dysplasia occurs more often in females than in males. This is probably due to the fact that more females are kept for breeding than males, hence a greater number are X-rayed and found to be dysplastic.

Exercise

There are two schools of thought on how or if exercise affects hip formation. Some believe that puppies should receive all the exercise they want, thus promoting strong pelvic muscles that will hold the hips in place while growing. Others believe that exercise should be restricted, thus avoiding trauma to bones, ligaments and tendons.

HEART DISEASE

Congenital heart disease is a recognized problem in the Newfoundland breed. There are several heart problems that can affect the Newfoundland and many other breeds. They are patent ductus arteriosus, pulmonic stenosis and aortic stenosis.

Aortic stenosis is an obstruction of the outflow from the left ventricle, most commonly occurring in the subvalvular position.

Subvalvular aortic stenosis, commonly referred to as SAS, is most often found in the Newfoundland, Golden Retriever, Rottweiler, Boxer and the German Shepherd Dog.

Studies that have been done in the Newfoundland indicate that the condition is inherited. Like hip dysplasia, the exact mode of inheritance has not been determined. SAS is believed to be a polygenic trait or an autosomal trait with modifiers. Dogs that are examined and found to be clear of it can still produce it.

It is not present at birth but develops as the puppy grows. A litter of puppies should have their hearts checked by a board-certified cardiologist at nine weeks of age or older. This is done as a screening to find the more severe cases, as a very mild case of SAS may be missed at this young age, even by a qualified cardiologist.

A general practice veterinarian with knowledge and a good ear may be able to hear and detect heart abnormalities in young puppies, but will not have the resources available for an accurate diagnosis.

All adult dogs should be examined by a board-certified cardiologist before being used for breeding. Dogs from a litter with a high incidence of heart problems should not be used for breeding. While heart problems are certainly not found in all litters, you never know when it may appear.

Heart problems are like hip dysplasia—if you aren't looking for them, you probably won't find them unless the condition is severe.

Breeders should not make the statement that their dogs don't produce heart problems unless they are having their puppies and adults cleared by a cardiologist. The only way to be is certain is by using a cardiologist. Hip dysplasia was not a problem until X-raying for hip dysplasia became a common practice.

The Newfoundland breed is not that old. Accordingly, almost all pedigrees can easily be traced back to the same few dogs. In other words, our genetic pool is not that large. Because of this, Newfoundlands from any bloodlines have the possibility of producing inherited heart defects. It is only by continually checking that we will know.

EYES

Entropion is the turning in of the eyelid, allowing the eyelashes to rub on the cornea and causing pain and inflammation. It is more common in the lower lid. It can be unilateral or bilateral. It may be inherited, or secondary to conjunctivitis or injury. Surgery is required to correct it. Ectropion, an outward turning condition of the lower eyelid, causes irritation and inflammation of the haw. It may be inherited or secondary to eyelid or nerve injury. Surgery is necessary to correct it.

In third eyelid prolapse or "Cherry Eye," a mass of red tissue suddenly appears at the inside corner of the eye. It occurs more often in young, growing dogs, affecting one eye at onset, but the second eye usually becomes affected within several weeks. It is sometimes incorrectly referred to as harderian gland enlargement. Surgical removal of the entire gland is required.

If surgically corrected, the dog cannot be shown.

TAILS

Sometimes puppies are born with a kink or bend in the tail. This can be a very slight bend or bump, hardly noticeable, to a kink that is a complete right angle. There can be more than one kink in a tail.

Sometimes puppies are born with shorter than normal tails. There has been the rare occasion of a pup being born without a tail or only a stub.

THYROID

Hypothyroidism, or low thyroid levels, is caused by an underactive thyroid gland. The thyroid gland controls many functions of the body. This seems to be a problem that is becoming increasingly common in all breeds of dogs, including mongrels.

PANOSTEITIS

Panosteitis is a painful inflammation of the long bones occurring in young, growing puppies, usually between the ages of four to twelve months. It is commonly referred to as wandering lameness because it usually shifts from one leg to another over a period of several weeks or months. More than one leg can be involved at the same time. It is self-limiting. Excessive amounts of calcium or protein in the diet are believed to promote panosteitis.

OSTEOCHONDRITIS DISSECANS (OCD)

Osteochondritis dissecans is caused by a flap of cartilage in the shoulder or stifle that breaks off and dies before it is fully calcified. Small pieces will often reabsorb if the dog's activity is severely restricted. It is important to avoid further injury to the joint. Surgery is sometimes necessary to remove larger flaps. Whether or not there is a genetic predisposition is uncertain.

BLOAT

Bloat (or acute gastric dilation/torsion) is the name of the condition when the stomach suddenly becomes distended with gas and/or fluids. In severe cases the stomach may twist, causing death. The cause is unknown. *Immediate veterinary care is crucial.* It is more common in the large, deep-bodied breeds like the Newfoundland. Avoid exercise immediately before or after a meal. Do not feed large amounts of food at one time.

"Kiss you, and you'll turn into a what?" Ch. Briny Deep's Captain Midnite investigating a prince under a spell. Bred by Claire Ives and owned by Sally Grasse.

8

Breeding the Newfoundland

"**R**EMEMBER you are dealing with living things whose fate is in your keeping. The responsibility for the welfare of the Newfoundland as well as the future of the breed is yours."

The above was written by the late, great Bea Godsol of Coastwise Kennels in an article on judging the Newfoundland, and passed on to me from another owner of a great kennel, Peggy Helming of Pouch Cove. Although it was written for judging dogs, it is appropriate for anyone breeding Newfoundlands to remember.

Breeding is not for the faint of heart. Sometimes I think breeders are bent on self-destruction—physical, mental and financial. Plan on a lot of hard work, sleepless nights, some bitter disappointments and don't ever plan on making a profit. But on the bright side is that pride and warm feeling you get when you look into the eyes of a trusting Newfoundland, or watch a beautiful dog you have bred go around the show ring, leap off a boat to "rescue" someone, or just sitting quietly with its family.

And I would be thoughtless if I did not add all the wonderful friendships you will develop because of puppies you have produced that have brought their owners so much happiness.

The most important concepts to bear in mind when determining if a dog is breeding quality is temperament and health and whether or not your dog closely meets the Standard.

Pet-quality dogs are just that and should not be used for breeding. Besides, why take the chance of jeopardizing your pet's life, as can happen with a female, or changing your male's personality? There is no reason to breed a pet-quality dog with the notion that you are only interested in producing more good pets, or that you will get another one just like the dog you have. Most puppies produced by the best dogs will end up as someone's pet. The general idea of breeding dogs is to improve the breed, not just produce puppies. Puppies produced from pet-quality parents are never an improvement for the breed.

In today's society, with the overpopulation of dogs, including purebreds, there is no reason for producing more unwanted dogs. If you want your children to witness the "miracle of birth," may I also suggest that you take them to a humane society to witness the agony of death.

Unfortunately, most dog breeders have no concept of genetics or how the genes are passed on from one generation to the next to make up an individual dog. You don't need a master's degree in genetics to breed dogs, but a basic understanding is certainly helpful.

Start with probably the most easily understood concepts of inheritance, which would be the inheritance of the coat color in Newfoundlands.

There are many good books on genetics, but the two I recommend to start with are *Practical Genetics for Dog Breeders*, by Malcolm B. Willis, and *The Inheritance of Coat Color in Dogs*, by Clarence C. Little, D.V.M., Sc.D.

Keep in mind that while breeding is based on genetic principles, genes are not that easy to control. Dogs have thirty-nine pairs of chromosomes, and there are more than 25,000 genes contained in each chromosome. So the genetic possibilities are endless.

Without question, a certain amount of success in dog breeding is a matter of luck. Luck to have the genes come together as you planned is nice for you, but totally random no less.

Also, when mentioning luck, I mean the good fortune of having gone to one breeder over another to purchase your first Newfoundland and getting off to a good start. Luck also touches experienced breeders that have sold a puppy into a pet home only to have a beautiful adult returned to them that becomes one of the great producers in the breed. Breeders who choose to mate two dogs without any bases for their selection, but end up producing a litter of beautiful dogs are yet another example of luck challenging science.

But luck cannot be depended on, and luck can run out. Don't ignore the scientific knowledge and veterinary technology available today. Breeding haphazardly will catch up with you in the end.

Too many novices get caught up in the sport of dogs before they realize that the first dog they purchased is not all that they could desire in a Newfoundland. If this happens to you, take the initiative to start over with a dog that is more suited for your purpose, a dog that will be a good foundation for your kennel. It will save you much time and money in the long run. The top breeders didn't start at the top—they were all novices at one time. It is only through knowledge and hard work and disappointments along the way that they got to a place of prominence.

It is important that you, as an aspiring breeder, be able to look at a pedigree and know the individual dogs listed. You should be able to bring a picture of each dog into your mind. Learn and make notes of each dog's virtues and faults. It isn't until after you have been involved in a breed for many years that you will be able to do this using only your own perceptions.

Go right to the owner of the dogs; don't rely on rumors spread by other breeders. If a breeder of a certain line doesn't tell you of the faults along with a dog's virtues, that person will not be much help to you. All dogs have faults. Not all have noteworthy virtues.

Breeders who honestly and openly discuss problems produced by their dogs, particularly health problems, risk getting labeled by others as having serious inherited problems in their lines. When breeders are screening for health problems and willing to be honest and tell you what problems their dogs have produced, you know that they are trying to produce quality dogs.

Keep in mind that when breeding dogs you must be concerned with the whole dog, not just one aspect. It doesn't matter how a good a dog's hips are, if the dog in question does not have the wonderful disposition or physical characteristics of the Newfoundland breed. It also doesn't matter how beautiful a dog is if it has a bad heart and should never be used for breeding.

Below is a philosophy that the late, remarkable breeder Kitty Drury felt firmly about and advised adherence to:

Coastwise Code

1. To pay special attention to bitches
2. To study grandparents rather than parents
3. To keep careful breeding records
4. Not to rush to every new stud with a name
5. To try to read a pedigree by breeding facts, not names
6. To put away all culls and weaklings at birth
7. Never to sell or give away an excessively shy or nervous dog
8. Never to sell any dogs the kennel cannot be proud of
9. To make good on any dog sold that may not turn out satisfactorily
10. To breed dogs for intelligence and disposition as well as physical perfection

TYPES OF BREEDING

Inbreeding is the breeding of closely related dogs, such as daughter to father, son to mother and sister to brother. It is the quickest way to set a desired type or characteristic within a breed. The dogs being inbred from must be superlative examples of the breed in both genotype and phenotype. Inbreeding is not for the novice and should only be used by the most experienced breeders. In the hands of a fool, inbreeding can be disastrous, but in the hands of an experienced breeder it can have dramatic results.

Linebreeding is a less intensified form of inbreeding. It is the breeding of less closely related dogs like half brother to half sister; granddaughter to grandfather; grandson to grandmother; niece to uncle; nephew to aunt; or cousins. Linebreeding is the safest way to breed and still be able to set the type and characteristics desired. It will just take a few generations of linebreeding to get the desired results consistently.

Outcrossing is the mating of unrelated dogs. Eventually, inbred or heavily linebred individuals will need to be outcrossed every three or four generations to bring some fresh influences into a line. Continually outcrossing will produce a confused pedigree, and you will not be able to predict the type or characteristics of the dogs produced from such breedings.

It is not true that inbreeding or linebreeding creates abnormal traits, physical or mental. It just brings what is hidden to the surface. The same abnormalities will be produced from two totally unrelated parents if they are both carrying the same gene.

Inbreeding and linebreeding do not create genes not already present, but they intensify and bring to the forefront both the desired and undesired recessive and dominant characteristics. When a characteristic is produced in a litter of pups that neither parent appears to have, it is not because inbreeding or linebreeding created it. It is because both parents were carrying the recessive for that gene.

Undesirable recessive genes can combine together even in dogs of outcross matings.

SELECTING A STUD DOG

It is important that you choose as a stud for your bitch a dog that will complement her strengths. Such a dog should not share the same faults that your bitch displays.

Make sure the stud you are considering has passed all the health requirements, such as having his heart and hips evaluated as an adult. He himself must be in good health. He must have the temperament desired. A dog with questionable temperament should never be used for breeding under any circumstance.

Don't pick a dog just because he is a big winner in the show ring or has numerous titles following his name. Titles do not denote a dog's ability to produce quality. Remember, phenotype is what a dog looks like, and genotype is the genetic makeup of the dog—one you see, the other you don't. Don't wait until your bitch comes into season to choose a stud dog to breed to. This should be carefully planned and not a hasty, last-minute decision.

Be sure you understand all the terms of the stud service contract and make sure that all parties have a signed copy.

All-time top producing sire of champions and ROMs, Ch. Pouch Cove Gref of Newton-Ark, ROM (Ch. Kuhaia's Rego, ROM, ex Ch. Pouch Cove Kasha Newton-Ark). Bred by Margaret Helming and Janet Levine and owned by Julie Heyward. *John Ashbey*

Ch. Kuhaia's Rego, ROM (Ch. Jack the Ripper, ROM, ex Ch. Edenglen's Lady Rebecca, ROM), bred by Janet Levine and Ronnie Farkas and owned by Ronnie Farkas. Rego's influence as a stud dog—and the linebreeding of Rego offspring—is responsible for the beautiful type and substance that we see on the top winning and producing Newfoundlands of today. *Graham*

BREEDING

Before we go too much further into breeding, please understand that this chapter will only scratch the surface on what you should know about the subject. It is however, particularly aimed at the special needs of Newfoundlands. There are many good books written on breeding and whelping. I would suggest that you read and learn all that you can before you even attempt breeding. It would take volumes to cover everything, but there is nothing like actual experience to guide you through breeding and raising a litter. Besides, I have yet to find the Newfoundland bitch that has ever read the textbook on how it should be done!

The next best thing to having that experience yourself is to have a good veterinarian and an experienced breeder friend, hopefully of Newfoundlands, that you can rely on for information and guidance. I had better add, at all hours of the day or night, because dogs never manage to do things when it is convenient for the people around them.

It is important that before the bitch is bred she be in good physical condition but not too fat and well exercised. She should be up-to-date on her vaccinations, be checked for parasites and treated if necessary.

Stud dog owners will require a prebreeding exam by a veterinarian that will include a test for brucellosis and a uterine culture.

The only time a bitch can be bred is during estrus, more commonly referred to as being in season or heat. A bitch is in season for approximately twenty-one days twice a year. The first signs of a bitch coming into season are swelling and licking of the genitalia and more frequent urination.

In large breeds like the Newfoundland, this usually occurs for the first time somewhere between ten and eighteen months of age. But it is possible for the first estrus to occur anytime after six months of age. Bitches should not be bred before their second season or at about two years of age. It is best not to delay the first breeding too long, as many bitches never conceive if they are much older at the first mating.

Newfoundland bitches usually cycle or come into season every six months. But some will cycle as often as every four months or as far apart as eight months. But six months is the normal time. Many bitches that come into season more frequently are not fertile.

An average-size litter for a Newfoundland would be about eight puppies. Six puppies would not be considered small, and ten puppies is not an exceptionally large litter in this breed.

It is commonly accepted that bitches should not be bred more often than once a year, particularly if they have had an average or larger than average-size litter.

The first nine or ten days of a bitch's season is referred to as proestrus. The first day of a bright red, bloody discharge is the first day of proestrus or season. The best way to determine the first day is by using a white tissue and swabbing the vulva.

During this time the bitch will be playful with other dogs but will generally

Foundation bitches for Pouch Cove Kennels: Am., Can. Ch. Kilyka's Jessica of Pouch Cove, CD, ROM (left), at age twelve, bred by Betty McDonnell and owned by David and Peggy Helming, and Ch. Kilyka's Becky Jo of Pouch Cove, ROM, at age nine, bred by Betty McDonnell and owned by Peggy Helming. Jessica and Becky Jo were half sisters out of the all-time top producing bitch, Ch. Shipshape's Sibyl, ROM.

Sweetbay's Chinaberry, CD, WRD, bred and owned by Julie and Ellis Adler of Sweetbay Kennels, is pictured nine weeks pregnant. Less than an hour after this photo was taken she whelped the first of eleven puppies.

141

not accept males for breeding. The color and amount of discharge slowly fades as the season progresses.

Estrus, or standing heat, is the second phase of the season and is when the bitch will allow the male to mount and breed her. This usually occurs about the tenth or eleventh day after the first red discharge and lasts until about the seventeenth or eighteenth day.

Ovulation and conception occur sometime during this period.

Bitches should be bred every other day until they refuse to accept the male. This will be a total of two or three breedings during that season. More bitches don't conceive because they are bred too early in the season than too late.

Bitches in season should never be allowed to run loose, nor should they ever be kept with a male while in season.

Do not keep a male and female together in the hopes that nature will take care of everything. You will never know if the dogs actually mated, and dogs can be seriously hurt this way. A young male can be ruined forever by having a bitch that is not ready to be bred turn on him.

Often, due to their size and heavy coat, you will have to assist Newfoundlands in the actual breeding. Some bitches will even try to sit or lie down during the tie. It is best to enlist the help of a more experienced dog breeder that will teach you how to help effect a mating.

Some of the earliest signs that a bitch is in whelp is a change in personality. Some bitches become extremely mellow and loving and want to be near their people constantly. The bred bitch's normal activity level may drop, but it is important that she receive moderate exercise to maintain good muscle tone for the upcoming whelping. If your bitch is one that stays active during pregnancy, do not restrict her normal activity until about the fifth week.

The vulva will stay somewhat enlarged after breeding. Between the twenty-eighth to the thirty-fifth day after breeding you may want to have your vet palpate your bitch to see if she is pregnant. With a bitch in whelp there will almost always be a vaginal discharge of clear mucous at about the fourth or fifth week after breeding.

A change in appetite is a good sign of pregnancy. Most Newfoundland bitches' appetites will increase during pregnancy. But there is the occasional bitch that may not want to eat for a week or two early in the pregnancy. Some bitches will have nausea, like morning sickness, although it can be at any time of day.

A good-quality kibble should always be fed. There is usually an increase in appetite starting at four to five weeks after breeding, and you should start increasing her food at this time. If she is not already on two meals a day, now is a good time to start. She may even need several smaller meals a day later in gestation. Do be careful not to let her get overweight at this time.

X-raying to see how many puppies there may not be advisable unless you cannot determine if the bitch is pregnant. In a large litter it is not easy to see all the skeletons on an X-ray, and breeders can be fooled into thinking there are fewer pups than there really are. X-raying should be reserved for use when absolutely necessary, not for a breeder's convenience. Just as in people, dogs should not be subjected to radiation unnecessarily.

The average length of gestation is approximately sixty-three days, or nine weeks. But it can also vary from fifty-nine to seventy days. The reason for the variations is that we count from the days bred, because we usually don't know the actual day of fertilization.

There are tests available that can be performed during the bitch's season that will show when a bitch ovulates or when she goes into diestrus (a sixty-day period following estrus), which will give a more accurate whelping date.

Pyometra, pus in the uterus, is a serious problem and can be fatal. It seems to occur most often about four to six weeks after a bitch has been in season. Some of the signs of pyometra are increased consumption of water, distended abdomen, vomiting and not eating. There are two kinds of pyometra, open and closed. With open pyometra there is a copious putrid discharge of pus from the vulva. It can sometimes be successfully treated, without spaying the bitch, with prostaglandin, which at this time is not approved for use in dogs. Closed pyometra can be more difficult to recognize as there is no discharge. The only way to save the life of a bitch with a closed pyometra is by spaying.

PRE-WHELPING PREPARATION

Make sure you are prepared well in advance of the whelping date. Most important is the selection of where in your home the bitch will whelp and the construction of a whelping box.

The whelping room should be in a warm, quiet area of the house but convenient to where you spend most of your time, to an outside entrance and laundry facilities.

Whelping boxes are customarily homemade from plywood or fiberboard, and sealed with polyurethane. For a Newfoundland a box that is a minimum of four by six feet in size so that the bitch can lie out flat on her side in comfort is needed.

If you are going to keep the puppies in the whelping box longer than three weeks of age, you may want to consider making it eight feet long. Make it so you can partition it off to six feet while the pups are young, and then have the full eight feet when they are up and walking around.

Height should be about eighteen to twenty-four inches, with a door so the bitch can get in and out easily. Be sure to include a puppy rail approximately five inches high and five inches wide around the inside walls so that a puppy will not get squeezed between the bitch and the side of the box. Puppies should not be confined in a solid-walled box after six weeks of age.

Items you will need for whelping and raising a litter should include the following:

Newspapers, lots of newspapers. Do not use those with colored print. Newspapers are used to line the whelping box and puppy area. When the pups are getting around well you will want to lay newspapers on the bottom of the pen and then shred some on top.

Blankets. You should have at least three. The ribcord bedspreads in double-bed size work well. They wash and dry easily and don't pill from the puppies' feet like blankets do.

Towels—hand towels for drying newborn puppies and large bath towels to lay under the bitch during whelping and for a few days after. There is quite a bit of fluid and discharge during whelping and for the first ten days after. Be ready.

Dental floss to tie around the base of the puppies' cords immediately after birth.

Thermometer for taking the bitch's temperature before and after whelping.

Scissors and hemostatic forceps to cut and clamp the cord in case the bitch doesn't, and most of them won't! Be sure to have alcohol for sterilizing scissors and forceps.

A scale for weighing the puppies at birth and every day for the first several weeks. This is especially important for a novice breeder, as it can be very difficult to tell if a puppy is gaining well until you develop a feel for it. It is important to make sure the puppies are gaining steadily. Human baby scales are generally used, and the weights from one breeder's scale to another will vary considerably, so don't be concerned if your pups do not weigh what someone else's pups weighed at birth. Puppies usually lose a few ounces the first day after whelping.

Colored knitting yarn or rickrack to put around each pup's neck so you can identify each one. It can be very difficult to tell one black pup from another black pup. Yarn will have some stretch to it, rickrack will not. Make sure that you tie it snug enough so that the pup cannot get a foot caught up in it. Be sure to tie it in a square knot and to change it daily. Yes, that is how fast Newfie pups will grow during the first few weeks.

Chart to mark the delivery time, sex, birth weight, color and markings, yarn color, comments and note whether or not each pup was born with its placenta.

Vetrap bandaging tape, to be used to protect the bitch's tail and keep it clean during the whelping.

Make sure you have everything ready a couple of weeks before the due date. Introduce the bitch to her whelping box ten days before she is due. Encourage her to get in the box and lie down. Show her what a nice place this is to be. Of course when you leave the room, so will she. As the day of whelping gets close, you will more than likely find her in closets pulling everything out and trying them for size. Better yet is the bitch that goes outside under the deck or porch to dig a hole in the ground. Don't be upset—it is a very natural thing for a bitch to do.

If your bitch needs a bath, do it at least a week before she is due, using a mild, natural shampoo. If she gets her legs or underbelly muddy close to the due date use plain water to wash her off.

WHELPING

It is a good idea to contact your vet to remind him that your bitch is going to be whelping soon. Make sure he or she will be available day or night, usually night. Why do they always have to wait until the middle of the night?

It is helpful to have someone with you during the whelping so someone will always be there to watch the bitch and help take the bitch out between pups. You will want to change papers and blankets several times during the whelping. Some bitches are very neat and some make a real mess. Many bitches will tear up the newspapers and blankets and can make a real shambles out of the whelping box.

Several days before the actual delivery you will probably notice the bitch's abdomen drop. The hip and back bones will protrude, giving her loin area a sunken appearance.

One of the best signs of imminent labor is a drop in body temperature. Start taking her temperature a week before she is due so that you have an idea of what her normal temperature is. Take it every twelve hours after the bitch has been resting. Normal should be between 100 and 101 degrees F. There will be some variations in temperatures, so don't become alarmed if you see it go down and then come back up. When the temperature drops to between 98 and 99.5 degrees F. and remains steady for a few hours, you can be pretty sure that you will have puppies within twenty-four hours. There are some bitches with which you can never seem to catch the temperature drop.

As whelping draws near, most bitches will refuse to eat, but then there are those that will never miss a meal, and a couple hours later start having puppies. As I said, they have not read the book on how it should be done.

Most bitches will find a dark, quiet, out-of-the-way place to nest, if they haven't already selected it. Or they will start pacing from room to room or asking to go outside. If you feel that the whelping is going to start soon, take her out on a leash to avoid her crawling into a small space you will have difficulty getting her out of.

The bitch will start panting, then stop and rest and pant some more. She will seem uncomfortable, get up and dig and push things around with her nose, then lie back down and go through the whole process again. Some bitches will even go so far as to repeat this process for days before. And just when you think she is really going to have that first pup, she will lie down in her favorite spot and go to sleep. Some bitches will give you these false starts for days.

It is best to confine her to the room you have everything set up in for the whelping, although I have had some bitches that were absolutely not going to have a puppy unless it was in the spot they picked. Some bitches can really be persistent about this. If the spot is even remotely reasonable, it may be best for all concerned to let her have the first pup there. Then take mother and pup and put them in the whelping box. She may try picking up the pup and taking it back to where she had it, but you will have to be persistent. Be assured, a bitch will not leave her pup. But then again remember that bitches never read breeding books.

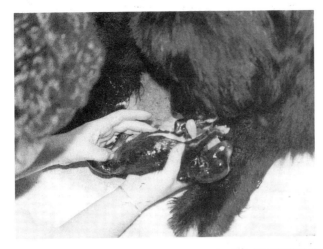

Ch. Benhil's Uptown Girl, ROM ("Molly") and newborn puppy with the allantoic sac still on.

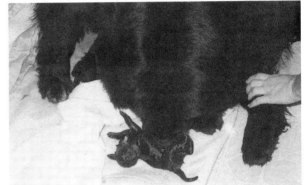

Molly is vigorously licking the puppy to stimulate breathing.

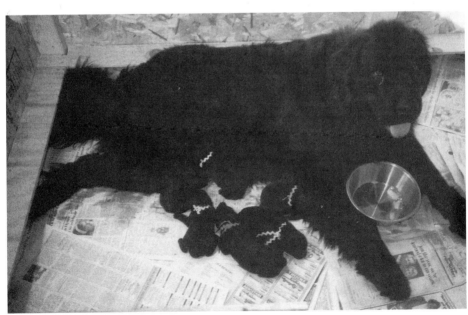

Molly taking a rest. Each pup has been weighed and a different-colored rickrack collar has been placed around its neck for identification.

Make sure the box is lined with plenty of newspapers and covered with a blanket and towels to absorb the fluids that are expelled during whelping. Believe me, some can really make a mess, and then there are those that do not believe they should have to clean up after themselves or the pups.

Contractions will start off slowly, usually coming in groups of several together and then a rest period of ten or fifteen minutes. When the pup is actually coming down the canal and ready to be delivered, the contractions will be harder and closer together. Some bitches will stand up to deliver a pup. Some will prefer to sit during labor and then slowly lift their rear as they have the contraction that pushes the pup out. Try to let her be in the position that is most comfortable for her—she will know what is best.

Sometimes when a puppy starts down the birth canal the bitch may feel the need to relieve herself and want to be let outside. You can take her out on a leash, and she should be taken out several times during the whelping, but make sure you have a towel with you. It never fails that when you go out without a towel (and flashlight at night) she will drop a puppy in the yard. It can be very difficult to pick up a wet newborn puppy without a towel.

The time has come to tell you that some Newfoundland bitches are not always the greatest whelpers or mothers compared with other breeds. I have had some bitches that were excellent and would handle everything themselves, remove the sac, sever the cord and lick the puppy dry. A really good mother is so intent on taking care of the puppies she will not let you have a chance to do anything for her. Then I have had some that couldn't have cared less how or if the sac came off the puppy or if the cord got cut. And you will have to do everything for them if the pup is to survive.

As the puppy nears the vulva and is ready to be expelled, the bitch will start to frantically lick herself, licking up the fluid and licking the puppy.

When the first pup arrives, refrain from touching the pup and give the bitch a chance to open the sac.

There are two sacs, the outer one that is filled with amniotic fluid and the allantoic sac, which closely surrounds the pup. Sometimes one or both sacs will rupture as the pup is born. Or the bitch may rupture them by licking. The bitch will eat the sacs immediately and probably sever the cord at the same time. Most pups are delivered in their sac, but it is not unusual to have the pup expelled without the sac. Most pups are born anterior, or front first, but it is not at all unusual to have them presented posterior, or rear first.

It is best if you let the bitch sever the cord with her teeth, as this will crush the cord, resulting in less bleeding than if the cord is cut. If the placenta comes out with the pup, she will probably eat this also, given the opportunity. Some breeders will only let the bitch eat a couple of the placentas and remove the rest before she has a chance to eat them.

If the placenta is retained and the cord is still in the vulva, she will pull it out. If the placenta does not come out at this time, there is not much you can do about it. It may be pushed out later. In any case, it is important that all the placentas be expelled. Make note of how many placentas were passed.

The time between puppies can vary from a few minutes to several hours, with the bitch taking rests between deliveries.

If your bitch doesn't immediately start licking the pup, use your finger to open the sac and pull it back from the puppy's nose and mouth. She may get the idea and start licking the puppy. If she doesn't start to lick the pup, you can then wipe the pup's muzzle with a towel and give Mother another chance to take over.

If your bitch is still not going to take care of removing the sac, severing the cord and stimulating the pup to breathe, you will need to do it for her.

Grasp the puppy and the placenta, if the placenta is presented with the puppy, in a towel. Remove the sac and wipe the pup's nostrils. Then briskly rub the pup to stimulate breathing. Don't worry about hurting the pup; newborns are not as delicate as you think!

After you have rubbed the pup dry and the pup has started breathing and crying, you can remove the cord. Before you cut the cord, clamp it to prevent bleeding about an inch from the pup with the forceps. Tie dental floss on the base of the cord.

Examine the puppy, checking for cleft palates and kinked tails. Weigh the puppy and fill the information in on your chart. Now place the yarn or rickrack on the pup.

Now it is time for the pup to nurse. It is important that newborn pups nurse soon after birth. If the pup does not nuzzle the teat and nurse without help, you will need to help it. With one hand, grasp the pup around the back of the neck, using your thumb and finger to press gently on the corners of the mouth, forcing the pup to open its mouth. With the other hand, squeeze the teat to express some milk. Put the pup's mouth on the teat to nurse. Make sure the pup is nursing.

During the whelping, you may want to offer the bitch a little ice cream or chicken noodle soup. You may give her some water, but be careful not to let her have too much, as some bitches vomit during whelping.

It is helpful to get the bitch up several times during the whelping and take her outside. That is also a good time to change the papers and blankets. Do not put the bitch out unattended.

Until you have whelped several litters, it is best to have your veterinarian check the bitch to be sure all the pups and placentas are out. After all the pups are born, the bitch will be tired and generally go into a very deep, relaxed sleep. With experience you will be able to tell the difference between this deep sleep and those naps she takes between pups.

For the first few days after whelping, bitches do not want to leave the whelping box. Some bitches must literally be dragged out of the whelping box to go out to relieve themselves.

Be sure that the bitch is licking all the pups in the litter, as this is necessary for them to digest their food and to relieve themselves.

Healthy puppies will twitch when they are sleeping.

Puppies like to lie together in a nice little pile. If the puppies get too warm, they will cry and spread out all over the box, trying to find a cooler place. This will make it difficult for the bitch to get in the box to lie down.

Four-week-old Pouch Cove pups.

Six-week-old pups from Greer Newfoundlands.

Ch. Teddy Tug's Lady Gabrielle with two of her four-month-old pups. Bitch pup on left is Carillon's Spring Break, and male pup is Carillon's Upper Classman, Best Puppy in Sweepstakes at the 1993 National Specialty. Owners: Mark and Joanne Chilcoat.

If the puppies are too cold, they will cry and fight to get down to the bottom of the pile to keep warm.

Sometimes the milk supply does not come in abundantly until several days after whelping. Feeding bitches cornbread after whelping will help increase the milk supply. It is normal for the bitch to pant while nursing puppies.

Many bitches do not have a good appetite immediately after whelping and may need to be coaxed into eating. You may want to try to add chicken noodle soup, canned meat dog food or hamburger mixed with the kibble.

Take the bitch's temperature a couple of times a day for the first week to be sure she does not develop an infection. Remember, a nursing bitch will have a slightly elevated temperature. If the temperature goes higher than 103 degrees F., call your vet.

It is important that the litter be watched closely day and night for the first few days to be sure the bitch does not lie on the pups and smother them.

During the first twenty-one days of life, the only things that are important for young puppies' survival are warmth, food, stimulation and sleep.

At twenty-one days the puppies can hear, see and relate quite well to their surroundings. From this time forward environment will play a big role in the psychological development of each puppy.

The brain and nervous system become fully developed between three and seven weeks of age. It is important that puppies be with their mother and littermates until at least seven weeks of age so they learn how to socialize properly with other dogs. Dogs that are removed from the litter before seven weeks of age usually have difficulty getting along with peers and will pick fights. At this age puppies will have play fights. If, therefore, the bitch doesn't correct a bully in the litter, the breeder should.

It is very important that each puppy be socialized by humans at this age. Each pup should have individual attention every day. It is important to hold and talk to each puppy individually. Starting at three weeks of age, cradle each pup in your arm on its back and talk to it. Do not be quiet around your litter. It is important that they experience different sounds such as those from various household appliances, telephone conversations—anything they would normally hear in daily life.

Three weeks of age is also about the time to start feeding your litter. You can soak the puppy food in water until it is soft and then mash it up and add more water until it is of loose, gruellike consistency. Or you can powder the dry food in a blender and then add water. The pups will usually be wearing more than they eat. Let Mom in afterward for cleanup. You should only feed the pups once a day until they get the idea. Keep a shallow dish of water available for them. Gradually decrease the amount of water you mix with the food as they get better at the food pan.

Have a composite stool sample checked by your veterinarian at three weeks of age. It is important that puppies be treated as soon as possible for any worms they may have.

By six weeks of age the puppies should receive the first of their vaccinations.

The next important period in a pup's life is between seven weeks and twelve weeks of age. This is the time when dogs learn to bond with humans and receive individual attention so they will learn to become self-confident and should start looking to a human as alpha leader. Dogs will become shy if not given individual attention during this period.

It is not wise to keep pups from the same litter together all of the time during the developmental period. One will become the leader and the others will become followers, lacking self-confidence.

At ten or eleven weeks of age they should have their preliminary heart checks before going to their new homes.

Am., Can. Ch. Seaward's Blackbeard, ROM. "Adam" is the all-time top winning Newfoundland in the history of the breed, with 31 all-breed Bests in Show, twice winning the National Specialty and multiple Bests of Breed at regional Specialties. Adam is the only Newfoundland ever to win Best in Show at the prestigious Westminster Kennel Club. Pictured left to right are the late breeder-judge Mrs. Maynard K. Drury, Gerlinde V. Hockla, Adam's handler throughout his career, trophy presenter Mrs. William Kurth, lifetime NCA member and Newf fancier, and his owner, the late Elinor C. Ayers, owner of Seaward Kennels. *John Ashbey*

9

Showing the Newfoundland

COMPETING in conformation or breed classes at a dog show is a way of proving the physical quality of your dog. It is in fact a beauty contest. Dogs are judged on how well they compare to the ideal Newfoundland as described in the Standard.

Before deciding to enter your Newfoundland in a dog show, it would be advisable to have him or her evaluated by someone knowledgeable on Newfoundlands who can and will give you an honest opinion. Learn your dog's faults and virtues and be honest with yourself. Do keep in mind that there are no perfect dogs.

Attend a few dog shows without your dog before actually entering so you can learn the proper procedure. Or find someone knowledgeable who is willing to guide you through learning how to show your dog.

Watch how the professionals set their dogs up. Learn ring procedures— they do not vary much from one ring to the next. You can handle your own dog in the ring or you can hire a professional handler to do it for you.

It is very rewarding to handle your own dog to its championship. Try to find conformation or handling classes that you can enroll in with your dog. Even with classes to attend, it will take a while before you become really skilled in showing your dog and comfortable in competition.

TRAINING YOUR DOG

Your dog will need a training (choke) collar and lead of the proper length. The collar should fit tightly around your dog's neck, with no more than two inches of slack when the collar is drawn tight. Your leash should be a short nylon show lead, preferably black, about two to three feet in length.

Start with your dog on your left side and teach it to stand quietly at your side. Do not worry about where your dog's feet are at this time.

Place the collar as far up on the neck and throat as you can. The collar should be right behind the dog's ears. Be sure to get the excess skin on the throat out from under the collar, so you have a smooth fit without extra skin being drawn up under the collar.

Grasp the collar on the back of the dog's neck with your left hand and pull it up. Be sure not to pull it so tight that the dog is choking—just tight enough to hold its head up. Use your right hand to help position its head, so that the bridge of the muzzle is level and its nose is not pointing up. Some dogs find it very comforting if you lightly scratch them under the chin while holding them in this position.

While holding its head up with the collar, tell it to "stack, stand, pose" or whatever word you decide to use as its command to stack in the ring. Unlike in the obedience ring, you can talk to your dog in the conformation ring.

Hold the dog in this position for a short period, but don't overdo it or it will start pulling away. Keep repeating this over and over until it gets the idea that it is to stand still until you release it from the stack command. Remember to always keep the dog on your left side and also between you and the judge.

Now that you have your dog standing still while you hold its collar taut, it is time to start placing its feet in the proper position. Slip your right hand under the collar on the back of the dog's neck, fingers pointing toward the dog's rear. Hold the head up while you reach over the dog. With your left hand, grasp the dog's left front leg just below the elbow. Pull up until it is up just off the floor and rotate the leg until the foot is pointing forward and is straight down from the elbow, then place the foot back down on the floor.

Change hands with the collar and do the same thing using your right hand to position the right front leg.

Switch back to holding the collar with the right hand. Reach over the dog and grasp the dog's left rear leg around the hock. Now rotate the hock until the toes are facing straight forward, and place the foot back on the floor with the hock being perpendicular to the floor. Do not pull the rear legs too far out behind it. Then place the dog's right rear leg the same way, being sure to have the two rear legs the proper distance apart, about the width of the dog's body.

Be sure that you do not overstretch the dog. It is important that the legs are not too far out in front or behind the dog. It must be stacked in a comfortable position or it is going to shift.

Believe me, while you are working on placing one leg, your dog will be busy moving those you have already placed. Do not lose your patience—remember that this is to be fun for both you and the dog. Practice makes perfect.

Training your dog to stand properly in the show ring is extremely important. David Helming is shown here making the most of "Wimpy," Ch. Mooncusser's Reef of Pouch Cove, ROM.

It is imperative that your dog gait smoothly on a lead. Winnie Wesseltoft is shown here moving Ch. Amity's Bearfoot of Pouch Cove, ROM.
Søren Wesseltoft

After you have the dog stacked, have someone approach it and run hands over its head, down its back and down the legs.

If you are showing a male, they should lightly feel the testicles. Judges must check all male dogs for two normal testicles.

It is important that you teach your dog to allow its front teeth, or bite, to be shown to the judge. Keeping the jaw closed, reach over the dog's muzzle, and with your thumb on one side and your index finger on the other, slide the upper lip up and back slightly until you can see the way the upper and lower teeth fit together.

Some judges will check the bite themselves and others will ask you to show them your dog's bite.

The first time a judge ever told me to "show me your dog's bite," I didn't know what he meant. I was shocked that he would think my dog would bite, and I proudly told him, "My dog won't bite."

GAITING

Controlling a Newfoundland that is excited by all the other dogs and everything that is going on around it is not always easy.

Hold the lead in your left hand, and extend your arm out straight to the side. With the collar right up behind the ears and a fairly tight lead, hold the dog's head up and walk in a straight line.

After you and the dog can walk in a straight line, try moving it at a trot.

Do this over and over until you and the dog move well together, without its trying to cross in front of you or trying to pull you. Be sure your dog keeps gaiting and does not break into a run.

Then practice going counterclockwise in a big circle. Make sure you have control. You will need to be able to slow it down so it doesn't run up against the rear of the dog in front.

When all the dogs move together in a big circle, some of them think it is a race and get out of control. Your dog may want to turn around and play with the dog behind. You don't want to allow either.

Now you need to practice gaiting your dog in a "down and back" and a "triangle" pattern.

If your dog is already moving well on a lead, it will not be difficult for it. But you will need to learn the proper way to turn so that your gaiting flows smoothly without your having to stop and get yourself into proper position again.

When the judge asks you to do a triangle, take the dog straight away from the judge, down the side of the ring, turning at the corner without breaking stride, and continue straight to the next corner. Slow the dog down a little as you approach the corner. You will need to make a tight turn because you will need to move diagonally back to the judge. The best way to do this is to run the dog right into the corner and then quickly turn to your right, making the dog come around you so that you can continue back to the judge on the diagonal. As soon

Ch. Flying Cloud's Yankee Spirit, a lovely bitch shown winning an all-breed Best in Show (Ch. Flying Cloud's Far Hill, ROM, ex Ch. Nashau-Auke's Maid of the Mist). Bred by Jane Thibault and owned by Vic and Vickie Nebeker. Spirit also won four regional Specialty Bests of Breed, has numerous Group placements, including a second at Westminster, and selects at National Specialties.

Ch. Ferryland's Abby of Newton-Ark, ROM (Ch. Kuhaia's Rego, ROM, ex Ch. Ferryland's Black Beauty), bred by Richard Swan and owned by Robin Seaman and Janet Levine. Multiple Group placer and Best of Opposite Sex at the National Specialty.

as you make this turn, look to see where the judge is standing so that you are heading in a straight line. Remember the judge is trying to see how well your dog moves, and if you are pulling the dog from right to left and all over the place, movement cannot be seen.

For a ''straight down and back,'' move the dog straight away from the judge. This can either be down the side of the ring or down to the diagonal corner. Stop when you reach the end of the ring and turn to your right, bringing the dog around you, then look at the judge and gait back to him.

It is important that you stop your dog in the desired spot when returning to the judge. Judges don't usually appreciate getting run down by a Newf or having to step back so they can see how squarely the dog's feet come to rest when it stops. So when returning to the judge, slow down and glide your Newfoundland into a nice stop. If you stop the dog too abruptly, it will not stop with its feet in the right place. The dog should stop so that its feet are placed in the same position as when you stack it.

RING PROCEDURE

Allow yourself plenty of time to get to the ring early so you can pick up your numbered armband from the ring steward and watch a few of the classes before yours so you know the judge's ring procedure.

Most judges usually follow the same basic ring procedure. All the dogs competing in the class enter the ring together. The steward will tell the handler of the first dog into the ring where to stand, and all the other dogs are lined up behind the leader—in show position. Before judging begins, the judge and the steward will walk down the line, each checking armband numbers.

At the start of judging the judge will usually look at all the dogs and then ask the class to go once or twice around the ring as a group, stopping back where they started.

The judge will usually examine the first dog and have it move individually, repeating the process for each dog.

When you return to the judge after you move your dog individually, he or she will probably send you to the end of the line. Do not cut across the ring to get to the end of the line; you are now going to get another chance to move your dog for the judge. Using the whole ring, gait your dog smartly around to the end of the line.

Some judges may examine each dog while they are standing in line and then have them move individually.

After all the dogs have been examined and gaited, the judge will ask everyone to take the dogs around the ring in a group. Sometimes this happens when the judge makes placements, pointing to the dogs in the order that he or she is placing them. This is called ''picking them on the fly.''

The judge may, on the other hand, select the dogs he or she likes best and place them accordingly at the front of the class and then ask them all to be taken around the ring together again before pointing to the ones selected.

Best in Show and Best in Specialty show winner Ch. Skipjack's JB of Gladshire (Ch. Skipjack's Double Dare, ROM, ex Ch. Gladshire's Black Watch), with breeder/owner/handler Christine Griffith.

Be sure to keep an eye on the judge in case you are asked to bring your dog to the front of the line or if certain dogs are being picked out of a large class.

Remember the judges are given a set amount of time to judge all the dogs entered under them, and they cannot wait around for you to get your dog set up.

Be sure always to conduct yourself in a sportsmanlike manner. Finally, even if you are not happy with the judge's decision, be sure to say thank you if you get a ribbon and leave the ring with dignity. Not everyone can be a winner, but everyone can act like one.

CLASS PROCEDURE

All breed shows offer classes for dogs (males) and classes for bitches. The classes are:

6 to 9 months puppy dog
9 to 12 months puppy dog
Dogs 12 to 18 months
Novice Dog
Bred by Exhibitor Dog
American-Bred Dog
Open Dog
Winners—for the first place in each class

The first-place winner in each class comes back into the ring to compete for Winners Dog (WD). The dog that is designated Winners Dog wins the points toward its championship. If the Winners Dog was the dog that won the open class, then the second-place dog from that class will be called back into the ring to compete for Reserve Winners Dog (RWD). If for any reason the Winners Dog is disqualified, the dog that was selected as Reserve Winners Dog would be awarded the points.

The classes for the bitches is exactly the same. After the Reserve Winners Bitch award is given, the champions or specials come into the ring to compete for Best of Breed.

The Winners Dog and Winners Bitch also compete for Best of Breed and the Best of Opposite Sex. The winners stand in line behind the champions, Winners Dog always standing in front of the Winners Bitch.

The judge will select a dog/bitch as Best of Breed (BOB). Then the judge will pick the best of the opposite sex as best of Breed. That dog/bitch is awarded Best of Opposite Sex (BOS).

The judge will then decide between the Winners Dog and Winners Bitch which one of the two is better. That dog/bitch will be awarded Best of Winners (BW). Best of Winners can be very important in determining the number of points won. Best of Winners is entitled to the same number of points won by the other winner, whichever is greater. An example would be that if the Winners Dog had won four points and the Winners Bitch had only won two points and

The beautiful brown Ch. Manitouloa's My Bear Kodiak, Best of Breed at the 1992 National Specialty, multiple all-breed Best in Show winner and multiple regional Specialty winner. Bred, owned and handled by Kathy Shelden and co-owned with William and Patricia Connolly.

Ch. Topmast's Star Bright, ROM (Am., Can. Ch. Topmast's Pied Piper, ROM, ex Topmast's Star Dust), was Winners Bitch at a regional Specialty. She was bred by Margaret Willmott and co-owned by Joan Bendure and Jane Thibault, and is shown with handler Tom Glassford.

the Winners Bitch was designated Best of Winners, she would get four points instead of two points.

The Best of Breed goes on to compete in the Group. There are seven groups, and the Newfoundland is in the Working Group. There are four placements give in each group. The dog winning first in each group goes on to compete for Best in Show. Championship points are awarded to Winners Dog and Winners Bitch. Points awarded are based on the number of dogs or bitches competing that day. The country is divided into different regions, and the points for each breed can vary from one region of the country to another. If you win Best of Breed or Best of Opposite Sex over champions, you can also count them into the number of dogs needed for points.

To become a champion a dog must win 15 points, under three different judges, and two of these wins must be majors. Majors are wins worth three, four or five points. The maximum number of points you can win at one show is five points.

It is also possible for a class dog to pick up points by winning Group One.

Before you start exhibiting at dog shows, it is advisable to get a copy of "Rules Applying to Registration and Dog Shows," available from the American Kennel Club.

BAIT

Bait is a treat used to get the dog's attention and show expression. You will need a dog that is well trained and does not start jumping all over when it sees the bait.

This is something that you work on at home. Every time you give your dog a treat, tell it to stand. If it sits it doesn't get the treat—it's that simple.

Stand in front of the dog and hold the treat up to your mouth, pretending that you are going to eat it. He will naturally bring his ears forward at attention, begging for a piece. Talk softly to him and slowly move your hand toward him as if you are going to give it to him, then pull your hand back. Keep his concentration on the bait. Give him a piece. Then get another and do the same thing again. Do this over and over until your dog will stand with ears forward.

Liver is the bait most commonly used. Dogs love it, it has a strong-enough smell to get their attention and you can put it in your pocket without making a mess.

Liver Treats

1 pound sliced liver (beef or pork)
2 dashes garlic powder or salt

Place liver in a medium-size saucepan, add garlic, cover with water and bring to a boil. Simmer until liver is done. Drain off the water (this can be saved and used to moisten your dog's dry food). Rinse the liver under cold water and pat dry with paper towels. Place on an oven rack under a low broiler just until dry on that side. Turn it over and dry the other side. Do not let the liver get hard. Cut into small pieces. Can also be frozen.

Some things you will want to take to the show are: crate, grooming equipment, water and bowl, chair, entry and time schedule, towels.

Be sure to dress properly to show your dog. Men wear casual slacks with a blazer and a tie. Women wear a casual dress or a skirt with pockets (for comb and bait) and blouse. Make sure you have sensible shoes for running. Women should not have excess jewelry that is noisy.

You will also want to have a small drool towel. The small terry hand towels work best. Your drool towel can be tucked over your waistband or put in your pocket.

Plan to go to the show and spend the day. You will meet lots of nice people that share the same interest as you do. Too many exhibitors leave right after their breed is done being judged. Plan to stay and watch the groups and Best in Show judging. You can learn a lot from watching the pros.

Newfoundland pups quickly grow into large adults. "Yankee" and five-week-old pup.

Søren Wesseltoft

10

Choosing and Raising
a Newfoundland

<hr>

THE PURCHASE of any breed of dog is a serious decision to make. But with a breed the size of the Newfoundland, there are even more factors to consider.

Newfoundlands, like any other breed, should only be purchased from a reputable breeder. The well-motivated breeder, operating with a fine bloodline, would never sell a puppy until and unless he or she approved of the home and met the family trying to acquire a puppy. Generally, the reputable breeder only has the one breed—sometimes a second. This breeder's sole objective is breed improvement with no thought to financial gain. He or she will flatly refuse to sell a puppy to any home deemed unsuitable for any reason. If you really have your heart set on a Newfoundland, understand what is involved and have the right environment for providing a happy home, the breeder you want to buy from will recognize this and help you.

Most importantly, a responsible breeder will not consider his or her involvement ended once your check is in the bank. The breeder you should seek out will always be there to help, advise and give you the benefit of their knowledge and experience.

IS A NEWFOUNDLAND THE BREED FOR YOU?

Do you realize how large an adult Newfoundland is? Do you have the space and time a Newfoundland requires? Are you willing to spend time grooming? Do you own other pets that would not accept a new addition to the household? Does a Newfoundland fit your life-style? Do you have a fenced-in area to confine a dog the size of a Newfoundland? Is the whole family agreeable to a Newfoundland? Who will be responsible for the daily care? Does anyone in the family have allergies to dogs? Who is going to be responsible for training? Can you afford the puppy and the equipment and vaccinations that are necessary to properly take care of a dog? Do you want a Newfoundland for conformation showing, Obedience competition or water work, or just to have a wonderful pet? All these questions need to be answered before you even begin to look for a puppy.

CHOOSING THE DOG

How to Select a Breeder

To obtain a list of Newfoundland breeders, contact the American Kennel Club for the name and address of the Newfoundland Club of America's general education chairperson or the corresponding secretary. The American Kennel Club registration and breeders' referral services are located at 5580 Centerview Drive, Raleigh, NC 27606-3390.

It is important to keep in mind that just because a member is listed on the Newfoundland Club of America's Breeder List, it is not an endorsement by the Club of that breeder. The Newfoundland Club of America is only supplying you with a list of members that breed their dogs and pay to have their names on the list. If there are unresolved grievances against a breeder, he or she will not be allowed to be listed. There are also NCA members who are breeders who choose not to be included on the breeders' list and can usually be found by contacting the regional Club in your area. Be a wise shopper and educate yourself before you start your search for a puppy.

You can also locate breeders by attending a regional Specialty or an all-breed dog show. In the latter case, be sure to find out in advance what time Newfies are going to be shown, but remember that it is best to wait until after the judging is completed before you approach an exhibitor for information. Before judging, they will be busy getting their dogs ready for the ring and may even be nervous. Afterward they will be glad to talk to you about their dogs.

Keep in mind that just because a certain dog won on a certain day, that it is not necessarily the best dog. Dog show judges are only judging what they see before them and what, in their opinion, best meets the Standard. Approach the exhibitors whose dogs you like best. In the Newfoundland breed it is important to keep in mind that biggest does not always mean the best.

Call your local kennel club, boarding kennels and veterinarians for names of breeders. It can be convenient to have your breeder close by for future help. Even if your vet doesn't have a breeder client, which most won't, he or she may have a client that is a Newf owner that you can contact.

You will generally not find experienced breeders advertising in the local newspapers, as they usually have a list of people waiting for their puppies. Their puppy sales are usually referrals from previous buyers, other breeders and veterinarians. Don't expect to be able to go out on the weekend and come home with a new doggy friend. Buying a puppy is not like doing the weekly grocery shopping. It is a lifetime commitment to the pup you bring home, a dog that you will be spending every day with for hopefully the next ten to twelve years. Take your time and carefully research and talk with all the Newfoundland breeders that you can. Phone as many breeders as possible. Make sure you have told them exactly what you want in a dog—male or female, pet, show or breeding.

Good breeders will be interested in discussing Newfoundlands with you, not just in selling you a dog. They will tell you all about the breed. They will point out the reasons you may want to own a Newf and the reasons the Newfoundland may not be the breed for you. If they don't mention any drawbacks of owning a Newfoundland, such as size, shedding and drooling or health problems, then you had better find another breeder who will.

Don't let any breeder sell you a "dry-mouthed Newfoundland." All dogs of the giant breeds, and Newfoundlands that are bred to look like a Newfoundland, have a tendency to have a wet mouth or drool occasionally. Males, due to their larger size and more massive heads, are more inclined to drool than females. The mouth of any Newfoundland will be dry most of the time. Newfoundlands slight in stature and lacking in proper head type are less prone to drool.

Breeders should tell you the precautions they have taken to produce healthy puppies. The breeder you purchase a puppy from should be available to guide you throughout the life of the dog. You should feel comfortable talking with the breeder.

Avoid any breeder who tells you he or she has never produced a puppy with a bad heart or with hip dysplasia. Either the breeder isn't looking for these problems or hasn't done much breeding, or is being dishonest. Problems can and will show up in any bloodline.

Once you have talked to several different breeders, make appointments to visit the kennels you are considering purchasing a puppy from. That is the best way for you to meet breeders and see their dogs and facilities. Besides, after they meet you they might decide that they don't think you would make a good Newfoundland owner.

Expect to be cross-examined as to what kind of home you have to offer a Newfoundland. The breeder who doesn't question your reason for wanting a Newfoundland, what you expect from your dog and where the puppy will live, is obviously not interested in the pups' future. That is a breeder who will not be available should a health or training problem arise. The ideal way to purchase a puppy is to be able to personally visit the kennel.

It is also possible to buy a good puppy from a breeder who lives across the country by having the puppy shipped to you. This will add to your cost, as you will have to purchase an airline crate and pay the shipping charges. If you must have a puppy shipped to you, don't select a particular breeder just because he or she advertises experienced shipping. All the experience in the world doesn't necessarily mean a thing once the pup is in the hands of the airlines. Besides, most breeders have experience shipping dogs. But don't be surprised if some breeders refuse to ship their pups.

Questions to Ask the Breeder

When will puppies be available? Are the puppies American Kennel Club registered? Will the registration papers be full registration or limited registration? Can you pick the puppy or will the breeder pick the puppy for you? What is the difference between show, breeding and pet-quality puppies? How does the breeder determine that difference? Does the breeder give a health contract? Does he give a veterinarian-signed health certificate or vaccination record with each puppy? Does he give a written feeding schedule? Does he send home a supply of the food and water the puppy is currently eating and drinking? Does he require a deposit? If a deposit is required, will a prompt refund be made if a pup isn't available? Ask for a copy of any contracts or agreements before making any decisions to purchase a puppy. Inexperienced puppy purchasers should not get involved with breeding, showing or co-ownership agreements. All agreements should be in writing, with both parties having signed copies. If you don't understand something, don't hesitate to ask.

Visiting Breeders

Make an appointment to visit a breeder you are interested in purchasing a dog from. Don't show up on a breeder's doorstep without an appointment and expect a royal welcome. Dog breeders are usually very busy people.

Plan on spending at least a couple of hours. Bring the whole family so the breeder can meet you as a family. It will help the breeder decide if he has a puppy for you.

Expect to see the area where the dogs live. While it need not be a palace, it is imperative that it be clean. The runs should be spacious and clean. Don't be alarmed if there is an occasional fresh stool in a dog's run.

The dogs should be clean and well groomed. They should be happy and eager to see you. Breeders who are proud of their facilities and dogs will be happy to show you all their dogs. Pay special attention to the puppies' parents. The sire may not be at the kennel unless the breeder also owns him. Ask at least to see a picture of him.

Most exhibitors and breeders start in dogs by buying a puppy for a family pet. After owning and learning more about their breed and the sport of dogs, they become involved in exhibiting and breeding. This may be you in a few years.

Deciding What You Want

The two biggest decision most buyers need to make is whether they want a male or a female and what color they should get.

Blacks are by far the most popular, while Landseers are, for the most part, more physically active than blacks.

Some grays will develop a problem with balding on the ears and sometimes on the feet. Grays with this balding factor tend to have thinner coats and are usually prone to skin problems. This is certainly not true of all grays; many grays have beautiful coats. But this balding does not generally show up until after the pup is about four months old. I have never seen or heard of this in any of the other colors.

Males are larger and perhaps a bit bolder than females. Both sexes make devoted pets.

Females come into season twice a year. Some males are always in "season," that is, always looking for that elusive mate and can be more difficult to control around other dogs. Females tend to be a bit calmer and more homebodies than males. Females are also slightly smaller than males.

All dogs not being used for breeding should be neutered at the proper age. Neutering prevents testicular cancer, and will greatly reduce the chance of prostate cancer and perianal tumors in males. Spayed females will not be as prone to mammary cancer or pyometra. Veterinarians are now promoting that dogs be neutered by six months of age. This may be fine for a small breed that is physically mature before age one, but Newfoundlands should not be neutered as young as the smaller breeds. Newfoundlands need more time to grow and mature physically so they will grow to the full physical stature that is the heritage of the breed.

The age of sexual and physical maturity will vary from dog to dog. Most male Newfoundlands reach sexual maturity somewhere between ten and sixteen months of age, and females are sexually mature after their first season. Neutering does not make a dog fat. Food and lack of exercise make a dog overweight.

If you select a male puppy, be sure that he has two testicles. Dogs with a retained testicle cannot be shown and should never be used for breeding. They will have to be neutered to prevent testicular cancer.

Selecting a Puppy

Don't purchase a puppy on the spur of the moment or because you feel sorry for it. Don't purchase a puppy from pet-quality stock.

Poor-quality breeders will only produce more poor-quality pups. If bad "breeders"—I hesitate to call them breeders because they are really only puppy producers—had a difficult time selling pups, they would soon quit producing them.

An excessively high price is not indicative of quality. But a low-priced pup is usually not a bargain either. A poor-quality, bargain puppy may end up costing you more in the long run, if it has health problems. Puppies from experienced, ethical breeders are usually medium priced and will generally fall in the same price range as that of other breeders of the same kind.

Black is the most popular Newfoundland color. The other colors—Landseer, brown and gray—are not rare, and such puppies should not cost any more.

169

Take a copy of the Standard along with you to check for conformation and markings. A Newfoundland puppy should look just like an adult except for size. Personality should be the most important characteristic of a pet puppy.

Knowledgeable breeders will go over each puppy with you, pointing out the puppies' attributes and faults. They will be able to describe each pup's personality to you.

Sit down on the floor or ground to play with the puppies. The puppies should come over and crawl into your lap. Avoid any puppy that is shy or does not respond to people, and also, unless you are experienced in raising and training dogs, avoid any puppy that appears overly aggressive with its littermates. This could be the sign of a dominant personality. Cradle the puppy on its back in your arms—it should have eye contact and be relaxed and content to be held.

Ask the breeder for permission before picking up a puppy. Never pick up a puppy by the front legs or the scruff of the neck. Use both hands, placing one hand on the puppy's chest and the other behind its back legs to support the weight.

It is normal for a puppy's coat to have a dusty appearance near the skin. The coat should be thick and soft.

Legs should be straight and well boned, never crooked or refined.

Newfoundlands should have dark eyes. Adult eye color can be very difficult to determine in a young puppy. If the eyes look light at eight to ten weeks, chances are they will be even lighter in the adult. Look at the parents' eye color. If their eyes are light, the puppy's eyes probably will be too. Be sure to check the eyelids for entropion (rolling in) or ectropion (turning out). In most cases these will need surgery to be corrected, although entropion and ectropion do not seem to be as common problems as they once were.

Pick a puppy that is in balance or proportion. A pup with good structure and balance will gait (trot) freely and easily with its head up. Don't pick a puppy just because you like its head or because it does or doesn't have certain markings. You need to look at the puppy as a whole and not for just one trait.

Tail carriage can be difficult to judge in young puppies. Young puppies have a tendency to carry their tails up, instead of properly straight out behind them when moving. It is important to feel for correct tail-set. Avoid, for show, any puppy that carries the tail rolled over the back.

Check the bite for a scissors (upper incisors closing tightly over lowers) or level bite (upper and lower incisors will meet edge to edge). An undershot mouth (the upper incisors behind the lower incisors) is not likely to correct itself with age. The lower jaw sometimes has a tendency to grow slightly more than the upper. An overshot jaw, the reverse of an undershot, may have more of a chance of correcting itself as the pup grows, but don't bet on it if the puppy is meant for show or breeding. If the front teeth are off more than the thickness of a nickel, there is little chance of a perfect bite as an adult.

The puppy's head and muzzle should be broad. Snipey or pointed muzzles do not improve with age.

Ticking, small black spots in the white coat of a Landseer, is usually not apparent in a young puppy, unless it is going to be heavily ticked as an adult.

It's hard to resist a Newfy pup. "Jake and Thunder" pups at eight weeks of age.   *Søren Wesseltoft*

A typically angelic Newfoundland pup will become a holy terror if not properly trained. Sooner or Later of Pouch Cove pictured at ten weeks of age.   *Søren Wesseltoft*

Amity's Admiral Ramsey at three months of age.

171

Remember, ticking increases with age. Ticking is usually found on the legs. In heavily ticked dogs it will also be in the white coat on the body.

When you leave the breeder with your new puppy you should have the following:

1. American Kennel Club registration papers properly filled out
2. Complete feeding schedule and instructions giving amounts and brand to feed
3. Veterinarian-signed health and vaccination certificate. Schedule of vaccinations the pup should still receive, and when and with what the pup was last wormed
4. Signed copy of any contract entered into between the breeder (seller) and purchaser
5. Three-or four-generation pedigree
6. Enough food for the first few days

HOUSING

You will need to decide where your dog is going to live before you bring your puppy home. If it is going to be an indoor dog, decide what rooms in the house the dog will be allowed in, where it will sleep, where it will be confined when no one is home. If the dog is going to be outside a good part of the day or at night, you will need to provide proper living quarters.

A fenced area to confine a dog is essential.

Ideally, your yard should be fenced so your dog can be safely confined and still have room to run and get exercise. I would hope that anyone intelligent enough to read a book would never consider chaining a dog.

Dogs cannot be allowed to wander loose. Remember, it is always the biggest dog in the neighborhood that gets blamed for everything. Plus it is against the law to allow a dog to run free. It is liable to get hit by a car, stolen or even poisoned by a disgruntled neighbor. Many people are afraid of dogs—especially very large ones. If your yard is not fenced, you can construct a kennel run for your dog. With today's busy life-styles it is important to have a fenced area for the dog when you are not at home—a place where it can get sunshine and fresh air and will be able to relieve itself as necessary. Six-foot-high chain link is the best fencing for confining a Newfoundland. Most Newfs would never try to get over a six-foot fence. Fences less than six feet high are not adequate for keeping out unwanted male suitors if your female comes into season. It may be also difficult to confine a male Newfoundland behind a fence lower than six feet if he detects a bitch in season in the neighborhood.

The run should be a minimum of eight feet wide by twenty feet long. Chain-link fencing can be purchased in freestanding panels that bolt together. The freestanding panels are great if you have to move, because they are easy to take apart and move with you. If you decide to move the pen to a different location in the yard, its portability is a real plus.

The "Helming Hound Hut"

Notes: 1. Siding is textier 1-11 material over insulated frame
2. Either 2"x 4" or 2"x 3" framing
3. Inside of house 3/8" or 1/2" plywood/plyscore over insulation
4. Roof & house floor - 1/2" plyscore
5. Floor should be sealed with wood preservative
6. Roof is standard shingles on tar paper
7. Window(optional) is Plexiglas
8. Doorway opening inside dimensions - 17"x 27"
9. Deck should be treated lumber

3'-10"

2"x 6"

2"x 4" (Flat for clearance)
(Typical 16" O.C.)

5'-2"

Stone

4"x 4" (Typical)
(Treated)

Note: Base stringers should be
treated lumber - adequate size
(4'x 6") to support house and deck.

17"x 27"

Variable
(2"x 4" Deck - Spaced 1/4")

4'-0"
(Outside)

Use plastic membrane under floor

12" Extension
over house
w/rounded corner

3'-6"
(Floor to Roof)

Doghouse with deck affords shade and protection. The "Helming Hound Hut" designed by David Helming.   *D. Vitale*

173

If you decide to go with the freestanding panels, you can just place railroad ties on the ground and set the panels on top of them. This will keep the fence off the ground, and the railroad ties will hold in the gravel you will need for a base. Freestanding chain-link kennels are also very salable if the day comes when you no longer have a dog.

Some people find it more aesthetically pleasing to construct a rail or board fence and then attach wire fencing on the inside. It is also important to check the zoning for fencing requirements, particularly if you live in a residential area.

In your dog run or pen you will need a surface that provides good drainage and one that makes cleaning up after the dog easy. Gravel is the ideal surface. Gravel provides the best drainage for urine and rain, and it makes picking up after your dog easy. It is important that you pick up after your dog once or twice a day. I use and recommend crushed limestone, as the alkalinity keeps down any urine odor. You will have to replace some of the gravel every year as you will lose some when picking up after the dog and some will work down into the ground below. Runs should be hosed down frequently, particularly in warm weather.

The run must be disinfected regularly. A mixture of three parts water and one part household bleach should be used. Mix in a garden sprinkling can and saturate the gravel. Let this sit on the run for an hour before hosing thoroughly. Be sure to keep the dog out of the area until it is rinsed. Another good sterilant is Borax washing compound, available at your grocery store. Sprinkle the run with water and then sprinkle the powder all over the run. Lightly sprinkle again to dissolve the powder. Let it stand for an hour and then do a thorough hosing to flush any remaining Borax into the soil below. Be sure to keep your dog off the area until it has been thoroughly hosed. There are also many commercial products on the market for just this purpose. You can usually find them at a local feed or pet supply store or order from a mail-order catalog.

Grass quickly turns to dirt and mud, making it most unsuitable for keeping a dog on for any length of time. Even in a large yard you will quickly be able to see where the dog spends most of its time lying or walking. The grass will become trampled and die out, leaving a dirt path or larger barren area.

Newfoundlands should never be kept on cement or dirt. Cement is hard and unforgiving. Dogs kept on cement, particularly large dogs, are prone to skeletal injuries. A puppy's feet will splay, and it will likely go down in the pasterns from standing on cement. Adult dogs will be prone to calluses on the elbows, which are not only unsightly but can eventually lead to water on the elbow or abscesses. Urine will trickle across a cement run and stay on the surface. The dog will walk through it and then carry a very unpleasant odor of urine. Urine will bleach a black dog's hair to brown and stain a white dog's hair yellow. When bitches squat to urinate, the hair on their hindquarters and tails are likely to come into contact with the urine, making for avoidable odor problems. Smooth cement does not provide a good surface for footing and can become very slippery when wet or icy.

Hopefully your Newfoundland will spend most of its time in the house with family members when they are home. Why have a dog that always lives out in the backyard? The more time the dog spends with the family, the more sociable and better trained it will become. Don't misunderstand, all dogs should have a safe outside area where they can be confined when you are not at home. But your dog also needs to be a part of the family.

If your dog is going to spend long hours outside in its run alone, another canine companion is a good idea, but this is no substitute for human companionship. After all, dogs are pack animals; they want to feel that they belong. Take a lesson and don't shut the dog away from family life.

Crate Training

Dogs were originally den-dwelling animals that lived in packs. They used dens for protection, and as safe places to raise their young. They never soiled in or near their den. If a dog is properly crate-trained, it will think of the crate as its den. A dog will not soil its crate if it can help it. This proves that most dogs still maintain the "den instinct."

A crate is a safe place to confine a puppy or dog when no one is available to supervise. Never confine a dog to its crate for punishment.

Confining a Newfoundland to a crate is not cruel—think of it as a dog bed with a door. Most dogs spend between fourteen and sixteen hours a day sleeping. Don't, however, misuse the crate by expecting a puppy to spend long hours without being allowed out to relieve itself.

There are basically only two different types of crates. Heavy-gauge wire crates and solid-sided fiberglass airline crates that are also used to ship dogs. Wire crates are available that fold like a suitcase, which makes them easy to transport and store. Wire crates are preferred for Newfoundlands because they allow for adequate ventilation and are available in many sizes.

Purchase a crate the size you will need when your puppy is full-grown. The crate should be twenty-four inches wide, forty-eight inches long and thirty-six inches high.

The puppy should sleep in the crate at night and for naps.

Crates are a great help in housebreaking a puppy. Start crate-training your puppy as soon as you bring it home. Place a towel or old blanket in the crate.

The idea behind using a crate for housebreaking is to confine the pup to an area just large enough for him to lie down in comfortably. If you give a puppy a large area, it will use one end as a bathroom and the other to sleep in. This ruins the whole theory of confining it to a small area. If you have purchased a crate that will be big enough to use as an adult, you can block it off to the proper size with a piece of plywood or an empty cardboard box of proper size.

Decide where you will place the crate. It is nice to have the crate in a quiet corner of the room you will be spending the most time in. Dogs do not like to be isolated. Remember to always take your puppy outside to relieve itself before placing it in its crate.

At first your puppy will probably object to being confined in a crate, and start whining and crying to be let out. This is normal. The important thing to remember is not to give in and let the pup out just because it objects. If you do submit and let it out of the crate, you will be rewarding it for causing a ruckus. Also, the puppy will learn to yelp and cry to get what it wants. And it will only do it again the next time you put it in the crate, so you must persevere. It is better to have the puppy yelling in its crate than loose in a room soiling the floor and chewing on anything it pleases, such as electrical cords or the kitchen cabinets. In all probability it is going to vocally show its displeasure at being confined and alone. Some people will move the crate into the bedroom at night so they can hear when the pup needs to be let out to relieve itself.

HOUSEBREAKING

As mentioned earlier, dogs are den animals. And den animals have a strong desire to keep their area clean. Even as young as at three weeks of age, puppies will sleep and eat at one end of the whelping box and toddle to the other end to relieve themselves.

Newfoundlands are easy to housebreak, if a few simple rules are observed. Do not give a puppy the freedom to wander throughout the house. Confine it to one or two rooms to start. Use baby gates if necessary. Make sure you and the puppy are in the same room at all times. If you or some other responsible adult can't be watching it, it should be in its crate. Housebreaking cannot be left up to young children, but they can help by taking the puppy outside. Consistency is the key to all successful training programs.

A young puppy cannot be expected to go too many hours before it will need to relieve itself. Start out by taking the puppy outside every hour until you know its needs. Watch for the puppy walking around sniffing the floor or starting to circle. This is a sign that it is looking for a spot to relieve itself. Quickly pick up the puppy and take it out to its designated area.

Remember the important times that a pup needs to be taken outside: within ten to fifteen minutes of eating or drinking, immediately upon waking, after playing hard, and the last thing you do before retiring for the night. You may want to withhold water from the puppy after seven or eight P.M., to help him get through the night.

Always go outside with the puppy to be sure that it has done its business. If you put the puppy out by itself, you will not know whether it did what it was supposed to or not. If not, it is sure to have an accident when it comes back in. Do not play with or distract the puppy when it is outside for this purpose. When the puppy has finished, reward it, *outside*, with petting and praise or a small doggy treat. If you reward your dog when it comes in the house, it will think it is being rewarded for coming in, not for relieving itself in the proper place. Plan on getting up a couple of times in the middle of the night for the first week or two to take the puppy outside. After that, both you and the pup should have a schedule. Very few young puppies can make it through the night. The age at

A bitch pup, Ch. Mooncusser Strike the Main at six months of age, bred and owned by Sue Jones.

ale pup, Ch. Benhil's Stillwater Gulliver at seven ɔnths of age, bred and owned by Joan Bendure and lan Lint.

Immature Landseer male at seventeen months, Benhil's Sir Lancelot, owned by Christopher Altier. *Hoag*

177

which a puppy can do so will vary. As a puppy grows it will need to go out less frequently. Puppies will probably have a few accidents before you both get into the routine. If you catch the puppy in the act, yell "No" sharply and loudly. Immediately pick up the puppy and take it out.

It is important that you do a thorough job of cleaning up any puppy accident, as any odor left behind will attract the puppy back to the same spot.

For urinary accidents on carpet, use a good-quality paper towel to blot up as much urine as possible. After you have soaked up the urine, it will be necessary to clean the carpet. There are many products on the market just for this purpose. If you don't have a commercial product, you can mix up a solution of one-third white vinegar to two-thirds water in a spray bottle. Spray heavily, rub into the wet area and blot some more. Another home remedy is a good-quality club soda. It will not leave your carpet sticky. Before using any product on your carpet, be sure to test it.

FEEDING

The breeder you purchase your pup from should give you a written feeding schedule listing brands and exact amounts of dog food you should feed.

With today's technology in dog-food production, very little needs to be added for puppies of the giant breed. Many breeders use and recommend the addition of sodium ascorbate (vitamin C) and vitamin E to a dog's diet. If you are feeding a quality food, an all-around vitamin supplement is not necessary, as the calcium and vitamins A and D they add are more than adequate in commercial dog foods.

Do not take it upon yourself to alter the diet the breeder gave you with your puppy without first consulting with the breeder.

It is very important that you follow your breeder's feeding regimen, as he or she should know best how this particular line of dogs grows. If your breeder has given you a specific diet to follow, and an experienced breeder will, do not let anyone change it, including your veterinarian, unless your dog has a dietary problem. Unfortunately, most veterinarians do not raise any breed of dog, particularly a giant breed, and most are not knowledgeable in dog nutrition. Through trial and error, most Newfoundland breeders have found the best type of diet for growing pups is a good-quality food that does not contain excessive amounts of protein, fat and caloric content. Those high-protein, high-fat and high-calorie foods may be all right for the smaller breeds that expend a lot of energy.

The Newfoundland's metabolism, however, does an excellent job of converting food into growth and energy. Because of the way a Newfoundland's metabolism utilizes its food, breeders have generally found that it is best to put Newfoundland puppies onto adult dog food at around four or five months of age.

Enjoying great popularity today are the natural diets consisting of a lamb and rice base preserved with vitamin E. They appear to alleviate the some of the ever-increasing skin problems that seem to be becoming common in all breeds of dogs today.

Fresh water should always be available except when at night during the housebreaking phase.

Overfeeding your puppy and promoting rapid growth is not going to make your Newfoundland any larger than its genetic makeup will allow him to be. Forcing rapid and excessive growth on a young puppy only enhances your pup's chance of developing skeletal problems.

Following is a diet for those that may not have received one with their puppy. Feeding schedules may be adjusted to fit your schedule and to help in housebreaking.

FEEDING INSTRUCTIONS

Eight Weeks to 10 Weeks: 4 meals a day

Morning: ½ cup of dry puppy food mixed with a small amount of warm water. Add a vitamin supplement only if recommended by your puppy's breeder.

Noon: ½ cup of dry puppy food

Evening: ½ cup of dry puppy food mixed with a small amount of warm water.

Bedtime: ½ cup of dry puppy food

The amount of food from this meal may be added to those above to aid in housebreaking. But most puppies should be about ten weeks old before they leave the breeder for their new homes.

Increase or decrease all amounts gradually as necessary. Fresh water should be available at all times. DO NOT LET YOUR PUPPY GET FAT!

Ten Weeks to 3 Months: 3 meals a day

Morning: 1½ cups of puppy food mixed with water and vitamin recommended by breeder

Noon: 1½ cups of dry puppy food

Evening: 1½ cups of puppy food mixed with water

Increase or decrease all amounts gradually as necessary. Fresh water should be available at all times. DO NOT LET YOUR PUPPY GET FAT!

Three Months to 5 months: 2 meals a day

Morning: 2 to 3 cups of dry puppy food with water and vitamin recommended by breeder

Evening: 2 to 3 cups of dry puppy food

Increase or decrease all amounts gradually as necessary. Fresh water should be available at all times. DO NOT LET YOUR PUPPY GET FAT!

5 Months to 1 Year: 2 meals a day

Morning: 3 cups of adult dry food with a protein level around 24% and vitamin recommended by breeder

Evening: 3 to 4 cups of adult dry food mixed with water

Water to dry food ratio: ¼ cup water per 2 cups dry food. The above amounts of food are only a guideline. Some puppies utilize their food differently than others. The amount of exercise a puppy receives will make a difference in the amount of food needed for your particular puppy. Dogs that live in cold climates, and outdoor dogs, will need more food to keep warm than a house dog or one that lives in a warm climate. Adjust your puppy's food accordingly.

Check the ribs every day. You should be able to feel them easily. There should be a light covering over the ribs. Puppies need to grow muscle mass and bone structure, *not fat*! Keep your puppy lean and muscular to avoid any potential growth problems. As puppies' bones are soft while they are growing, it is harmful for them to carry excess weight. Fat dogs are not healthy dogs. Because you are feeding your puppy a well-balanced food, do not add any vitamins or mineral supplements, except the ones the breeder you purchased your pup from instructed you to use. *Your veterinarian should not change your puppy's diet in any way without the prior knowledge and approval of the breeder.*

Hard, large biscuits may be given as a treat. They are also excellent for keeping your dog's teeth clean of tartar. After five months of age your puppy can be placed on adult food. Your dog may only want one meal a day but it is better to keep it on two meals a day until its first birthday, if possible.

Never feed your pup immediately before or after exercise.

COLLAR AND LEASH TRAINING

Start your young puppy with a collar as soon as you bring it home. Your puppy's first collar should be a flat nylon buckle collar. They are available in adjustable lengths, with a quick-release buckle that makes it easy to put on and remove. The quick-release buckles are fine for young puppies. As your dog grows, you will need to use a regular flat nylon collar with a metal buckle because the quick-release buckles are not strong enough to hold the weight of a growing Newfoundland. Make sure you adjust the collar properly—two fingers should fit under the collar. If the collar is too loose, your puppy will pull out of it.

Do not use a choke collar for training until your puppy knows how to walk on a leash. Choke collars are for training only. A dog should never be left unattended with a choke collar on.

For a leash, purchase a six-foot soft nylon, cotton or leather lead. Never use a chain leash, as they are hard on your hands and noisy, and a good pull from your Newf will cause the leather loop to break.

After your puppy has become accustomed to wearing its collar, you can attach the leash. Follow your puppy around as it sniffs and explores, talking to it and occasionally offering a small treat. Stoop down, hold your arms out and call your puppy to you in a happy tone of voice, using its name and the command "come." Use the leash if necessary to coax the pup to you. When it comes to you, give it a treat and pet it and tell it how good it is.

Slowly start using the leash to guide the dog in the direction you want it to go, talking and offering little treats along the way. After about a week your puppy should be proudly walking along on its leash.

OBEDIENCE

It is important that all dogs learn the basic commands of Sit, Stay, Down, Off and Come. Because a Newfoundland puppy quickly becomes such a large dog, proper training at a young age is important. Today there are Puppy Kindergarten or Obedience classes that specialize in training and socializing young puppies. It not only gives you the incentive to work with your dog daily, but also gives your dog the opportunity to socialize and learn how to act around other dogs and people. Enroll in one as soon as your pup has had all its necessary vaccinations.

You can start teaching your puppy to sit as soon as you bring it home. Hold a treat, with your index finger extended, in front of the pup's nose. As soon as it smells it, slowly draw it back and up over its head, saying "Sit" over and over. The puppy will follow the smell and sit so that it can reach the treat. Repeat this exercise over and over until the pup starts to sit as soon as it hears the Sit command and sees your hand in front of its nose. Soon all your pup will need to see is your finger and hear the word "Sit."

Put your pup in the sitting position in front of you. Holding a treat in your hand, let the puppy smell it and then draw the treat down to the floor in front of the pup. Repeatedly saying "Down," hold the treat down on the floor with your thumb. As soon as the pup is lying down, let it have the treat. You will be amazed at how quickly your pup will learn the Sit and Down commands.

Start eliminating the treats by giving one only occasionally, but be sure to always verbally praise and reward with a pat.

Never allow your pup to jump up on you with its front paws, even when it is small. The puppy will soon be big enough to knock an unsuspecting person down. If you don't allow this in your young pup, it does not usually become a problem with your adult Newfoundland. If your pup gets overexcited and forgets its manners, yell "Off" and quickly bump it in the chest with your knee. Remember to use the command Off and not the command Down. Down is the command you give when you want your dog to lie down. The word "Off" is used when you want your dog to get off an object or person.

Come is probably one of the most difficult commands to teach a dog. With your dog on its leash, call it to you, happily saying its name and the word "Come" together. Give a little tug on the leash to guide the pup to you. When it gets to you, offer it a treat and make a big fuss over it by petting it and exclaiming how good it is. Never call a dog to you to punish it. It will soon learn not to come at all. And do not do this off leash until you are absolutely certain that the pup will obey. If your dog does get loose and won't return, do not chase him. Dogs enjoy being chased—to them it is a game. I have yet to see an owner who can outrun a dog. Instead, call the pup's name to get its attention and then try running in the direction you want it to come. Even if the puppy has taken off, when you do catch it do not punish it. Suffering verbal or physical abuse will only teach it that it does not want you to catch it.

Be sure to make training a good experience for your dog. Do not lose your patience. If you do, put the dog away and train when you are in a better frame of mind.

A young puppy's biting on your hands, sleeves or pant legs is normal but not acceptable behavior. When your puppy bites at you, startle the puppy by loudly yelling "No" into its face. Then hand it one of its toys that it can chew on. Never play tug-of-war with your puppy. It only teaches it to use its mouth to play with you and that biting is permissible. Provide your puppy with plenty of dog toys to chew on. There are many that are made for being chewed, such as hard rubber or nylon toys. Never give your pup an old shoe—it can't tell the difference between an old shoe and a new shoe.

SWIMMING WITH YOUR NEWF

Some Newfoundlands will enter the water for the first time and take right off swimming. Others may be hesitant and just need a proper introduction to the water. It is usually helpful if another dog that is an experienced swimmer accompanies yours in the water that first time.

Start the dog in a calm lake or pond where the entrance into the water is gradual. When introducing the dog to the water for the first time, it is best if you actually accompany the dog into the water. The first and most important rule when playing or doing water work with your dog is that you should always wear a life jacket. An inexperienced or tired dog may try to climb onto you to for security or to rest.

Hold on to the dog's collar as you enter the water. Just as the dog is about to get in water deep enough to have to swim, place your free arm under the dog's loin to help lift the rear. Most dogs entering the water for the first time will have a tendency to paddle excessively with the front legs and walk on the bottom with the rear legs. When the dog is relaxed and stroking confidently, you can remove your arm.

11

Grooming
the Newfoundland

THE NEWFOUNDLAND coat is not hard to care for with regular grooming sessions that any owner can handle. The frequency of grooming depends on how much coat your individual dog carries. Some bloodlines carry very profuse coats.

Dogs kept primarily outdoors in a kennel will develop a much heavier undercoat than a dog that lives indoors. Newfoundlands shed profusely in the spring and fall. Like all double-coated breeds, they will loose small amounts of hair daily. Breeds that shed are inclined to have a "doggy odor" if not kept clean.

Unspayed females will usually blow, or lose, some coat previous to coming into season. Spayed females and neutered males do not shed as much, but most will develop a coat that grows very long. Grooming sessions should begin when your dog is a young puppy and made into a pleasant experience for both dog and owner. Do not subject your dog to hours of grooming at one time. If a lot of time is needed, be sure to give your dog periodic breaks.

Regular grooming will not only keep your dog looking nice but will also help keep the skin and coat clean and healthy. It is important that the air get down to the skin. Poor grooming or no grooming will cause the coat to become dirty and matted, which can cause skin problems if not corrected.

When Newfoundlands are shedding or blowing coat, they are more inclined to chew on themselves, causing a sore or "hot spot."

How frequently your Newfoundland will need to be groomed or bathed will depend on the amount of its coat and your dog's life-style. If your dog is a house dog that only roams around a manicured yard, it will stay relatively clean. If your dog has acreage to run on and a pond to swim in at will (Newfie heaven), you will have to groom it more often.

You can generally keep a Newfoundland's coat in good condition with a weekly brushing with a slicker brush. Regular grooming will prevent mats from forming. Weekly brushing will also remove any dead coat that would otherwise be shed onto your floor, carpeting, furniture and clothes.

If money is not an object, you can use a professional pet-grooming salon. Many professional groomers are not willing or do not have the facilities to work on a dog the size of a Newfoundland. I would advise that, after you find a professional willing to work on your Newf, you take the dog in for an estimate prior to making an appointment. Without having an idea of the cost, you may be astounded by the bill when you pick up your dog. If your dog's coat is matted, or if the dog is blowing a lot of coat, some professionals may take it upon themselves to decide that it would be easier on a dog and more economical for the owner to shave the dog down. Newfoundlands should never be shaved. You are not doing your Newf a favor by shaving it in warm weather. Shorthaired dogs have a much more dense coat that protects them from sunburn, heat and insects. The only time shaving would ever be in order would be if the dog was so matted it would be cruel to attempt to comb the coat out. A shaved dog should be kept indoors until enough coat grows back to afford protection.

EQUIPMENT

The proper equipment to groom your Newf will certainly make the job easier. Mail-order pet-supply catalogs have the largest selection and the best prices for grooming aids.

A grooming table that the dog will stand or lie on is helpful but not necessary. It is much easier for the person doing the grooming to be able to stand while working on the dog.

You can either purchase a grooming table or build a sturdy one of wood. The table top should be twenty-four inches wide, and the length should be a minimum of thirty-six inches up to forty-eight inches long. Heights can vary, but most purchased tables are thirty inches high. The table top should have a carpet or rubber mat covering to give the dog secure footing. Make sure the table is sturdy so the dog will feel even more secure.

Dogs that enjoy being groomed are usually eager to get on the grooming table. Depending on the height and stability of the table, most Newfs will jump on the table without assistance. Others will put their front feet on the table and ask for some help getting the rear onto the table. The dog should be trained to both stand and lie on the table.

If you don't have a table, you can sit on the floor or ground to do your grooming. That plan works best for a young person with a supple back. Given a choice of grooming on the floor or on a table, an experienced Newfie fan opts for a table, supple back notwithstanding.

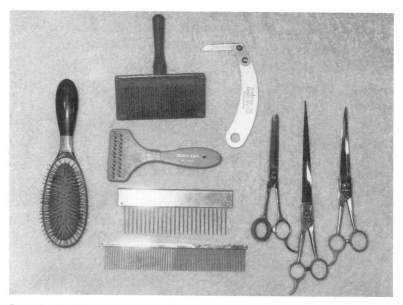

Grooming tools from center **top**: slicker brush, mat splitter, scissors (left to right), thinning, straight, curved, **bottom**: combs—greyhound, large comb, Resco coarse, rake; pin brush is on left.   *C. Lange*

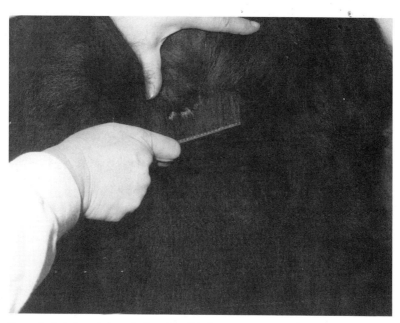

Separate hair to get down to the skin. If hair is tangled or matted you will need to start at the end and work toward the skin. Be sure hair is combed out all the way down to the skin.   *C. Lange*

GROOMING TOOLS

Grooming tools useful for working on a Newfoundland will include:

Medium-sized flat slicker brush
All-steel coarse comb, with teeth about ¼ inch apart and 1½ inches long
Rake
Spray bottle
Coat conditioner
Straight scissors
Dog nail clippers
Ferric sulfate powder or styptic pencil
Dog shampoo

For show grooming, additional grooming items would include:

Hair dryer, preferably one made for use on dogs
Pin brush
Thinning scissors
Curved scissors

GROOMING TECHNIQUES

Brushing

Care must be taken to brush the coat from the skin out. Many first-time Newf owners make the mistake of brushing only the outer layer of hair, which will not get the dead hair and tangles out.

First spray the section of the coat you are going to brush with some coat conditioner or moisturizer diluted with water. This will help prevent the coat from breaking and help condition it at the same time.

Start brushing on the back leg, working from the bottom to the top, and from the rear of the dog to the front. Grasp the slicker brush in one hand. With your free hand lying flat against the dog, lift and push the hair in the opposite direction of its natural growth, until you can see the skin. Run the brush through the hair directly below your hand. When that section is fully brushed, slide your hand upward, releasing more unbrushed hair. Continue working in this manner around and up the leg.

Be careful when brushing between the dog's rear legs that you do not inadvertently brush the scrotum or vulva. It is wise to use your free hand to shield the genitals from the brush.

It is important to keep removing dead coat from your brush as you work. This is easiest done with the use of a comb. If you encounter any mats, first try removing them without cutting them out. There are several ways to remove mats. If the mat is not too large or tight, you may be able to separate it with your fingers into several small mats, which you can then brush through. You can also try to break down a large mat by holding the comb vertically and just pulling a few teeth on the end of the comb through it. If the hair is tightly matted, use the scissors to cut vertically through the mat several times. Then try brushing or combing it out. If the mat is thick and covers a large area, you may have to cut horizontally across the mat and then brush from the center of the mat out.

You can also buy a mat comb or mat splitter. These are available in several models and can make a tedious job much easier to handle.

After the rear quarters are done, begin brushing the back in the same manner. Start at the base of the tail working forward. Continue on to the ribs, chest and front legs. Pay particular attention to the area between the front legs and ribs. Use the comb on the hair under and behind the ears. This hair is very fine and has a greater tendency to mat.

It is usually easier to do the belly and tail while the dog is lying on its side. Work from the tip of the tail to the base. After the dog has been totally brushed with the slicker, run a comb through the coat to be sure that all mats, tangles and loose hair have been removed.

Care of the Nails

If your dog's nails touch the floor when it stands or walks, they will need to be cut. There are many different types of nail trimmers on the market, but they all work equally well.

The important thing in trimming the nails is not to cut into the quick, a very sensitive area inside the nail. If the quick is cut too deeply it will not only be very painful to the dog but will also cause the nail to bleed. Be sure to have your styptic pencil or coagulant powder handy.

Dogs with white feet may have white or transparent toenails that make it easy to see the quick. The quick will appear pink, and you will easily be able to see how far you can cut.

In black nails the center will be whitish-gray. Make sliver-like cuts until you see an area in the center that is black and moist looking—that is the quick. If the nails are excessively long, you will not be able to cut them back to the proper length at one time. You will have to take them back gradually by cutting them often. Newfoundlands have front dewclaws that are usually not removed, so be sure you do not forget to cut the nails on them. Some owners feel uncomfortable about cutting their dogs' nails. If possible, find someone who can show you how it is done. Veterinarians or professional groomers will usually cut the nails for a nominal fee. Once a dog has had a bad experience with having its nails cut, it will be very reluctant to sit still for it the next time.

Care of the Ears

It is important that ears be kept clean. Dampen a piece of cotton with isopropyl alcohol or hydrogen peroxide and gently wipe the inside of the ear. Do this several times, using clean cotton each time, until the cotton comes out clean. Then, using a clean, dry piece of cotton, dry the ear. If you choose, you can purchase commercial ear-cleaning products. A clean ear does not have any odor.

The Newfoundland's pendant ear does not allow air to get into the ear. Any warm, moist, dark place lacking air circulation is a great place for bacteria to grow, thus causing ear infections. To help eliminate this problem, we keep the hair that grows on the side of the head, directly under the ear opening, cut very short. To do this, hold the ear flap up from the top of the head, holding your straight scissors pointing up or down cut the hair as short as you can. This will allow more air to get to the ear and eliminate hair that mats easily.

Bathing

Newfoundlands will generally need only a couple of baths a year, unless they are being shown.

Do not bathe your dog unless it has been thoroughly brushed. A Newfoundland with a heavy coat that has not been throughly brushed will be a matted mess if so treated.

Most owners will not have an indoor area suitable for bathing a Newfoundland. I would not advise using your personal bathroom! If you do, you may be facing hours of clean-up and the possibility of a clogged drain. If you bathe your dog in an inside tub or shower, be sure to have a basket or screen in the drain to collect the hair. Even a well-combed-out dog will lose more coat during the bath.

Weather permitting, a bathing area outside will be the easiest. Some owners prefer using a children's wading pool for outdoor bathing. If possible, connect a hose with a nozzle to a warm water supply. Warm water will penetrate the Newfoundland's heavy, sometimes oily coat better than cold water. You can however, use cold water—your Newf won't mind.

Be sure to have a place to securely fasten the dog and that everything you will need is in easy reach. Shampoo, coat conditioner, sponge or cloth for washing the dog's face and some old towels.

Holding the nozzle close to the skin, wet the dog as much as possible. Do not spray the dog's face. Use your wet sponge or cloth to wash the face. Be sure to wash under the ears but be careful not to get any water in the ears. It is not easy to get a Newfoundlands' coat thoroughly wet. After the initial wetting, you will find that adding a little shampoo will help the water to penetrate the coat. Spray small amounts of water onto the coat and squeeze through with your other hand. This will help distribute the shampoo through the coat and get the skin totally wet. Add more shampoo. Do not rub or swirl the hair; squeeze the shampoo through the hair, and be sure you have shampoo all the way down to the skin. After the shampoo has been worked through the entire dog, let the dog stand for about five minutes before rinsing. Again, make sure the source of the water is close to the skin and begin rinsing. Start at the front and top and work back down. Make sure all the shampoo is rinsed out of the coat. Shampoo

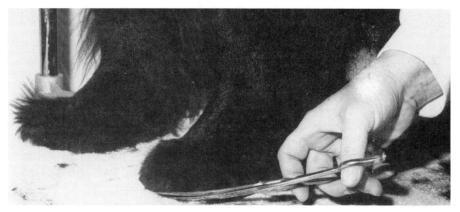

Scissor around outer edge of foot so the hair is neat and does not touch the floor. *C. Lange*

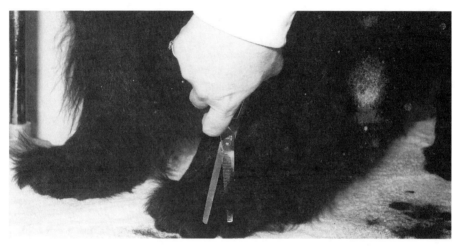

With thinning scissors pointing downward, scissor excess hair from top and sides of feet. Foot should have a rounded cat paw shape when done. Be sure the dog is standing when you are scissoring the top of the feet. *C. Lange*

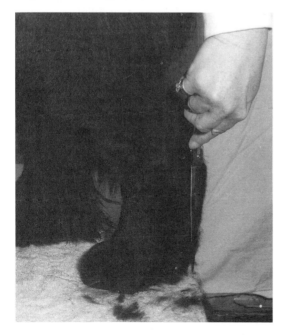

Straight scissors can be used to scissor the excess hair from the hocks. Hair should be left approximately one inch long or longer. With the scissors pointing downward, scissor around the hock to give a neat appearance

C. Lange

189

allowed to remain in the coat will make the coat look dull and can cause itching. Coat conditioner or creme rinse is not necessary, but it will help to repel dirt and discourage tangles.

After the bath is complete, it is best to put the dog in an area where it can run around and shake off the excess water.

Towels hasten the drying period, particularly if you do not have a dog dryer. You can also use your own hand-held dryer on the warm or no-heat setting. If you are going to blow-dry the dog, brushing and lifting the hair with a pin brush will make the task go faster.

After the dog is dry, brush or comb the dog again to make the coat look its best and to remove any little tangles that you may have missed earlier.

Trimming

Newfoundlands are trimmed for neatness. All trimming can be done with a straight scissors. A thinning scissors, however, does make it easier to blend the hair and avoid cut marks. With the thinning scissors you will need to make many cuts, working from the base of the hair out. Always hold your scissors so they cut with the way the hair naturally lies, never across the hair. Comb the hair as you trim.

With your straight scissors, cut the hair on the bottom of your dog's feet flush with the pads. This will give the dog better traction on smooth surfaces, reduce the amount of dirt and water coming into the house and prevent ice balls from forming between the toes in the winter.

Stand the dog on a smooth, flat surface. Use your straight scissors (or curved, if you have them), and cut all the way around the edge of the dog's foot so that no hair hangs over onto the table. Now with your slicker brush, brush the hair on the dog's foot up, and with scissors (thinning scissors if you have them) pointed down toward the surface the dog is standing on, trim around the foot. Now with the scissors, blend the excess hair to round the foot into the shape of a cat's paw. When you are finished you should have a nicely rounded foot, not four individually defined toes.

Trim the hock hair if it is excessively long. Again holding the scissors pointing down, trim around the hock to the desired length, usually not more than an inch long.

To trim the ears, start by cutting around the ear. Lift the ear to cut the hair that is behind the fold. Do not cut into the short, thick hair. Just cut the long hair that hangs below the edge of the ear. This can be done with a straight scissors. Blend the edge with thinning scissors, or angle your straight scissors to remove the blunt edge.

Now with the ear in its natural position, scissor the hair on the flap of the ear to give a neat appearance.

Most pet owners like the big bib of hair on the front of the Newfoundland's chest. If your dog is a messy drinker, or drools a great deal, you may want to trim some of the hair off. If the hair is constantly wet it may mildew or become sour-smelling.

Cut off long hair that hangs below the ear with straight scissors. Pull ear forward to expose entire lower edge. Use the thinning scissors to taper the hair on the edge. With the ear lying naturally, thin the excess hair on the ear flap from the bottom edge to top.

C. Lange

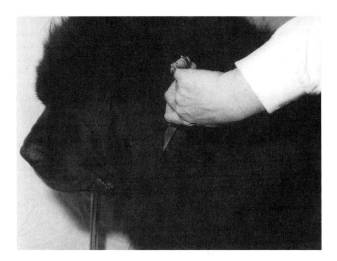

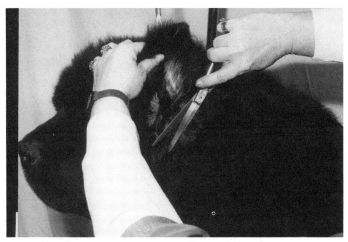

With straight scissors pointed down, cut the hair below the ear opening as short as possible. This will allow the ear to lie flat against the head and allow freer air circulation. *C. Lange*

Trimmed ear. *C. Lange*

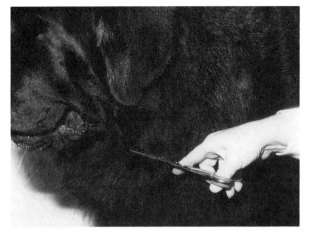

The hair from the dog's throat and bib should be trimmed for neatness. To avoid cut marks in the hair, use thinning scissors. When you become more adept at scissoring, you will be able to use straight scissors. For best results have the dog stand during trimming.

C. Lange

If your dog has excessive hair around his neck, you will want to trim the hair shorter to define the neck. This is particularly necessary for show dogs, as excess hair will give the appearance of a short neck.

C. Lange

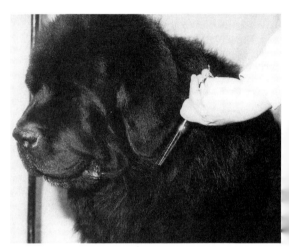

Visualize a line from the back of the ear's base to about the middle of the shoulder. Trim the hair below this line and around the neck, including the throat; trim down to the point of shoulder. Trim the hair to the length needed to give the appearance of neck length and shoulder layback desired. *C. Lange*

With a straight scissors angled to follow the way the hair lies naturally, cut to the shape and length you want.

To make the coat easier to care for on spayed bitches and neutered dogs, we sometimes give them what is called a "puppy cut." Scissor the hair all over to about two to three inches in length. Remember not to cut across the hair. Always keep your scissors pointed in the direction the hair naturally lies as you cut. Your results will be better.

SHOW GROOMING

In keeping with its working heritage the Newfoundland was always shown naturally. Only the ears and feet were trimmed for neatness. Prior to the 1970s, the flatter coats did not lend themselves to sculpting. Today's profuse coats can sometimes make a dog's body appear unbalanced—neck too short, body too long, poor toplines and many other blemishes that do not really exist.

Showing in conformation is a beauty contest. Exhibitors use every advantage they can to make their Newfs more competitive. It is particularly important if the dog is going to be in Working Group competition.

Some people have a natural eye to evaluate where and how the dog appears out of proportion. Do not just start to cut unless you have this talent. Instead, have someone who knows your dog tell you where to trim to enhance the picture.

Always use a thinning scissors and always cut the hair in the direction the hair naturally lies. The coat color on a brown or gray Newfoundland usually has many different shades—lighter closer to the skin and darker on the ends. Be very careful when scissoring to take the excess hair out from underneath to avoid creating patches of lighter hair where it should be dark.

For excessive hair on the throat, sides of neck and shoulder, which can give the appearance of a short neck, use your thinning scissors to shorten the hair. The purpose is not so much to thin the coat in this area but to shorten the hair to give length to the dog's neck. Have an imaginary line from the back of the base of the ear to about the middle of the shoulder. Trim the hair below this line, around the front of the neck, to the other side. Do not trim the hair above this line.

Too much hair on the shoulder above the elbow can give the appearance of short front legs when viewed from the side. To avoid this look, use your thinning scissors to shorten the hair above the elbow. This will make the elbow appear higher than it really is, thus making the front leg appear longer. Make sure the hair is smoothly blended.

To avoid having the dog appear out at the elbows, trim off the excess feathering down the side of the front leg. This will also make the bone appear more massive.

Some dogs have steep shoulders or have the appearance of steep shoulders due to excess hair. To check if your dog has the proper shoulder layback, put one hand on the withers and the other on the point of the shoulder. The line between the two should be well laid back, not too steep.

Excessive feathering on the elbow and side of the leg should be removed. Carefully using straight scissors, or thinning scissors, trim the hair to the same length as the shorter hair on the side of the leg. This will remove the excess hair on the outside of the elbow and leg that can make your dog appear out at the elbows when moving. *C. Lange*

Excessively long or thick pants hair on the buttocks can make your dog's body appear longer than it should be for his height. You can achieve the look of a shorter body by either cutting the hair shorter with thinning scissors or thinning the hair and combing it down until you get the desired look. *C. Lange*

If your dog looks too steep in the shoulders, shorten the hair in a straight line from the point of shoulder to where the withers should be for proper layback. This line needs to be approximately an inch or two wide, depending on the dog. Always make sure you blend the hair into the neck. When the dog is standing, this gives the appearance of the shoulder having more layback.

The topline should be level. You will find that many Newfoundlands have a more profuse coat starting at the loin and extending over the buttocks. This gives the dog the appearance of being low in the shoulder or running downhill.

To correct this, start while drying the dog by brushing the hair down. Blow-dry the hair so it lies as flat as possible in this area.

If the hair still stands up too much, you will need to thin it out. Lift up a small patch of hair, and with thinning scissors, starting near the body on the underside, make several cuts, moving the scissors each time. Comb flat to remove the cut hair and see if you have taken enough out. It is better to take a little at a time. You can always cut more, but you can't put it back on. This hair should be thinned out enough so that it will lie down giving the proper, desired shape. Be careful not to remove so much hair that the base of the tail sticks out. If the dog is long-bodied, shortening the length of hair on both the chest, shoulders and rear will help make the dog appear more compact.

Excessively thick hair on the back of the buttocks can make the dog's body appear longer than it actually is. Put the thinning scissors, with the point angled down, deep into the coat, and work your way out and down the hair. Comb to remove the cut hair. Continue doing this until you have achieved the desired look. Again, you can always take more hair off, but you can't put it back on.

To make the hair on the rear lie flatter, mist lightly with water and pin a towel tightly around the rear. Do this in the grooming area; do not take your dog up to the ring this way.

All the scissoring and trimming you do will not fool a good judge. When a judge puts his or her hands on the dog or watches your dog move, he or she will know the dog's true conformation.

Bubbelinas Dekanawida Squaw, noted producer of some beautiful champions in Denmark, is doing what Newfs enjoy doing most of all, swimming and retrieving for the fun of it. Bred by Liv Fridtjofsen, Squaw is owned by Einar Paulsen. *Søren Wesseltoft*

196

12

The Newfoundland
as a Working Dog

MOST OF US think of our dogs as loyal companions and friends who are always ready to come at our beck and call. And, although most of our canine charges have member status in our families, they are seldom called upon to perform tasks any more difficult than fetching slippers or bringing in the paper. This is a significant change from the not-so-distant past when a dog's worth to its master was determined by its usefulness as a worker. A good dog worked for its keep, and many breeds were developed as working dogs. This is especially true of the Newfoundland and is something that any owner, or potential owner, should understand about the breed: the Newfoundland is a working dog.

The Newfoundland's strength, size, physical hardiness, intelligence, even, docile temperament and innate need for human companionship has made it one of the best suited, of all canine breeds, to assist its human masters in an amazingly large number of tasks. Newfoundlands have been generally used as draft animals, pulling three-or four-hundred-pound sledges or carts laden with firewood, timber, coal, fish or a wide range of merchandise; retrieving game; hauling in heavy fishing nets; guarding children at play; rescuing people from drowning; searching for missing persons—even locating dead bodies under water.

The island of Newfoundland is where this breed has been extensively used in its role as a working dog, especially during the nineteenth and early twentieth centuries. In 1824 it was estimated that the town of St. John's was the home of as many as two thousand working Newfoundlands. These dogs were used in teams or singly, and it has been claimed that the labor of one Newfoundland could provide at least subsistence for its master.

The fact that a team of dogs, usually three to five in number, could be harnessed to a sledge with a load ranging from three hundred to five hundred pounds, draw it for miles without a driver, with no undue strain, to their destination, and then return home under their own guidance, made them particularly useful draft animals.

Until the 1940s, larger teams, averaging about seven, were used to transport the mail from rail junctions to Newfoundland's more remote outposts over terrain that would defeat the efforts of the most hardy ponies or packhorses. The British Crown recognized the Newfoundland's service by placing its portrait on one of this country's postage stamps.

During the era of the sailing ships, Newfoundlands were customarily employed as "ship dogs" on vessels plying the waters of the Atlantic and Mediterranean. Their unequaled swimming ability, exceptional intelligence and natural lifesaving instinct enabled them to rescue many of their human charges from watery graves. Many times a Newfoundland was dispatched from the deck of a ship breaking up in pounding surf to swim ashore with a communication line, enabling those on shore to rig a boatswain's chair and bring the crew to safety.

During World War II, the U.S. Army used Newfoundlands as pack animals, and they saw service in the defense of the Aleutian Islands. *The Army Technical Manual* of 1943 described the Newfoundland as "a massive, powerful dog. Water-resistant coat equips him for cold and wet weather. An excellent pack dog, he possesses also talent for rescuing drowning persons."

Most of these dogs were trained for three months during the harsh winters that are typical of Fort Robinson, Nebraska, or Fort Remic, Montana. Along with obedience training, they also learned to haul heavy loads. This training served their masters well when these Newfoundlands were sent to Alaska and the Aleutians. Winter storms in this remote part of the far North are so fierce that visibility is often reduced to inches and the windchill can go to below minus 100 degrees. They packed their cargo through deep snowdrifts, in subzero temperatures that froze their leather leashes solid.

Regularly, these dogs safely guided the soldiers back to their base through howling gales that could come up in a matter of minutes, with literally no warning.

Many of the army camps in the Aleutians were several miles inland from the landing areas, and Newfoundlands were depended upon to haul heavy sacks of supplies, often working for more than ten hours without a break. They did this, "steady and uncomplaining. At the end of the day the dogs acted as if they had been out for a leisurely stroll in Central Park."

Newfoundlands were so perfectly suited to this harsh environment that they frequently slept outside of their kennels, seeming to prefer a blanket of snow to more conventional shelter. The only extra protection they did require was rawhide boots, which were used to protect their webbed feet from the sharp, jagged ice.

But since World War II the Newfoundland's role as a working dog has changed significantly. No longer are they commonly used as draft or pack animals for commercial purposes, and their role as "ship dogs" ended along with the era of the sailing vessel.

Nowadays working Newfoundlands, in addition to being family members, furnish a valuable service as search and rescue dogs.

But fanciers of this working breed have recognized the need to preserve the characteristics that have made it such an invaluable companion and workmate to its human masters. The Newfoundland Club of America has developed tests to promote water rescue skills and draft work. Through these competitions the dogs can win various titles such as WD (Water Dog), WRD (Water Rescue Dog), DD (Draft Dog) and TDD (Team Draft Dog).

The American Kennel Club sanctions a number of Tracking and Obedience events. AKC Obedience titles a dog can earn are CD (Companion Dog), CDX (Companion Dog Excellent), UD (Utility Dog), TD (Tracking Dog) and TDX (Tracking Dog Excellent). The ultimate Obedience title that can be achieved is OTCH, or Obedience Trial Champion.

Aside from promoting the desirable behavioral characteristics of the Newfoundland, these events are also excellent places for Newfoundland owners (along with their dogs) to socialize with others, exchange ideas, give and receive advice and simply have a good time.

OBEDIENCE

Since obedience is a key element in the nature of a working dog, it is natural that participation in Obedience Trials are a popular endeavor with many Newfoundland owners. Newfoundlands may not be as agile as some of the smaller breeds, but if properly trained they will work at the pace their trainers set. They are steady and happy performers, particularly if trained with patience and kindness.

Obedience competition has three different levels or classes. Each level becomes decidedly more difficult, involving high and broad jumps, retrieving articles and scent discrimination. The Novice class is for dogs working on their title for Companion Dog (CD), the Open class is for dogs working on their Companion Dog Excellent (CDX) titles, and the Utility class is for dogs working toward the Utility Dog (UD) title.

Contact the American Kennel Club for a copy of the booklet of rules *Obedience Regulations*.

To obtain any of the AKC Obedience degrees, a dog needs three qualifying scores, or "legs," in each class to win each Obedience title. The legs must be won under three different judges. Dogs do not compete against each other to earn legs. To qualify, a dog needs a score of more than 50 percent of the available points in each exercise, and a final score of 170 points or more. A perfect score is 200 points.

Awards are also given for High in each class and an overall High in Trial.

Finally, there is the Obedience Trial Champion (OTCH) title, which is the highest Obedience title a dog can win. An OTCH is awarded on the basis of points won by placing first or second in Open B and Utility B classes. The title requires 100 points. The dog must win at least three first places under three

Can. OTCH Sweetbay's Bailey UDT, Can. UD, WRD, DD. Bred and owned by Judi and Ellis Adler. Bailey shows the fine form that earned her the advanced utility title in both the United States and Canada.

OTCH Sweetbay's Gretl, TD, shown with owner/trainer Nanette Wiesner. Gretl was the first Newfoundland to earn a perfect score of 200 and only the second Newfoundland to attain her OTCH. *Milton G. Klipfel*

200

different judges, with at least one first place in each class. Points are given based on the number of dogs competing.

Only two Newfoundlands to date have garnered the OTCH title. The first was OTCH Barbara Allen's Jessie, WD, owned and trained by Bob Wallace and achieving her title in 1982. The second was OTCH Sweetbay's Gretl, TD, owned and trained by Nanette Wiesner, whose Obedience accomplishments would more than do credit to any breed. Gretl was the first Newfoundland ever to achieve a perfect score of 200. She was the Newfoundland Club of America's top Obedience dog for the years 1986 though 1990—an amazing accomplishment for any dog and its owner.

In 1991, upon her retirement from active competition, Gretl was given a special award for her years of outstanding achievement.

According to Nanette, "many obedience enthusiasts have begun to view the Newfoundland in a whole new light. A large breed can indeed possess the same capabilities as those more common breeds currently dominating the obedience ring. Newfoundland trainers might have known this all along, but I hope Gretl helped to contribute to some of this enlightenment in others."

WATER TRIALS

Newfoundlands have an inherent lifesaving instinct that makes them natural water lifeguards. While some other breeds possess this trait in varying degrees, no other breed has this characteristic to the extent that the Newfoundland does. The Newfoundland is the consummate water dog.

One of the most rewarding experiences a Newfoundland fancier can experience is to watch a Newf perform at a Water Trial. They work with their owner with enthusiasm, courage and eagerness to perform the tasks at hand.

Various regional Newfoundland clubs sponsor Water Tests, which are sanctioned by the Newfoundland Club of America through the Working Dog Committee. These competitions are divided into Junior and Senior divisions, which consist of progressively more difficult exercises.

Since this is not a training manual, I'm not going to describe water dog training in any great detail, but I will summarize some of the basic considerations all friends of the Newfoundland need to be mindful of.

Water Test training is fundamentally the same as any other type of training for your Newfoundland. It should be done consistently. Each exercise or task should be taught in increments—that is, broken down into simpler steps that the dog can learn more easily. Conduct training under conditions where you have your dog's attention—taking care not to drag out a training session beyond your dog's attention span. (Newfs, as bright as they are, get tired, bored or distracted over a period of time.)

Many Water Test skills can be taught on land, and many trainers suggest that this is where one should begin in the first place. Basic control—heeling, sit-stay, retrieving—are obvious ones and form the essential basis for the other more complex tasks. A dog who has not consistently learned to come on command is going to have a hard time responding to a steward who is sitting in a boat fifty feet from shore.

A novice can obtain guidance from the regional Newfoundland clubs that conduct Water Tests and water-training workshops. Seek advice from experienced trainers when starting out. They can provide a wealth of information, prevent you from making serious training errors and save you and your pet much time and frustration.

If you are serious about water work, whether for play or competition, I would advise purchasing one of the several water-training manuals available. *The Newfoundland Club of America Water Test Training Manual*, written by and available from the working dog committee of the NCA, and *Water Work, Water Play*, available from the author, Judi Adler, Sweetbay Newfoundlands, of Sherwood, Oregon, are both excellent books.

Junior Water Training

The equipment necessary for junior water work are:

Collar and leash
2 bumpers, one with an 8-foot floating line
Boat cushion
2 life jackets, one for the trainer to wear and one for the dog to retrieve
75 feet of floating line
Protective footwear for the trainer

The Junior Division exercises consist of the following:

Basic Control—a three-part exercise consisting of basic control commands. The dog must heel properly, respond to Stay and Come commands, and, as part of a group, Down and Stay as their handlers cross the ring, wait for one minute and remain down until their handlers return. Dogs that have a CD (Companion Dog) title are exempt from this exercise.

Single Retrieve—an exercise where the dog has ninety seconds to retrieve a boat bumper that its handler has thrown at least thirty feet from shore into the water. The dog must retrieve it and return it to the handler on shore.

Take a Line—a timed, three-minute exercise in which the dog has one minute to take a seventy-five-foot rope, with a knotted end, from its handler on shore and then, within two minutes, swim to a steward who is treading water about fifty feet from shore. The dog must swim close enough to the steward so that the steward can take hold of the line.

Drop Retrieve—another timed exercise in which the dog has two minutes to retrieve a boat cushion or life jacket, which a steward in a boat fifty feet from shore has quietly dropped into the water on the seaward side of the boat. The handler, who is on shore, directs the dog to fetch the object, and the dog has two minutes to retrieve it and deliver it to its handler.

Tow a Boat—an exercise wherein the dog pulls a boat a distance of fifty

"Water Kids": Nashau-Auke's Boomer on left and Nashau Auke's Reba McIntyre, owned by Regina Pavao. Boomer was bred by Jane Thibault, and Reba was bred by Jane Thibault and Pam Langdon.

Enjoying themselves after a successful water trial are Teddy Tug's Marcus Tullius, WD, owned by Aura and John Dean (left), and Mooncusser's Piper Pouch Cove CD, WRD, DD, owned by Nancy McKee and Peggy Helming.

Ch. Shadybrook's Try For An Oscar, CD, WRD, ROM, about to take a line from owner/trainer Richard Krokum. "Josh" is bred and owned by Jeri and Richard Krokum.

feet, in wading-deep water, parallel to the shore. The dog must do this within ninety seconds.

Swim with Handler—in this exercise both the dog and handler swim out from shore together. Upon a signal from the judge, the handler commands the dog to return to the shore. The handler then grasps hold of the dog, which then tows the handler to shore. This must be accomplished within two minutes.

Senior Water Training

Equipment necessary for senior water training is the same as for the junior division, with the addition of a life ring with a length of line attached suitable for the dog, underwater retrieving articles, such as a wiffle ball weighted with pebbles or a small canoe paddle. The use of a rowboat with a sturdy platform is also required.

Senior Division exercises are more challenging and consist of the following:

Underwater Retrieve—an exercise in which both handler and dog go into the water together and wade out to where the dog's underbelly touches the water surface. The handler then tosses a weighted object three feet from the dog. The dog retrieves it by either submerging its head to grasp the object or pawing it to shallower water and then picking it up and delivering it to the handler. There is a three-minute limit on this exercise, and the handler can throw the object as many times as desired during this period.

Life Ring—a more challenging exercise that utilizes the Newfoundland's lifesaving skills. Three stewards tread water seventy-five feet from the shore and are positioned thirty feet apart. One of them mimics a drowning swimmer— thrashing and calling for help. The dog takes from its handler the knotted end of a rope that is tied to a life ring and then, at the handler's order, delivers the life ring to the "drowning" steward and tows him in to shore. The dog must do this within three minutes.

Retrieve Off a Boat—requires the use of a boat positioned fifty feet off shore with a platform where both the dog and handler are seated. The handler throws the oar at least ten feet from the boat and the dog has two minutes to voluntarily retrieve it and deliver it to the handler or steward.

Directed Retrieve—an exercise during which the dog must retrieve two objects, a boat cushion and a life jacket. The articles are placed on the shore side of the canoe, fifty feet from shore and fifty feet apart. The judge selects which object is to be retrieved first and the handler directs the dog to it. The dog must retrieve that object and return it to the handler and then retrieve the second object within four minutes.

Take a Line/Tow a Boat—an exercise in which two stewards are in a boat positioned seventy-five feet from shore. One steward, sitting in the bow, calls the dog, which is waiting onshore. The dog takes a short line attached to a bumper from its handler and must swim out to the boat, approaching close enough for the steward to grasp the line. The dog must then tow the boat to shore and pull it until the hull touches bottom. The time limit for this exercise is three minutes.

Anchorage's Navigator, CD, TDI, CGC, shown doing the tow-a-boat exercIse with owner/trainer Ann Burlingame. Navigator is bred and owned by Ann and Norman Burlingame. *Beth Dykstra*

VN Ch. Riptide's Brown Kodiak Bear, WRD, DD, also the canine star of the movie *Police Academy II,* shown doing the Retrieve Off a Boat exercise. Bred by Virginia and Grant Hoag of Riptide Kennels, Kodi is owned and trained by Kathie Cullen.

Ch. Sweetbay's Dylan, CDX, Can. CD, WRD, shown earning his WRD title with owner Judi Adler. Dylan is bred and owned by Judi and Ellis Adler.

Rescue—a direct test of the dog's innate lifesaving instinct and skill. In this exercise the dog and handler are in a boat located fifty feet from shore. The handler jumps from the boat and the dog then has thirty seconds to dive into the water to rescue the handler. The handler may call the dog. The dog must swim directly to the handler and tow him or her either back to the boat or to shore.

Training your dog for successful competition in water tests is a serious endeavor but nevertheless very rewarding. It will strengthen the bond between you and your Newfoundland and introduce you to a new group of friends who share your interest in and love for the breed.

Dogs qualifying in the Junior Division are granted the WD (Water Dog) title. The WRD title is granted to dogs that qualify in the Senior Division.

NEWFS TO THE RESCUE

It might come as a surprise to some to learn that the Newfoundland is an outstanding search-and-rescue dog, every bit as capable as the fabled Saint Bernard or the legendary Bloodhound. Many people owe their lives to the New-foundland's air scenting (not to be confused with tracking) ability. Its keen sense of smell, endurance and, above all, its superior intelligence, coupled with proper training, make it an excellent search-and-rescue dog.

Newfoundlands are air-scenting dogs, so they typically work with their heads up in order to detect an airborne scent. They do not need some article of clothing or personal effect of the person who is the object of their search. It seems that they have a natural instinct for locating the source of human scent and, working without a lead, the handler simply follows and trusts the judgment of the dog. Newfoundlands are all-terrain, all-weather search dogs that also posses an uncanny ability to locate bodies under water.

Search-and-rescue Newfoundlands have their own training academy. It is called the Black Paws Search, Rescue and Avalanche Academy. The training academy itself and the National and International Headquarters are located in Bigfork, Montana.

Black Paws was founded by Susie and Murphy Foley. Despite the fact that the academy has been in existence only since 1986, there are Black Paws–trained "Newfoundland" search dog teams and organization chapters throughout the United States and in other countries. Black Paws is a nonprofit organization. All training, equipment and emergency responses, as well as any other expenses, are paid for by the member dogs' owners and handlers. It has the unique distinction of being the one and only Newfoundland search dog organization in existence today.

The academy accepts only purebred American Kennel Club–registered Newfoundlands from all over the United States and foreign countries. The course takes one week, and its size is limited.

The dogs and their handlers are trained in the areas of air scenting, locating lost individuals, locating submerged corpses and finding avalanche victims. And, since most of these dogs will be part of a Search And Rescue team (SAR)

Black Paws Search, Rescue and Avalanche Academy founders Susie and Murphy Foley. In the bow of the raft is student Nicolette Dobson with her Newf, Alano's Dark Shadow. Shadow is on a "search low" command, seeking human scent.

Black Paws Search and Rescue members, Nancy Furhrer with Teddy Tug's Ivy and Sam Butler with Sir Zachery of Butler Farms. Dogs and owners are outfitted in their search gear.

requiring the use of various means of transportation and equipment, they are also trained with chair lifts, repelling gear, draft dog equipment, helicopters and boats, including rubber rafts. The owners must possess both Red Cross First Aid and CPR cards and be in good physical condition.

Black Paws search dogs, owned by the Foleys, were used by Utah authorities in an attempt to locate the bodies of a number of victims of the infamous serial killer Ted Bundy. Although the Newfoundlands were not initially successful, the authorities plan to use them in any subsequent searches. Their initial failure was due, most likely, to the inaccuracy of Bundy's directions—they were simply searching in the wrong areas.

In another more remarkable but less publicized case, Chelsie, one of the Foleys' Newfoundlands, found the scattered and highly fragmented bones of a hunting camp caretaker over one year after his disappearance. The remains were found on a remote mountainside that was littered with animal bones. Susie Foley writes in the *SAR Dog ALERT* that Chelsie was able to distinguish human from animal bones: "She would curl her lip and reluctantly take [a] human bone in her mouth, then drop it, but would not take the animal bone. Definitely an ability I didn't expect to be used in this manner."

There have been many cases of people found by Black Paws–trained dogs. Unfortunately, more victims are found dead than alive. I will not give any more cases, as it is not the intent of the members to publicize the details of tragedy.

Foley has also noted that Newfoundlands are particularly well suited for finding and recovering avalanche victims. Their extremely acute scenting ability and innate lifesaving instinct make them superior to other breeds—they are faster, in many cases, than electronic locator beacons. Newfoundlands will also dig a rescue hole directed to the buried victim's face, thus reducing the danger of suffocation.

Susie Foley says that all Newfoundlands can be trained to perform as search-and-rescue dogs. She feels that the instinct is strong in all Newfoundlands, regardless of bloodlines. I am glad to see that, through the efforts of the Foleys and other dedicated owners, this noble breed is gradually being restored to its rightful place as the premier rescue dog. But I must also stress that the decision to train your Newfoundland as a search-and-rescue dog is a very serious undertaking requiring time, dedication and money. You are volunteering your Newfoundland and yourself to provide a vital service, the demands of which can be time-consuming, creating personal inconvenience and, in some cases, real danger. But if you are up to it, one would be hard pressed to think of any endeavor that could be more rewarding for you and your dog.

TRACKING

In tracking, a dog must show its ability to track a human scent over a set course.

The track is laid on a course of between 440 to 500 yards in length. It is

Can. OTCH Sweetbay's Bailey, UDT, Can. UD, WRD, DD, pictured in tracking harness with favorite glove. Bailey earned her tracking title at the first-ever for-Newfoundlands-only tracking test, held as part of the 1985 NCA National Specialty in Litchfield, Connecticut. Judi and Bailey flew in from Oregon to participate in this test. Bailey is bred and owned by Judi and Ellis Adler.

divided into "legs," or sections with corners. At the end of the track the dog will find a well-scented article left by the tracklayer. The article is generally a glove, and the dog gets to keep the prize.

A tracking course for the TDX test is between 800 and 1,000 yards long. There must be obstacles along the way, such as streams, fences or possibly a road to cross. There are four articles to locate. They can be items such as a billfold, shirt, shoe—anything that bears the scent of the tracklayer. One article is placed at the start of the track, two more along the track and the final article at the end of the track. Again, the dog is usually allowed to keep the final article.

Two books on tracking that are particularly recommended are *Go Find!*, by L. Wilson Davis, and *Training Tracking Dogs*, by William R. Koehler. Both books are published by Howell Book House.

DRAFT TEST COMPETITION

The purpose of these competitions is to encourage and demonstrate the capability of the Newfoundland to perform work involving hauling and the necessary, related skills that would be required in real work situations: primarily pulling and maneuvering a cart or wagon. There are two draft titles that can be earned: Draft Dog (DD), for dogs competing individually, and Team Draft Dog (TDD) for teams of two or more dogs working together. All exercises are off lead. A draft dog must show its willingness to be hitched, perform basic commands and pass through a course showing the dog's ability to maneuver the apparatus, culminating with pulling weight-loaded apparatus on a cross-country course of at least one mile.

If you are interested in participating in this competition, contact the Newfoundland Club of America for regulations, equipment guides, training information and locations of Draft Tests.

Again, as in any other competition, it will require time and effort on your part to be successful. Enjoy the thrill and satisfaction of working with your Newfoundland and the camaraderie of working with other Newf enthusiasts. Like all working activities, it will strengthen the bond between you and your dog. It is also an activity that can easily be enjoyed by the entire family. Most Newfs love to pull, and for small children there is nothing more fun than being towed in a cart by the family dog.

BACKPACKING

With all the emphasis on health and the environment today, backpacking is a great way to enjoy the company of your Newf and the beauty of nature at the same time. Of all canine breeds, the Newfoundland is probably best suited to serve as a backpacking companion. It possesses a combination of endurance, strength, intelligence and a lifesaving instinct.

Am., Can. Ch. Ebunyzar's Salty Tang, DD, ROM, multiple Group winner shown pulling a cart with his breeder/owner Hannah Hayman.

Ch. Edenglen's Brigantine Yankee and Golliwog's Katrinka Too Much, crossing a stream while backpacking with owner Alan Riley. Many Newf owners find backpacking a great way to enjoy the outdoors and also the companionship of their dogs. Brigantine and Katrinka are owned by noted authors JoAnn and Alan Riley.

214

The reason for bringing your Newf along on a backpacking expedition is for companionship and fun, not to employ your pet as a beast of burden, despite its strength and willingness to work. In fact, particular care must be taken in training, equipping and conditioning your pet.

When on the trail, your dog must be under control at all times. Remember that you are sharing the trail with others who may not appreciate the attentions of a very large dog that resembles a bear.

Also keep in mind that your Newf will have more maneuverability with a lighter load, and this can be especially important when fording streams or traversing steep rockfalls.

Balanced, properly fitted packs are also an essential consideration. They must not put too much stress on your dog's back and also be comfortable for the dog to carry.

If you are interested in backpacking with your Newf, I highly recommend the following books: *Taking Your Dog Backpacking*, by Newfoundland owner Alan Riley and available through the NCA Working Dog Committee, and *Guide to Backpacking with Your Dog*, by Charlene G. LaBelle. This is a detailed guide that includes everything from training and outfitting to ''keeping the bugs away.''

Newfoundland owners should understand that their pets are working dogs, that they delight in performing useful tasks for their human masters. While many Newfs are quite content to hold down the carpet, they appreciate and thrive when challenged with any task that makes use of their innate working skills.

Mooncusser's Thurston Howl with his owner, Cindy Spinden, backpacking up Mt. Washington in New Hampshire.

The monument to Boatswain, Lord Byron's Newfoundland companion, on the grounds of Newstead Abbey in Sherwood Forest.

"Boatswain"

13

The Newfoundland in the Limelight

$\mathbf{T}$HE FOLLOWING APPEARS on a monument in the garden of Newstead Abbey. It is a tribute to Boatswain, a Newfoundland owned by the English adventurer and poet, Lord Byron:

EPITAPH TO A DOG

NEAR THIS SPOT
ARE DEPOSITED THE REMAINS
OF ONE
WHO POSSESSED BEAUTY
WITHOUT VANITY,
STRENGTH WITHOUT INSOLENCE,
COURAGE WITHOUT FEROCITY,
AND ALL THE VIRTUES OF MAN
WITHOUT HIS VICES

THIS PRAISE, WHICH WOULD BE UNMEANING
FLATTERY
IF INSCRIBED OVER HUMAN ASHES,
IS BUT A JUST TRIBUTE TO THE MEMORY OF
BOATSWAIN, A DOG
WHO WAS BORN AT NEWFOUNDLAND
MAY, 1803
AND DIED AT NEWSTEAD ABBEY
NOV. 18, 1808

When some proud son of man returns to earth,
Unknown to glory, but upheld by birth,
The sculptor's art exhausts the pomp of woe,
And storied urns record who rests below;
When all is done, upon the tomb is seen,
Not what he was, but what he should have been.
But the poor dog, in life the firmest friend,
The first to welcome, foremost to defend,
Whose honest heart is still his master's own,
Who labours, fights, lives, breathes for him alone,
Unhonour'd falls, unnoticed all his worth,
Denied in heaven the soul he held on earth:
While man, vain insect! hopes to be forgiven,
And claims himself a sole exclusive heaven.
Oh man! thou feeble tenant of an hour,
Debased by slavery, or corrupt by power,
Who knows thee well must quit thee with disgust,
Degraded mass of animated dust!
Thy love is lust, thy friendship all a cheat,
Thy smiles hypocrisy, thy words deceit!
By nature vile, ennobled but by name,
Each kindred brute might bid thee blush for shame.
Ye! who perchance behold this simple urn,
Pass on—it honours none you wish to mourn.
To mark a friend's remains these stones arise;
I never knew but one—and there he lies.
—LORD BYRON

Like many others who have written about the breed, Lord Byron was obviously impressed with his black Newfoundland's (Boatswain has been inaccurately portrayed in the famous Madame Tussaud's Wax Works as a Landseer) outstanding qualities of appearance, physical strength, temperament, character and intelligence.

Boatswain lived with the young Byron at Newstead Abbey, which was the family's ancestral residence. He was his master's constant companion, always accompanying him on Byron's daily walks through the Abbey's woods and fields. On the many rainy days that typify England's wet maritime climate, Boatswain lay at his master's feet by the fireplace in the Abbey's library as the poet composed his verse and wrote his essays.

Byron was notorious for parties, sometimes lasting several days. Boatswain would have no part of this and retreated to the quiet of nearby Sherwood Forest, where he remained until Byron's less civilized human companions departed and the Abbey returned to normal.

Thomas Moore, in his *Life of Byron*, sheds more light on the generous nature of Boatswain's character. The poet's mother had a Fox Terrier, Gilpin, who fought daily with Boatswain, and their fights were so violent that it was feared that Gilpin would eventually be killed. For his own safety Lady Byron sent Gilpin to live with one of the Newstead tenants. Shortly thereafter,

Byron left for Cambridge and Boatswain was left to the care of the Abbey's servants.

One morning Boatswain caused considerable alarm throughout the household by disappearing without a trace. But that same evening—and, I'm sure much to the relief of the Abbey's staff—Boatswain returned with his old, but now former, enemy, Gilpin, in tow.

Boatswain had gone into Newstead and somehow found Gilpin and brought him back home. From then on, and despite the Terrier's ornery nature, the two were the best of friends. Boatswain, in typical Newfoundland fashion, even defended his little charge from their less amiable canine neighbors.

Upon Boatswain's death, Byron declared that he himself, his favorite butler of many years and the Newfoundland would all be buried under the same monument. But this didn't suit the butler's plans for eternity and he quit immediately saying, "Your lordship will be buried in the Westminster Abbey. That only leaves Boatswain and myself to be buried under the monument. At Judgment Day what will they think of me On High when I rise from the same grave as a dog? No, thanks, I am leaving." Apparently, this poor man failed completely to understand Byron's intended compliment.

Lord Byron met his end in Greece, and Lyon, another Newfoundland, was at his side. His affection for Lyon seems to have equaled that which he had for Boatswain: "Thou are more faithful than men, Lyon. I trust thee more."

Lyon watched over his master's deathbed and was later returned to England, where he remained in the care of one of the late Lord's trusted friends.

The Newfoundland has been a favorite of other historical figures, including Sir Walter Scott, Charles Dickens, Robert Burns and Richard Wagner (who once introduced his Newfoundlands to his friends as "nature's own gentlemen").

Queue was Samuel Adams's "shaggy Newfoundland" and is featured in Jean Fritz's children's book, *Why Don't You Get a Horse, Sam Adams?* The dog, reflecting his master's politics, took particular pleasure in harassing the British redcoats.

George Washington and Benjamin Franklin were also reputed to have owned Newfoundlands.

The first Newfoundland to figure prominently in the show ring, Nero, was owned by the Prince of Wales (later Edward VII). He won first prize at Birmingham in 1864 and at Islington in 1865. Nero was described as a, "rich black dog, totally free from white, powerful, good tempered, fine framed, very massive in form, and with a sagacious expression." Queen Victoria was also a fan of the breed.

Bing Crosby was also a serious Newfoundland fan, and his interest went beyond ownership to breeding. He presented one of his kennel's pups to President Franklin Roosevelt as a gift to the children of the Warm Springs Foundation.

Robert Kennedy's Brumis

If any Newfoundland can claim true celebrity status, it was Brumis, owned by the late Robert Kennedy. And despite the fact that the Kennedys were virtually

Robert Kennedy and his Newfoundland, Brumis.

Boomer Esiason, quarterback for the New York Jets, and his two wide receivers, Ebonewf's Charlie Bear, on the left, and Ebonewf's Raider Bear. Both dogs were bred by Louise Esiason of Ebonewf Kennels.

symbols of the Democratic party, Brumis was so well known that even the Republicans couldn't resist the temptation to exploit this dog's notoriety by throwing a tongue-in-cheek "Dog Daze Party" in his honor. Although it was in good fun, some of it was a bit on the acerbic side, such as one poster, which read: "All Animals Are Equal but Some Are More Equal Than Others."

Brumis had the run of the Justice Department halls when Kennedy was U.S. Attorney General. Probably more than once his master had to search the hallways whistling for him after he had slipped out of the Attorney General's fifth-floor offices. On one occasion he was found in the FBI section of the building.

Art Buchwald, in his satirical "Brumis the Great," writes that the name Brumis in Newfoundland means a prolonged meal eaten around two A.M. He goes on to say that Brumis treated Kennedy guests picnicking on the lawn of the Kennedy home as if they were so many fire hydrants. Buchwald also alleged that any Kennedy guest was in danger of losing all of his or her food to Brumis, who, he insists, grabbed the food off their plates.

As an example of such un-Newfoundlandlike behavior, Buchwald describes a meeting between Kennedy, Attorney General Nicholas Katzenbach and a Southern university president to discuss the desegregation issue. Brumis allegedly kept snatching ham and eggs off the university president's plate. This happened three times. Apparently, the Southerner was intimidated into agreeing with all of Kennedy's points.

There are several reports that Brumis also participated in swearing-in ceremonies. At the swearing in of N. A. Schlei as assistant attorney general, the big dog pushed aside Supreme Court Justice John Harlan, who was conducting the ceremony, and stood up, put his great paws on Mr. Schlei's shoulders and searched his face seriously, before letting him proceed with the oath. This drew applause from the witnesses.

In the 1964 congressional campaign Brumis appeared with his master on TV in Kennedy's successful bid for the Senate.

Two other Newfoundlands, Scruffy and, several years later, Poochie, joined the Kennedy clan. In 1975, keeping with its Newfoundland tradition, the family acquired Brumis II.

Kodiak—A Many-Sided Talent

Kodiak was a bronze Newfoundland who can claim movie-star status in addition to being the most titled bronze in Newfoundland history. He played Lou, a police dog, in the comedy film *Police Academy 2*. His owner, Kathie Cullen, has related to me how the director and cast couldn't believe how well trained this dog was—responding off lead to voice and hand signals only. But there was one catch: Kodiak, with typical Newf stubbornness, would take direction only from Kathie or a female friend of hers. He ignored the men on the set. He would also decide that a particular scene had been rehearsed enough and call it quits, refusing further cooperation.

Ch. Riptide's Brown Kodiak Bear (owned by Kathie Cullen), canine star of the movie *Police Academy II*. Copyright © 1985 by The Ladd Company (all rights reserved).

But it should also be mentioned, and not merely in passing, that Kodiak was a true hero. On May 28, 1983, he was given the Newfoundland Club of America Heroism Award for saving his owner's life. Kathie had fallen asleep late one evening with beef melts cooking on a gas stove, and her house had filled with smoke. Kodiak was outside but after sensing that she was in danger roused her by pounding on the front door. She awoke and was able to escape to safety.

The Literary Newfoundland

This breed has been very well treated in the world of canine literature.

Although the Newfoundland was bred as a working dog and used for such mundane and unremarkable tasks as pulling sledges laden with raw lumber, the dominant themes in the literature about this dog celebrate its intelligence, strength and innate character, which is so similar to the better aspects of human nature—honesty, integrity, loyalty, to name a few.

Many stories are historically based. Scannon, for instance, was a working member, in the literal sense of the word, not merely a mascot, of the Lewis and Clark expedition, which is credited with opening up the American Northwest. A monument to Lewis and Clark and Scannon stands in Great Falls, Montana to this day.

There are numerous accounts of the self-sacrificing bravery of Newfoundlands who have rescued their humans from disintegrating ships breaking up in the pounding surf on some rocky coastline, or children drowning in the churning current of some flooding river.

Almost all of the literature about the Newfoundland centers around the breed's humanlike intelligence, absolute bravery, consistently gentle nature, natural prowess as swimmer and innate lifesaving instinct.

The dog has made frequent appearances in historical literature, both fiction and nonfiction. There are also a number of children's books where it appears as the central, or one of the primary, characters.

Marie Killilea's beautifully illustrated children's book *Newf*, is the most recent addition to Newfoundland literature. It is a lyric tale of a "large black dog" that comes ashore on a remote coastline. He finds an abandoned fisherman's cottage "with tilting walls and a crumbling roof," where he befriends the cottage's sole inhabitant, a small white kitten. It is a powerful but simple and unsentimental story of bravery and love between two unlikely companions—a giant black dog and a little cat. This is a remarkable book that can be enjoyed by both children and adults. Ian Schoenher's illustrations are emotionally powerful, with an almost surreal quality about them. Part of their power derives from his extremely accurate portrayal of the Newf. He based his illustrations on photographic studies of Ch. Pouch Cove's Favorite Son ("Jacob") owned by Peggy and Dave Helming.

Killilea herself has considerable experience as a Newfoundland owner and is also the author of *With Love from Karen*. This book is a sequel to *Karen*, which is a moving account of her daughter's heroic struggle with a physical

A Distinguished Member of the Humane Society, painting by Sir Edwin Landseer. The white-and-black variety was given the name Landseer after the artist.

Saved, by Sir Edwin Landseer. Landseer's paintings of the white-and-black Newfoundland greatly enhanced the popularity of that color variation.

224

handicap. A good portion of *With Love from Karen* is a delightful and entertaining story of the addition of two Newfoundland bitches, Ocean Borne and Perigee Tide (both from Little Bear Kennels), to the Killilea household. Aside from being a fascinating portrayal of how caring for others, in this case two dogs, can help a handicapped person develop a solid sense of self-worth and overcome physical disability, it is an interesting, amusing and detailed account of some of the basic elements of life with two show-quality Newfoundlands.

Another fairly recent children's book (but one which may be enjoyed by adults as well) is *Casper to the Rescue*, by Colleen van Hemert and Jack Whitehead. The hero, Casper, is an Australian Newfoundland that is trained to be a water rescue dog. It is a simple story, but the photographs are charming, and it is an accurate depiction of the training of a water rescue dog.

Bob, Watch Dog of the River is another book for younger readers, the story of a Newfoundland that lived on the docks of London during the late 1800s. Bob, after saving twenty-three lives, was granted membership in the Royal Humane Society after rescuing the wife of one of its human members from drowning.

R. M. Ballantyne's nineteenth-century novel *The Dog Crusoe: A Tale of the Western Prairie* is an epic tale of the adventures of a Newfoundland dog and its master in the early American West. If you can wade through its complicated prose, which was typical of the style of that period, it makes for interesting reading.

Barney of the North is a short novella recounting the heroic exploits of a Newfoundland by Margaret S. Johnson and Helen Lossing Johnson. It is highly readable and beautifully illustrated, but you might have some difficulty finding a copy, since I am not aware of any recent printings.

Seasons of the Sea, by Monique Corriveau, is a fictionalized version of a biographical account of a family's last year on the island of Oderin, which is part of the province of Newfoundland. Pierrot, a Newfoundland, is one of the central characters.

In her anthology titled *Brave Tales of Real Dogs*, Eleanor Fairchild Pease recounts the story of the Scottish Newfoundland who rescued his Mastiff arch-enemy from drowning. She also describes other well-known accounts of Newfoundland bravery.

The Animal Story Book, which is a collection of animal stories compiled by W. H. Kingston, has several amusing Newfoundland tales. One of them concerns Neptune, who represented the epitome of honesty and canine intelligence. Every morning at eight o'clock he would take a basket containing a certain amount of money to a bakery shop, where the baker would replace it with the proper number of rolls, and Neptune would then return the basket, rolls intact and uneaten, to his master.

Another one recounts the tale of a Newfoundland who, after being bitten on the back of the leg by a smaller "cur," caught his tormentor and punished it by dropping it into the water off the end of the dock, but then rescued it just before it sank out of sight.

Another new book out based on true stories of life with a Newfoundland is *Great Balls of Fur*, by Jager.

A nineteenth-century collection, *Short Stories for School and Home Reading*, has the following vignettes about this remarkable dog:

DANDIE AND THE PENNY

A gentleman in Edinburgh had a Newfoundland dog, named Dandie, which seemed to know every word that was said to him Some of his master's friends used to give Dandie a penny if they happened to meet him. He would then go away to a baker's shop, and buy bread for himself. One of these gentlemen, when passing along the street, was met by Dandie, which trotted along by his side, looking up eagerly as if expecting his usual present. He then said to the dog: 'I have not a penny just now, but I have one at home.' Having returned to his house some time after, he heard a noise at the door, and when the servant opened it, in sprang Dandie to get his penny. In fun, the gentleman gave the dog a bad one. He went with it, as usual, to the baker's, but was refused his bread, as the money was bad. Dandie took up the bad penny, walked back to the gentleman's door, and scraped at it. When the servant opened it, he laid down the penny at her feet and marched off, seemingly feeling highly insulted at having such a dirty trick played upon him.

 . . . Dandie, however, frequently received more money than he required for his necessities, and took to hoarding it up. This was discovered by his master, in consequence of his appearing one Sunday morning with a loaf of bread in his mouth, when it was not likely that he would have received a present. Suspecting this, his master told a servant to search the room—in which Dandie slept—for money. The dog watched her, apparently unconcerned, till she approached his bed, when seizing her gown, he drew her from it. On her persisting, he growled, and struggled so violently that his master was obliged to hold him, when the woman discovered sevenpence-half-penny. From that time forward he exhibited a strong dislike to the woman, and he used to hide his money under a heap of dust at the back of the premises.

DANDIE AND THE BOOT-JACK

On one occasion Dandie's master came home rather late at night, and found all the family in bed. He wanted to take off his boots, but could not find his boot-jack in the place where it usually lay. After searching a while, he could not find in anywhere in the room. He then said to his dog: 'Dandie, I cannot find my boot-jack; go and seek for it.' The faithful animal, understanding perfectly what had been said to him, went and scratched at the room-door, which his master opened. Dandie set off to a distant part of the house, and soon returned, carrying the boot-jack in his mouth. He had found it under a sofa in another room, where his master had left it that morning. Dandie had remembered where it was, although his master had forgotten.

DANDIE AND THE SHILLING

One evening Dandie's master had some visitors at his house. One of them happened to let a shilling drop on the floor. It disappeared, and after the most diligent search, could not be found. The dog was sitting in a corner of the room, looking quite as if he knew nothing about what was going on. Turning to him, his master said:

English cigarette trading cards depicting Newfoundlands.

1988 trading card from J. P. Coats Thread.

Newfoundland cast-iron statues on the lawn of the Westfield, New York, Hospital. Cast at the Bartlett Hayward Company in the 1850s in memory of Canton and Sailor. Newfoundland lawn statues were popular during the Victorian era.

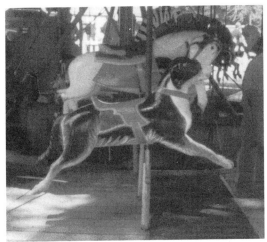

Carved Newfoundland on a merry-go-round, circa 1917.

One of the many types of cast-iron Newfoundland banks. Di Sellers Collection.   *Sellers*

Two Spelter models of Newfoundlands. Di Sellers Collection.   *Sellers*

Large Staffordshire Newfoundland. Di Sellers Collection.
Sellers

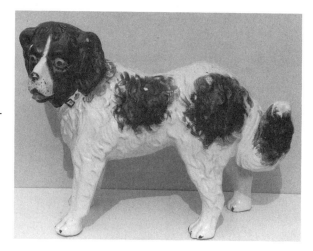

Pair of Staffordshire Newfoundlands with a spill vase (center) showing a Newf rescuing a
drowning child. Di Sellers Collection.   *Sellers*

229

'Dandie, find us the shilling, and you shall get a biscuit.' He had no sooner spoken, than the dog jumped upon the table and laid down the shilling. When it fell upon the floor, Dandie had picked it up without anyone seeing him, and had kept it in his mouth all the time they were seeking for it.

In the same collection there are also the two following short stories that illustrate the Newfoundland's bravery and prowess as a swimmer:

A BRAVE DOG

A vessel was once driven, by a storm, upon the coast of Kent. The waves were beating violently against the wreck, and she was sure to go to pieces very soon. The crew, consisting of eight men, took to the rigging, and were calling for help; but the waves were so high that no boat could be launched to try and save their lives. A crowd of people assembled on the shore, and among them a gentleman accompanied by his large Newfoundland dog. Fastening a line to a short stick, he put it in the dog's mouth, and told it to swim to the ship. The dog at once understood his meaning, and sprang into the sea, fighting its way through the foaming waves. It could not get near enough to give the men the stick it had in its mouth: so they made fast a rope to another piece of wood, and threw it towards the dog. It immediately dropped its own piece, and seized the one the sailors threw to it. With much difficulty it swam back through the surge and delivered it to its master. By this means a line of communication was formed with the vessel, and every man on board was pulled ashore safe and sound.

A PRICELESS DOG

A gentleman, returning from New Orleans in a steamer, was especially interested by a lady who was one of the passengers. She was the wife of a wealthy planter, returning to her father's house with her only child, to whom she was most devoted. While passing through the canal of Louisville, the steamer stopped for a few moments at the quay. The nurse wishing to see the city, was stepping ashore, when the child sprang from her arms into the terrible current which swept towards the falls, and immediately disappeared. The confusion that ensued attracted the attention of a gentleman who was sitting in the fore-part of the boat quietly reading. Rising hastily, he asked for some article of clothing which the child had worn. The nurse handed him a tiny apron she had torn off in her efforts to save the child as it fell. Turning to a fine Newfoundland dog that stood eagerly looking up into his face, the gentleman pointed first to the apron, and then to the spot where the child had sunk. In an instant the noble dog leaped into the stream and disappeared. By this time the excitement was intense; and some person on shore, thinking that both child and dog were lost, procured a boat, and started to search for the body. Just then the dog was seen far away with something in his mouth. Bravely he struggled with the waves, but it was clear that his strength was failing fast, and more than one breast gave a sigh of relief as the boat reached him, and it was announced that he was still alive. The dog and child were both brought on board. Giving a single glance to satisfy herself that the child was really living, the young mother rushed forward, and sinking beside the dog, threw her arms round his neck and burst into tears. Few could bear the sight unmoved, and as she caressed and kissed his shaggy head, she looked up to the owner of the dog and said: 'O sir, I must have this dog; take everything I have but give me the preserver of my child's life.' The gentleman smiled, and patting his dog's head, said: 'I am very glad, madam, he has been of service to you, but nothing in the world could induce me to part with him.' The dog looked as if he quite understood what they were talking about, and giving his sides a shake, laid himself down at his master's feet, with the expression in his large eyes that said plainer than words: 'No; nothing shall part us.'

The Newfoundland's consistently good press and the popularity of this breed with many in the celebrity crowd is due largely to the simple fact that this is a truly delightful animal. During the latter half of the nineteenth century and into the first decade of the twentieth, it was one of the most popular household breeds in the United States. The breed's legendary talents—lifesaving instinct, prowess as a swimmer, size and strength, and natural affinity for children— make it an ideal companion and baby-sitter, as Newfoundlands still are to this day.

There is a great deal of literature about various breeds, and most of it is quite favorable to our canine friends. And throughout my extensive reading and research, I have yet to find even one unfavorable tale or depiction of the Newfoundland dog. Few other animals, and dogs specifically, can come by celebrity status by virtue of their character alone. In this respect, the Newfoundland has few peers.

Royal Doulton 1978 Christmas plate, titled "Christmas in America." Di Sellers Collection. *Sellers*

A dramatic view of the Best of Breed ring at the 1989 National Specialty in Denver, Colorado.

Kohler

The Bred by Exhibitor Bitch Class at the 1985 National Specialty in Windsor Locks, Connecticut.

Søren Wesseltoft

232

14

The Newfoundland Club of America and Regional Clubs

THE NEWFOUNDLAND CLUB OF AMERICA, Inc., commonly referred to as the NCA, is the American Kennel Club–recognized parent club for Newfoundlands in the United States. The functions of the Newfoundland Club of America are many, and we are fortunate to have such an active parent club.

The purpose of the Newfoundland Club of America is to encourage and promote quality breeding of purebred Newfoundlands and to bring their natural qualities to perfection. The Newfoundland Club of America encourages preservation of the Newfoundland's natural instincts by developing and sponsoring working dog activities.

FORMATION OF THE NEWFOUNDLAND CLUB OF AMERICA

The first Newfoundland Club of America was recognized by the American Kennel Club on May 19, 1914. Very few records are available on this club except that they published a folder on the breed in 1926. The Standard they followed was very similar to the English Standard.

Sometime between 1922 and 1924 another breed club—the North American Newfoundland Club—was established. It never joined the AKC but set up a Standard that included a list of defects and faults. This Standard was also the first in the English language to emphasize the importance of undercoat. This club staged a Water Trial in Cornwall, New York, in 1929.

Committees were appointed in both the original Newfoundland Club of America and the North American Newfoundland Club to merge the two groups. Apparently a merger of the two clubs was not accepted by the memberships.

Most of the members eventually joined the Newfoundland Club of America, and the North American Newfoundland Club was dissolved.

The American Kennel Club read out the original Newfoundland Club of America as an organization for nonpayment of dues on February 7, 1928.

Our present Newfoundland Club of America was started at a meeting held at the home of Mr. and Mrs. Homer Loring in Boston, Massachusetts, on February 21, 1930.

The officers the first year were President, Mr. Quentin Twachman; Vice-President, Mrs. Vivian Moulton; Secretary, Miss Elizabeth Loring; Treasurer, Mr. Harold Ingham. The Newfoundland Club of America gained American Kennel Club membership and recognition as the parent club of the Newfoundland breed in May 1930. As an American Kennel Club–recognized club, the Newfoundland Club of America can hold American Kennel Club–sanctioned Newfoundland Specialty shows for conformation and Obedience competition.

In June 1930 the Honorable Harold Macpherson of Newfoundland was elected to the Board of Governors.

The following year the Standard was proposed. Meetings were held only once or twice a year. The membership was a small, dedicated group that gave freely of its collective time and money to promote the breed.

In 1947 Mrs. Elizabeth (Loring) Power of Waseeka Kennels became president and Mrs. Godsol, of Coastwise Kennels, was elected secretary.

In 1951 Mrs. Godsol, breeder, obedience trainer and professional all-breed judge became president. Mrs. Godsol's main contribution to the Club was communicating with Newfoundland fanciers in many parts of the world and urging them to carry on the work of improving the breed.

We have been fortunate in having had many knowledgeable and dedicated presidents to guide our club. A few of these illustrious leaders were Mr. Maynard Kane Drury, of Dryad Kennels; Mr. Harry Wisnell; Mr. Edward Wilson; Mrs. Maynard Drury; The Rev. Robert Curry; Ms. Elinor Ayers, of Seaward Kennels, Reg.; Mrs. Betty McDonnell, of Kilyka Kennels; Mrs. Louise Esiason, of Ebonewf Kennels; Dr. Thomas McGill, of Celtic Newfoundlands; and Mr. David Helming, of Pouch Cove Kennels.

NATIONAL SPECIALTIES

The first National Specialty show is reported to have been held in 1933 at the Morris & Essex Kennel Club in Madison, New Jersey.

Am., Can. Ch. Topmast's Pied Piper, ROM, was Best of Breed at the 1976 National Specialty, handled by breeder/owner Margaret Willmott of Canada. The outstanding quality of this dog sparked the interest that the Landseer Newfoundland enjoys to this day. *Tatham*

Ch. Barharber's Rosco of Pouch Cove (Ch. Barharber's Wilbur Wright, ROM, ex Ch. Motion Carried of Pouch Cove, ROM), bred by Margaret Helming and owned by Donna and David Barber, was a Best of Breed winner at the National Specialty.

National Specialty shows were held in 1940 and 1941 in conjunction with the North Westchester Kennel Club in Katonah, New York.

Mrs. Bea Godsol judged the 1941 Specialty, selecting Ch. Barnacle Bill of Waseeka for Best of Breed.

Despite the fact that no Specialties were held during World War II, breeding was only slightly curtailed. American Kennel Club records show that there were 178 Newfoundlands registered in 1940. This dropped to a low of 99 registrations during 1944.

But the increase started in 1945, with 175 dogs registered. Most years since World War II have shown a steady increase. In 1992 the American Kennel Club registered 3,153 individual Newfoundlands from 807 litters. Newfoundlands ranked in fiftieth place out of the 136 breeds recognized by the American Kennel Club. Fewer than half of all dogs actually eligible for individual American Kennel Club registration are registered.

At the Ladies' Kennel Association, the first postwar Specialty was held on Long Island in May 1948. The entry of forty-eight dogs was judged by Mr. Alva Rosenberg. Best of Breed went to Ch. Waseeka's Jolly Sailor Boy. Best of Opposite Sex was awarded to Dryad's Coastwise Showboat.

The Newfoundland Club of America has sponsored a National Specialty every year since 1948. The first independent National was held in 1967 at Lenox, Massachusetts.

The Newfoundland Club of America's National Specialty is hosted by one of its recognized regional clubs each year. It is the attraction of the year for most Newfoundland owners and exhibitors and the only time in the year that so many Newfoundlands are gathered in one place. Four days of activities are filled with daylong competition in conformation and working events, beautiful trophies and special awards to be won. Owners, breeders and fanciers from all over the world meet and forge friendships. Many booths filled with Newfoundland collectibles, artwork, jewelry, equipment for working dogs and a dazzling variety of Newfoundland memorabilia tempt the passionate shopper.

The NCA annual business meeting, educational presentation, awards banquet and auction are all part of Specialty activity. The National is held in a different area of the country each year. The 1990 National Specialty hosted by the Penn Ohio Newfoundland Club in Hudson, Ohio, had over seven hundred individual dogs entered—an all-time record for the breed.

Competition in conformation, including Puppy Sweepstakes, and Obedience are the main events at the National.

A Puppy Sweepstakes—conformation judging for dogs six to eighteen months of age—is usually judged by a breeder and run as an additional competition.

Junior showmanship competition is held for young handlers between the ages of ten and sixteen.

Sometimes the regional club hosting the National will feature a Water Trial, a decorative carting competition, and a Draft Test in conjunction with the big event.

Ch. Topmast's Orange Blossom Special winning Best in Sweepstakes at the 1985 National Specialty. Breeder/owner/handler Margaret Willmott. Judge: Joan Bendure.

Ch. Nashau-Auke's Nicholas Nickabee (Ch. Flying Cloud's Far Hill, ROM, ex Koki Kali De Nashau-Auke, CD). Bred by Jane Thibault and Jerry Zarger and owned by breeders with co-owner Donald Frubwald, winning Best of Opposite in Sweepstakes at the 1985 National Specialty.

The Newfoundland Club of America is a very active parent club maintaining many committees. General education, health and longevity, judges' education, rescue, Working Dog, and audiovisual are but a few.

PUBLICATIONS

Newf Tide is the Newfoundland Club of America's profusely illustrated bimonthly magazine. A subscription is included with membership in the Newfoundland Club of America, and it is also available by subscription to nonmembers.

Newf Tide publishes articles on health, breeding, water, draft and obedience training and regional club news. Different issues feature coverage of the National Specialty, the breeds' top producers and top show and working dogs for the year. Regional Specialty winners, new champions and dogs earning Obedience and Working titles are regularly pictured.

The Newfoundland and You, a pamphlet written and distributed by the Club, is intended to aid new and prospective Newfoundland owners.

The *Annual of Titlists* is published by the Newfoundland Club of America. Members pay to have their dogs' pictures and pedigrees published. A Newfoundland earning any American Kennel Club or Newfoundland Club of America title is eligible. It is sent free to all Newfoundland Club of America members.

REGIONAL CLUBS

The Newfoundland Club of America fosters the organization of regional and local Newfoundland clubs. Just as the American Kennel Club recognizes and sanctions parent clubs, the Newfoundland Club of America does the same with its regional clubs. The Newfoundland Club of America allows regional clubs to host American Kennel Club–approved Specialties and Obedience Trials. The Newfoundland Club of America also gives regional clubs permission to hold NCA-sanctioned Water Trials and draft tests.

Belonging to a regional club affords members the chance to get to know other Newfoundland fanciers, to exchange knowledge, and to hold Water Trial training classes, puppy matches and educational seminars. Many regional clubs participate in local parades and holiday activities. Regional clubs publish newsletters filled with useful information, and almost all regional clubs have Newfoundland Rescue Programs.

There are regional and local Newfoundland clubs sanctioned by the Newfoundland Club of America all across the country, including Hawaii.

Contact the Newfoundland Club of America's corresponding secretary to find the regional club nearest to you.

Stud Dog Class at National Specialty. Ch. Pouch Cove Gref of Newton-Ark with his get, Ch. Mooncusser's Dutch Treat, ROM, and (left) Ch. Mooncusser Sloop Aurelia.

Stephanie Sosa, NCA's top Junior Handler for 1990 and 1991, showing her Ch. Kilyka's Cozy at Dockmaster, co-owned with breeder Betty McDonnell.

WATER TRIALS

The first Newfoundland water trial was held in 1929.

Today most Newfoundland Club of America regional clubs host a Water Trial annually.

The Water Dog (WD) and Water Rescue Dog (WRD) title is awarded to any Newfoundland that successfully completes the exercises in the Junior Division and Senior Division respectively.

REGISTER OF MERIT (ROM)

The Newfoundland Club of America Register of Merit title was created to honor Newfoundlands that have proven themselves to be extraordinary producers of champions and working Newfoundlands. The title is used after the registered name of the dog or bitch and can be used only after official notification by the Newfoundland Club of America.

A dog receives its Register of Merit title when he has earned twelve (12) ROM points. A bitch receives her Register of Merit title when she obtains six (6) ROM points. Any Newfoundland that finishes its American Kennel Club bench Championship earns one ROM point for its sire and one ROM point for its dam.

A Newfoundland that earns its ROM title earns 1 ROM point for its sire and 1 ROM point for its dam.

For a sire to receive his ROM he must have produced ten (10) ROM and/or Champion offspring. For a dam to earn her ROM, she must produce five (5) ROM and/or Champion offspring.

One point is given to a sire or dam for its first American Kennel Club or Newfoundland Club of America working-titled offspring. Additional working titlists will be counted as earning an ROM point for their sire or dam only after a total of five ROMs and/or American Kennel Club bench champions have been credited. A formula for counting working titlist as ROM points for a sire or dam is: divide by 5 the total number of champions and ROMs, drop the remainder and add 1.

One Newfoundland can earn a maximum of 3 ROM points for its sire or dam. To accomplish this a Newfoundland would have to earn its AKC bench championship, an ROM title and one of the working titles.

VERSATILITY NEWFOUNDLAND (VN)

One of the most coveted Newfoundland Club of America titles is the Versatility Newfoundland (VN). This title is awarded to dogs that have garnered their AKC championships, an American or Canadian CD Obedience title, both WD and WRD Water titles and the DD Draft Dog title.

Ch. Shiprock Legacy Wheeler Dealer, CD, DD (Ch. John's Big Ben of Pouch Cove, ROM, ex Ch. Shiprock's Look To Liberty), winning Best of Breed at the 1993 National Specialty under Denny Kodner. Bred by Vicki and Ron Wakefield, and shown by owner Linda Morley, he is co-owned with Vicki Wakefield. *Tatham*

Ch. Jubilee You're The Top (Ch. Pouch Cove's Favorite Son, ROM, ex Jubilee's Anything Goes) was Winners Dog at the 1993 National Specialty. Bred by Julie Rigling, he is owned by Peggy and David Helming and Julie Rigling. *Tatham*

Ch. Cypress Bay Can Do Cassandra (Ch. John's Big Ben of Pouch Cove, ROM, ex Ch. Cypress Bay's Cosette of Tabu) was Winners Bitch and Best of Winners at the 1993 NCA National Specialty. Bred, owned and handled by Debra Thornton. *Tatham*

241

AWARDS

The Newfoundland Club of America gives certificate awards for all the Water and Draft Dog titles earned.

Newfoundland Club of America members earning an American Kennel Club championship on their dogs are given a medallion in recognition. The first Obedience title is acknowledged with a pin, and different gemstones for the pin are given for subsequent Obedience titles earned.

Rescue

The Newfoundland Club of America and the regional clubs promote and support a very active breed-rescue program. It is unfortunate that we even need such a committee. But it is a consequence of today's ever-changing life-styles and the fact that there are puppy mills and indiscriminate breeders whose only interest in Newfoundlands is monetary.

The program owes its success to Mary L. Price, who has done so much to advance rescue at both National and regional club levels. Many families have adopted Newfoundland puppies and adults who would have certainly been put to death had it not been for just such a program.

On left is Am., Can. Ch. Tarbell's Boaz and Am., Mex. Ch. Tarbell's Jethro winning first and second in Veteran Sweepstakes at a regional Specialty. Both dogs are owned by Ruth March of Tarbell Kennels.   *Ashbey*